HARVARD EAST ASIAN MONOGRAPHS
58

THE LITERATI PURGES: POLITICAL CONFLICT

IN EARLY YI KOREA

THE LITERATI PURGES: POLITICAL CONFLICT

IN EARLY YI KOREA

by

Edward Willett Wagner

Published by

East Asian Research Center

Harvard University

Distributed by

Harvard University Press

Cambridge, Mass.

1974

The East Asian Research Center at Harvard University
administers research projects designed to further
scholarly understanding of China, Japan, Korea, Vietnam,
Inner Asia, and adjacent areas. These studies have been
assisted by grants from the Ford Foundation.

Library of Congress No. 74-21777
SBN 674-53618-5

CONTENTS

v

PREFACE

This study was begun fully twenty years ago and was completed five years later, in 1959. The reader will join me, I trust, in regretting the very long delay in making it available. The fault is entirely mine and I can only plead the usual academic preoccupations. Fortunately, in the narrow perspective, next to nothing has been done in the intervening years to render this work outdated or, indeed, to add measurably to it. This is no reflection, surely, on the intrinsic interest and importance of the topic but rather suggests the still struggling state of the art in the study of traditional Korea.

The manuscript in its present form is little different substantively from the original dissertation version. A variety of editorial changes have made the presentation more lucid and readable, but there has been no attempt to undertake new research or add new material. Here and there, especially in the introductory chapter, I have recast certain remarks that seem to me now to have betrayed ignorance. And some amount of detail has been excised, in particular from the narration of the less central events of 1504 and 1519. Readers interested either in the earlier naïveté or in the fuller detail are invited to refer to the dissertation itself ("The Literati Purges—Case Studies in the Factionalism of the Early Yi Dynasty," Harvard University, 1959).

A note accompanying the bibliography discusses the sources I have used in this work and comments on other materials of potential value for a study of this sort. Appendix A presents an alphabetical list of major Yi dynasty central and provincial offices and posts. The list also includes other offices mentioned in the text. My renderings are meant to convey equally a sense of function and a sense of hierarchy; the literal meaning of the Chinese characters, consequently, often has been ignored. Appendix B lists all date citations appearing in the text and notes and gives the volume and page location in the *Sillok* for each date (see note on page 7).

Romanization of Korean sounds is in accordance with the McCune-Reischauer system. A general glossary provides Chinese characters for place names, terms, and the like. A separate glossary gives the characters for the names of all persons appearing in the text and notes.

In its different aspects and stages this study owes much to the counsel and help of a number of people. While doing research in Korea and Japan I turned especially to professors Yi Pyŏng-do, Han U-gŭn, and the late Takahashi Tōru for advice. Professors Yi Kwang-nin and Kim Ch'ŏl-chun also were helpful. Undertaken originally as a Ph.D. dissertation, the work benefitted from the direction of my faculty adviser, Edwin O. Reischauer. The encouragement of Benjamin I. Schwartz and John K. Fairbank was meaningful both initially and subsequently in the decision to publish the manuscript. To Professor Fairbank, in particular, I am grateful, for his faith in me and in the work, for his patience, for his time, and for his wisdom.

The technical preparation of the manuscript for publication, in both its routine and creative aspects, was undertaken by Lois Dougan Tretiak. She has done an immensely capable job and I am both pleased and thankful that I may acknowledge here my debt to her skilled services.

Finally, the manuscript owes more to my wife, Namhi Kim, than the mere total of her research and calligraphic contributions. Her high expectations for the development of the Korean studies field at Harvard raise a standard which, I hope, the *Literati Purges* will help to bear forward.

Cambridge, Massachusetts
Summer 1974

EARLY YI DYNASTY KINGS

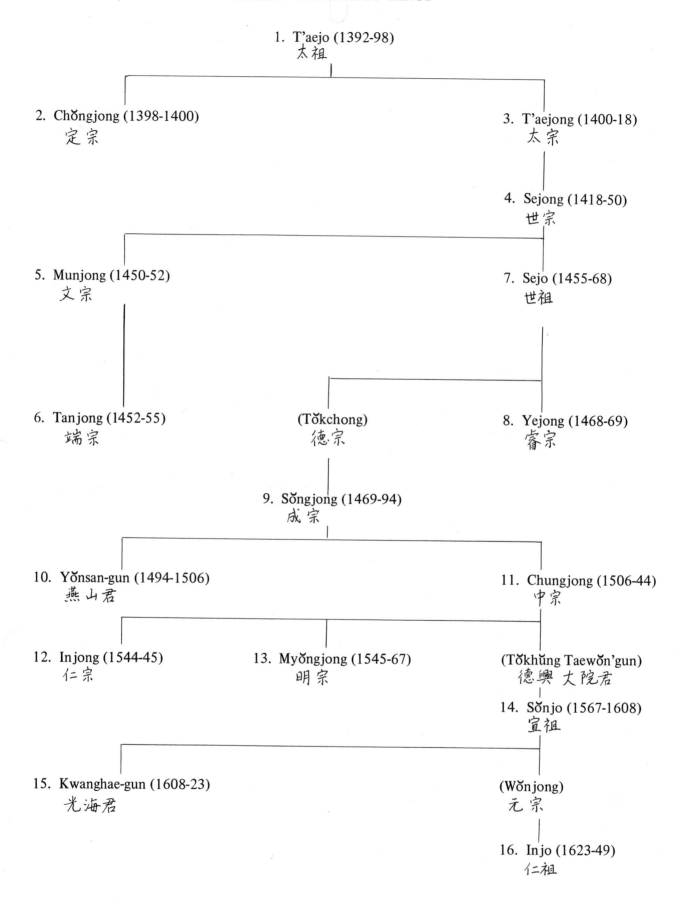

INTRODUCTION

Factionalism was the central political phenomenon of the Yi dynasty (1392-1910). Korean historiography employs the term *tangjaeng,* "factional strife," to designate this phenomenon. The traditional date marking the inception of the period of factional strife is 1575, the eighth year of the reign of King Sŏnjo (1567-1608). It was in this year, apparently, that the earliest designations of factional affiliation, the terms Easterner *(tongin)* and Westerner *(sŏin),* were first used. These terms denoted the supporters or sympathizers of two leading figures in the central government of that day and symbolized the division of a significant portion of the officialdom into two hostile camps. Subsequent factional divisions, subdivisions, and realignments are commonly said to have been lineally related, in every case, to these archetypes. By the end of the seventeenth century, the factional picture had been stabilized as alignments became more permanent. The end products of more than a century of redivision and realignment were four principal factions, the so-called Four Colors *(sasaek).* For another two hundred years, down to the very last years of the nineteenth century, this remained a living, operative term in the political vocabulary of Yi Korea's ruling elite.

A striking aspect of factional conflict in Yi Korea is the contrast between the depth of the factional division in the society and the shallowness of the issues under contention. Major disputes centered around such questions as the designation of an heir-apparent or the proper period of mourning for a deceased queen, or, still more transparently, conflict would be ascribed to personal animosities. In this light, Yi dynasty factionalism would appear to have been no more than a naked struggle for political power, motivated by desires for economic affluence and social prestige. This view likely is both too simple and too harsh, and in any case it leaves basic questions about Yi factionalism unanswered. In particular, how did lines of conflict come to be drawn as they were? Why did Yi dynasty factional divisions prove so enduring? In other words, why did factionalism become institutionalized in the latter half of the Yi dynasty and prove so stubbornly resistant to efforts to eradicate it?

These questions, in turn, pose others. What historical preconditions specific to Korea contributed to the development of factionalism in the Yi dynasty? And what immediate historical factors shaped the contours of the later phenomenon of factional strife? A satisfactory answer to the first of these latter two questions must be based upon an understanding of the main lines of development of Korean culture. The answer to the second question will be more easily sought in the study of the political history of the early Yi dynasty.

Yi dynasty factionalism did not spring into existence, unheralded, in 1575. For at least the preceding one hundred years the Yi central government endured almost unrelieved political turmoil, the manifestation, broadly speaking, of a struggle for control of the policy-making machinery. During this century of conflict there occurred, over a fifty-year period, four major explosions that were severe but temporary setbacks to attempts by the censoring organs—the Offices of the

Inspector-General, the Censor-General, and Special Counselors—to win the paramount voice in government councils. On each of these occasions, charges of factionalism, of clique forming, were leveled against numbers of government officials who were linked to the efforts to enlarge the policy role of the censoring organs. Korean history calls these four events *sahwa,* the "Literati Purges." The four *sahwa* are dated by the sixty-year Chinese cyclical system and, accordingly, are known by terms that identify the year in which each occurred: the *muo sahwa* (Purge of 1498; also called the History Purge), *kapcha sahwa* (Purge of 1504), *kimyo sahwa* (Purge of 1519), and *ŭlsa sahwa* (Purge of 1545). The Literati Purges—the first three of which are the subject of this monograph—were attempts to arrest the growing power of the censoring organs or to prevent the manipulation of the censoring organs for power-seeking ends. The purges thus were a particular manifestation in the early Yi dynasty of the general phenomenon of political factionalism.

Factionalism was implicit in the Yi dynasty political settlement. The monarchic institution in Korea always has been characterized by strict limitations placed upon the exercise of royal authority. Ever since the unification of the peninsula under Silla, the status of the Korean king had been that of *primus inter pares.* At the same time, the ruling *yangban* (official) class had preserved an unusually high degree of continuity—of freedom from dilution by new claimants to the privileges it monopolized and from the loss of these privileges. In practice, a ruling house had always lived together with the yangban class in an equilibrium that at its finest point of balance represented a kind of constitutional monarchy, but that more normally tilted between degrees of tyranny and of an ochlocracy of aristocrats in which the king was little more than a figurehead.

The Yi dynasty did not deviate from this pattern. The composition of the yangban class underwent little change in the transition from Koryŏ to Chosŏn (the formal name of Korea under the Yi). The new ruling house, forced to seek support among the less privileged segment of the yangban in order to seize the throne defended by the more privileged, derived the greater part of its appeal from its promise to reverse the end-of-Koryŏ imbalance within the yangban class. In the end, however, the Yi monarchs found themselves obligated both to old and new forces, with the result that political privilege might be claimed by a substantially enlarged upper class.

The new dynasty was not merely beholden to a large and diverse body of claimants to political preferment, but its very survival would depend upon the manner in which these obligations were met. Motivated thus by considerations of dynastic security, the founders of the Yi relied upon two contradictory political devices in their efforts to insure the continuity of the new royal house. One device was the Merit Subject *(kongsin)* system. The other was the adoption of Confucian morality, together with its corollary principles of political organization and practice.

Why were the two devices contradictory? Merit Subject status brought with it economic rewards of great magnitude. At the same time, however, Confucian dogma condemned the acquisitive instinct and approved instead simplicity and frugality. Merit Subject status offered unusual opportunity for political advancement, but Confucian doctrine recognized a different type of merit principle, one that would find its logical expression in a fairly administered examination system and in career advancement in accordance with manifest ability in the art of government. Merit Subject status most often was accorded in connection with succession disputes, which demanded the talents of many military men. But in character and education these would be the antithesis of the ideal Confucian civil administrator, who even favored the elimination of men of military training from duties logically and traditionally entrusted to them.

The special privilege and power attendant upon Merit Subject status provide the clearest example but the contradictions just noted were present in like degree no matter who occupied positions of first importance in the government. Whether they were Merit Subjects, kinsmen of a queen, those who had contracted marriage ties with the royal house, or simply career officials having no unusual advantages—men might be awarded large amounts of land or be enabled to wield great political influence, but they could not be given immunity against assault on their privileged position. Their enjoyment of high station was constantly challenged by agencies of the government staffed largely with men who were younger, more deeply committed ideologically, and less privileged. In particular, the censoring bodies represented the conscience of the state, ever vigilant against violations of an ideal set of ethical standards. Entrusted with broad powers both of policy evaluation and personnel scrutiny, the censoring bodies naturally focused their attention on the occupants of high positions.

Final victory in any clash between the censoring organs and the high echelons of the government could only be decided by the ultimate authority of the king. Those in power positions normally lacked cohesiveness and elan, and were further handicapped by the factor of ideological anomaly—they themselves were committed to tenets of Confucian doctrine that their very existence often flouted. On the other hand, the threat to the security of the throne that would be posed by their wholesale disaffection was tangible and immediate.

The censoring bodies, while lacking continuity on the individual level, derived both corporate continuity and a sense of mission from firm and acknowledged ideological underpinnings. Their cause was favored, too, by the intimacy and frequency of their contact with the sovereign. The doom they cried, however, often was amorphous, and their arguments to the throne lacked sufficient urgency to overcome a natural reluctance to disturb the existing order.

Yet such was the zeal and persistence of the officials of the censoring bodies—and such was the dynasty's commitment to the concept of remonstrance—that kings tended to accede to minimum demands until faced with ultimate choices. As a result, the history of the fifty years treated in this study is characterized by periods of steady accretion of power on the part of the censoring organs. But as their power grew, the censoring organs wielded it with decreasing wisdom and with increasing intolerance and partisanship, until the process was joltingly arrested by violent means. Such an event was a Literati Purge.

Chapter I

THE SETTING

The Yi dynasty more nearly represented a renovation than a new construction. The founders of the royal house of Yi boldly changed the pattern of their inheritance in some respects; land reform, adoption of Confucianism as a state creed, and abolition of privately maintained armed forces are cases in point. In other ways, however, the Yi dynasty was only a continuation of the Koryŏ by another name. In particular, although some redistribution of the apparatus of power occurred, the political balance remained essentially where it had been. At bottom, the founder of the new dynasty, Yi Sŏng-gye, had merely brought off a successful palace coup.

Yi Sŏng-gye was perforce a cautious innovator. He owed his throne not only to his own enterprise but also to the support of forces with deep roots of their own in the Korean body politic. The claim of these forces to political privilege was independent of that of the Yi themselves, and it was a claim that might well be filed elsewhere. In consequence, change had to come slowly and, although there was much solid achievement, the dynasty failed to attain significant forward momentum. Areas of decay appeared in the institutional framework before it was completed, and these acted to imperil the structure while it was still being built.

In its first half century and more the house of Yi was beset by a number of succession disputes. The political history of these years finds a natural focus on these events and on the development of political forces that were an outgrowth of them.

A vital corollary of the succession disputes was the creation of groups of Merit Subjects, men extraordinarily rewarded for services of unusual value to the state. For the most part, the Merit Subjects of the early Yi rulers were those who had rendered signal service in winning the throne by force for their sovereign or in maintaining him on it against the threat of force.

There existed, then, special bonds of loyalty and interdependence between a sovereign and his Merit Subjects, and these ties were strengthened by the nature of the rewards bestowed by the throne. Most immediate and tangible of these were land and slaves. Merit Subjects enrolled in the first class of merit received grants of land *(kongsinjŏn)* that yielded incomes greater than the stipends paid the highest rank in officialdom, and lesser degrees of merit were rewarded proportionately. From the very outset the hereditary character of Merit Subject land was acknowledged, an important exception to the cardinal principle of state ownership upon which Yi land reform was based.

Other emoluments and privileges were designed to insure the continued devotion of Merit Subjects and their descendants to their sovereign benefactor and his lineal successors. Merit Subjects were given the title of Great Lord *(puwŏn'gun),* or Lord *(kun),* and this was accompanied by promotion in rank. In addition, criminal acts of Merit Subjects traditionally were viewed with marked leniency. Their descendants, especially their direct heirs, would be favored by occasional promotions in rank and might advance in government service via the "protection" route, relieved of the necessity of qualifying in the examinations. Special privileges with respect to rites in honor of their ancestors were accorded Merit Subjects; certain badges of the royal esteem added to the prestige value of Merit Subject status.

It was only natural that the uniquely favored treatment accorded the Merit Subjects should enhance their role in the governmental process. Merit Subject status frequently served as an entree to higher government position. In fact, the four or five leading figures on each merit roster might normally expect rapid elevation to the higher eminences of the State Council while others tended to be employed at higher levels than before. Moreover, mechanisms existed enabling many Merit Subjects to participate in important government councils even though they did not hold duty posts.

In the society as well, Merit Subject status was accompanied by new opportunity. An upgrading in the level of marriage ties could be anticipated—sons or daughters of the reigning sovereign himself would fall to some, while others would succeed in betrothing their children to those of leading royal clansmen or government personages.

The Merit Subjects, then, made up a distinct and powerful force in the government. Their political instincts were pronouncedly conservative, being concerned with the preservation of enjoyed privilege. As the special prop of the sovereign who created them, Merit Subjects could scarcely be expected to constitute a force for change; yet they often were the authors of it. Theirs was a two-edged sword, quick to defend against encroachments on their privileges from either below or above. A king who owed his throne to his Merit Subjects had always to remember that king-makers are at one and the same time king-breakers.

The propriety of rewarding specific groups of Merit Subjects was a major issue in the background of two of the purges that are the subject of this study. Moreover, the roles of individual Merit Subjects in a variety of important events of the time also loom large in the record. A better understanding of these events will be gained by noting the circumstances of the creation of the various Merit Subject lists. It is convenient to do this in the context of a brief discussion of the history of the early decades of the Yi dynasty.

The founder of the new dynasty, Yi Sŏng-gye, had won wide repute for his military exploits against the Jurchen in the northeast and against Japanese marauders in the coastal regions of the south before he attained the stature of a dominant figure in the central government. Yi Sŏng-gye proved to possess political acumen as well when, acknowledging the rising power of the Ming, he turned back from the Yalu the army he was leading to support the Yüan and seized control of the government. Using his new power to replace the reigning monarch with one who was more docile, he ousted from the government those unsympathetic with his aims and set immediately to work on a drastic overhaul of the land-holding system. This achievement signaled the defeat of the Koryŏ royal house and of the forces that supported it, for it destroyed the economic foundations on which their power rested. A scant year after the enactment of land reform, Yi Sŏng-gye permitted his supporters to place him on the throne.[1]

One of the first acts of King T'aejo (Yi Sŏng-gye), naturally, was to reward the men most intimately associated with him in the founding of the new dynasty. Thus were created the "Dynasty Establishment" or, as I have called them, the T'aejo Merit Subjects (*kaeguk kongsin*). Initially, fortyfour men were enrolled in three classes of merit (1392.8.20),* and later at least eleven more names were added to the roster (1392.9.27 S, 11.19, 1398.12.15). In addition to other honors and rewards, those enrolled in Class One received grants of land ranging from 150 to 220 *kyŏl*[2] and from 15 to 30 slaves to work the land; those in Class Two received 100 *kyŏl* of land and 10 slaves; those in Class Three received 70 *kyŏl* of land and 7 slaves (1392.9.16 S). Moreover, T'aejo created a very large body of Minor Merit Subjects *(wŏnjong kongsin)*, apparently more than 1,000 (see 1392.10.9, 1393.7.22, 7.27, 7.29, 8.10, 8.15, 8.17, 1396.1.20). Some of these too were rewarded with land (as much as 30 *kyŏl*) and slaves.[3]

T'aejo was blessed with eight sons, the issue of two queens. Under the influence of his second queen, T'aejo wanted to designate her elder son as his heir but, encountering strong opposition from among his Merit Subjects (who made it clear that they were urging the lesser of two evils), he at length settled upon the younger son. This decision did not please the six sons of the first queen, one of whom, Yi Pang-wŏn, had particularly distinguished himself in the founding of the dynasty. Consequently, in 1398, claiming that he had uncovered a plot against himself and his brothers, Yi Pang-wŏn launched a coup in which the two sons of the second queen were killed, together with a number of Merit Subjects and others who had accepted Yi T'aejo's decision on the succession question. Refusing to put himself forward, Yi Pang-wŏn had an unambitious brother designated heir to

---

*Extensive use of the *Sillok* and the *Chōsen shi* has created a problem of attribution, since both are in the form of a daily record of the operations of the government. My solution has been to make citations in the form of numerical year, month, and day dates (e.g., 1519.11.15), which, enclosed in parentheses, I have inserted appropriately in the body of the text. The year figure represents the year of the Western calendar to which it roughly corresponds, while the month and day figures follow the lunar calendar system employed in the *Sillok*. References to the *Sillok* are distinguished from those to the *Chōsen shi* by the addition of a capital "S" following the date figure (e.g., 1519.11. 15 S). On occasion, the same date in both the *Sillok* and the *Chōsen shi* is cited. This is because of the *Chōsen shi* practice of collecting under one date-heading material on a single topic scattered under several date-headings in the *Sillok*. In my date citations, the prefixing of "i" to the month figure indicates an intercalary month (e.g., 1504.i4. 23).

Location of references to the *Chōsen shi* is a simple matter, since this source has converted the cyclical characters for the days into their numerical equivalents. The reader need only convert the year figure to the corresponding year of the reign in which it falls, whereupon he may quickly find the month and day in the appropriate volume of the *Chōsen shi*. References to the *Sillok*, on the other hand, are not so easily found. Fortunately, recent editions of the *Sillok* (one published by the Korean History Compilation Committee of the Ministry of Education, Republic of Korea, and another by the Gakushūin in Tokyo) have added reign year and month data to each page, so that the only problem remaining is the day. This, of course, is given in cyclical character form, and the reader will be required to refer to Appendix B, where *Sillok* locations of all date citations appearing herein are given.

the throne. Sick at heart at the strife among his sons, T'aejo now abdicated in favor of the new heir, who became King Chŏngjong (1398-1400).

The succession problem, however, was not so easily settled. The circumstances under which Chŏngjong had gained the throne called for the creation of another merit roster. Accordingly, twenty-nine men were enrolled as Chŏngjong Merit Subjects *(chŏngsa kongsin)* and were given land, slaves, and other benefits commensurate with those received by the T'aejo Merit Subjects (see 1398. 9.17, 10.1 S).[4] But some among the new Merit Subjects were dissatisfied with the level of their rewards and, in 1400, joined with another son of T'aejo in armed insurrection. Yi Pang-wŏn soon subdued the rebels, had himself named heir, and, at the end of the same year, accepted the throne offered him by Chŏngjong. Yi Pang-wŏn, King T'aejong, first rewarded forty-seven of his leading supporters by enrolling them in four classes of merit,[5] and then settled down for a long and constructive reign.

For fifty years Korea's destiny was ably guided by two of the dynasty's most brilliant monarchs, T'aejong (1400-1418) and Sejong (1418-1450). Mindful of the threat to the security and tranquility of the state inherent in the existing system of private armies,[6] T'aejong ordered these forces disbanded. With the aim of fostering the study of Confucianism and accelerating the acceptance of Confucian morality, he had movable type cast in copper and many books printed in this way. At the same time, he banned the long-popular texts on divination and geomancy, placed restrictions on the number of Buddhist temples and of monks, and repossessed large amounts of Buddhist land and slaves. Continuing a task begun in the last years of Koryŏ, T'aejong compiled and published two books of statutes, thus carrying further forward the rationalization of the legal system and of the institutional structure. It was also under T'aejong that the first steps were taken to bar the illegitimate sons of the yangban class from important public office and to ban the remarriage of widows. And it was T'aejong who moved the capital permanently to Seoul (1405).

In 1418 T'aejong disinherited his eldest son, who had displayed disturbing traits of character, and designated his third son, who became Sejong, as his successor. Then he abdicated and, until his death four years later, placed his prestige and counsel at the disposal of the new king.

Sejong's reign is best known for the development of the *han'gŭl* writing system, the remarkable Korean alphabet, but it was a period of great creative activity in many spheres. Sejong developed an existing institution, the Hall of Worthies *(chiphyŏnjŏn)* into a center of scholarly and scientific inquiry, carried on for the most part by dedicated younger men. The officials of the Hall of Worthies had played a leading role in the creation of *han'gŭl,* and they made similar contributions to a variety of other projects. Movable type was cast anew and printing techniques improved. Not only were texts of Chinese provenance printed, but important new Korean works appeared. There were, for example, histories, gazetteers, and books on farming, medicine, and music. A rain gauge was invented, as well as sundials, water clocks, and astronomical instruments of various kinds.

In the realm of economic policy, Sejong introduced important refinements in the land system. Agricultural land was divided into six grades, in accordance with quality, while nine degrees of crop year were recognized. Taxes, then, were to be assessed on a scale of land fertility and in the light of weather conditions as they affected the yield in a particular year. Sejong also reworked the compilations of statutes published by T'aejong, and so brought nearer the completion of the basic legal text of the dynasty, the *Kyŏngguk taejŏn* (National Code). And he carried on his father's anti-Buddhist policy, forcing the consolidation of existing sects into only two groups, destroying all but a handful of temples, and confiscating most of the temple land and slaves.

Sejong conducted a vigorous foreign policy as well. To put an end to the ravages of Japanese marauders, he sent a military force to Tsushima and, after a brief and successful campaign, worked out a treaty settlement whereby Japanese commercial activities were permitted on a reduced and controlled basis at the so-called Three Ports *(samp'o)* on the southeast coast. In the northeast he set up the Six Garrison Districts *(yukchin)* to block the depredations of the Yain (Jurchen) tribes, and in the northwest he established four new counties as a first step to opening the regions along the Yalu to colonization.

Sejong was succeeded by his eldest son, Munjong (1450-1452). Then, upon Munjong's untimely death, the throne passed to the boy Tanjong (1452-1455), and the dynasty once again was riven by a succession dispute. Tanjong's uncle, the second son of Sejong, was a vigorous and able man, but a man of inordinate ambition. Asserting that they were plotting with one of his younger brothers against Tanjong, he first killed two High State Councillors (Hwangbo In and Kim Chong-sŏ) who had been charged with safeguarding the inheritance of the young king. He then had himself appointed Chief State Councillor and, concurrently, Minister of the Boards of War and Personnel (1453.10.11). Not long content to rule in fact but not in name, in 1455 this prince accepted the throne left vacant by the dutiful abdication of his nephew, becoming the monarch we know as Sejo (1455-1468).

Sejo had promulgated one merit list to reward those who joined him in his initial move to power, the killing of Tanjong's highest ministers in 1453, and shortly after he ascended the throne he announced another. The forty-three men enrolled in the first instance, including Sejo himself, I have called the Sejo-Usurpation Merit Subjects *(chŏngnan kongsin),* and the forty-four men of the second list I have called the Sejo-Enthronement Merit Subjects *(chwaik kongsin).* The rewards in both instances were of the magnitude of earlier merit rosters (see 1453.10.15 S, 10.17 S, 10.18 S, 11.4 S, 1455.9.9 S). The record reveals that Minor Merit Subjects were enrolled in 1453 (see 1454.28), but there is no indication of the number. Something like 2,200 Minor Merit Subjects were named in 1455 (12.27 S); these, however, did not receive awards of land and slaves.

Sejo's path to the throne, it may well be imagined, was lined with disaffected officials. Those who miscalculated Sejo's strength and identified themselves with the cause of royal legitimacy were killed, banished, or otherwise punished. A large number of others viewed the new ruler with distaste on moral grounds. Some of these eventually found it possible to reconcile themselves to the new regime, but some, citing the ancient watchword that a subject does not serve two lords, turned their backs on the traditional career of public service. One such group that was especially widely revered for its expressions of loyalty to Tanjong came to be known as the Six Loyal Subjects *(saengyuksin)*. Still others who had remained in office after Sejo's usurpation plotted to restore Tanjong to the throne. The scheme was unmasked and a great blood-bath ensued (1456.6.2, 6.3, 6.6, 6.18), but the leading figures in the attempt, men who had served Sejong as officials of the Hall of Worthies, won undying fame as the Six Martyred Subjects *(sayuksin)*.[7] Before long, Sejo demoted Tanjong in title, calling him Nosan'gun,[8] and sent him into banishment (1457.6.21), but presently, after another abortive attempt against the throne, Sejo had him killed (1457.10.24). Sejo's crown was now secure.

Free to turn his attention to the affairs of government, Sejo made some notable achievements. A man of military bent, he pursued an active frontier policy and, by a combination of cajolery and force (including a joint campaign with Ming China), brought the incursions of the Yain to a temporary end and firmly established Korea's claim to its present northern borders. At the same time, he revitalized military training, published military texts, and stimulated the development of improved weapons. While he reversed aspects of the policy of suppression of Buddhism, even sponsoring the publication of sutras, he was also responsible for the appearance of a number of important technical and scholarly works, and he succeeded as well in completing the first two sections of the National Code.

At the end of his reign, in 1467, Sejo was confronted with an insurrection in Hamgyŏng province led by one of his military commanders, Yi Si-ae. The revolt, soon put down, prompted the creation of still another merit roster; the forty-four men enrolled at this time, in three classes of merit, I have called the Sejo-Pacification Merit Subjects *(chŏkkae kongsin)*.[9]

Sejo had but two legitimate sons; the first (Tŏkchong) died in youth, and he was succeeded by the second, known as Yejong (1468-1469). Scarcely had Yejong taken up his royal duties than a plot was reported against the throne. The Fourth Minister of War, Yu Cha-gwang, alleged that Nam I, a brilliant young former Minister of War who had played a leading part in quelling the Yi Si-ae revolt, was scheming to place a great-grandson of T'aejong on the throne. In the end, about forty men were executed, including a former Chief State Councillor, and Yu Cha-gwang was named at the head of a new merit roster. There were thirty-nine of these Yejong Merit Subjects *(iktae kongsin)*, and they were given the usual rewards in the usual amounts (1468.10.28 S, 10.30 S, 1469.5.20 S, 7.3).

Yejong passed away after only a year on the throne, leaving a single infant son. The problem of succession was solved by seating the younger of Tŏkchong's two sons, a boy of twelve, upon the throne under the regency of his grandmother, Sejo's queen. This was King Sŏngjong (1469-1494). Then, as a form of insurance against the outbreak of still another internecine struggle for the throne, a new roster of Merit Subjects was drawn up, the most numerous to that date. In all, seventy-three men were enrolled in four classes of merit and, in addition, 1,059 men were enrolled as Minor Merit Subjects in three classes (1471.3.27 S, 8.25 S). Although the level of rewards was substantially less than heretofore, on this occasion, for the first time, objections were raised to a royal desire to create a new group of Merit Subjects. Arguing that the recipients of these new awards had rendered no meritorious service, the Censorate repeatedly urged that the king nullify his action. These protests, however, went unheeded (1471.3.27).

At the outset of Sŏngjong's reign, then, when the story of the Literati Purges begins to unfold, there was a large number of Merit Subjects incumbent in offices of the central government or available for such appointments. In a span of less than twenty years, from 1453, five merit lists had been promulgated, with a total enrollment of close to 250 men. Present also, with claims to preferential consideration, were the sons and grandsons of the Merit Subjects enrolled in the first decade of the dynasty. And there were, in addition, literally thousands of Minor Merit Subjects. The extent to which the members of this privileged segment of the ruling class may have dominated the society of that day must be the subject of a separate investigation. But it is clear that they played a leading role, occupying, for example, many of the highest civil and military offices.

In the office structure of the Yi dynasty the normal division was made between the civil and the military ranks. Civil posts were filled by officials of the "east rank" *(tongban)* and military posts by those of the "west rank" *(sŏban)*. Taken together these comprised the "two ranks" *(yangban)* of the officialdom. In terms of hierarchy, all posts to be occupied by the yangban were assigned to one of eighteen grades of office rank. The highest of these was called Senior First Rank and the next was Junior First Rank, and so on, down through Junior Ninth Rank. Each official possessed a personal rank classified, essentially, according to the same scheme. In attestation of this, he was issued an office warrant, which he would forfeit only if convicted of a serious crime.

Normally, of course, a man first acquired personal rank when he first was appointed to office and there was always a close correspondence between personal rank and the rank of the post to which a man might be appointed. Promotion in personal rank, then, typically was achieved by winning appointment to a higher ranked post. There was provision, however, permitting service in a higher level post without a concomitant promotion in personal rank. Similarly, he could be appointed to a post one rank lower (but seldom more than one rank lower) than his personal rank. Appointment to a higher-ranking post was not the only means by which an official's personal rank might be raised. Extraordinary promotions were accorded for a variety of reasons, such as Merit Subject enrollment, marriage into the royal family, the rendering of distinguished military service, the winning of royal literary competitions, and the like.

The governing elite of the Yi dynasty, the "yangban" who held the ranked positions in the government, consisted overwhelmingly of men drawn from a hereditary aristocracy. Membership in this privileged class appears to have been based on historical factors that antedate the Yi dynasty; at any rate there is little evidence to indicate that the founding of the Yi brought with it any important increment to the already existing yangban lineages. And if dynastic change did not occasion change in the composition of the ruling class, it is not surprising that yangban entitlement remained essentially static throughout the dynasty. To be sure, access restriction was not so much a question of statutory as of customary law. But a variety of practices, both legal and social, kept the ruling elite apart, their lineages essentially inviolate. As the centuries passed, of course, large numbers of the burgeoning yangban population itself came to be effectively excluded from meaningful access to government position, and many eventually were submerged in the mass of the commoner population.

Even within the core of the yangban class there were the underprivileged. The foremost in this category were the clansmen of the royal house. It was a basic political doctrine of the Yi to isolate the members of the royal clan from the residual points of political power. However, those five generations or more removed from a sovereign ancestor were accorded fully equal treatment with respect to eligibility for the examinations and for public office. A second group, the illegitimate sons of yangban, were not readily permitted to sit for the examinations and were restricted in their opportunities to advance in office through other channels. Still more despised, the sons and grandsons of yangban women who had remarried were entirely disqualified from office.

On the level of the petty bureaucracy, of course, the privilege of governing was shared by another class, the "middle people" *(chungin)*. The elite component of this small group manned the technical posts which were tied in with the specialized examination courses, and another performed clerical duties, and the like, in the offices of the central government. In the provinces, a third group of *chungin* had hereditary rights to the administrative and clerical jobs in the establishments of the provincial governors and of the local magistrates. These petty bureaucrats were called the "local officials" *(hyangni)*.

There were two other broad social class groupings. The "commoners" *(sangin)* consisted, in essence, of the producers and taxpayers—the farmers, fishermen, merchants, and artisans. The "low born" *(ch'ŏnmin)* included the slaves owned privately and by the government, actors, shaman, *kisaeng* (female entertainers), and pariah groups. Members of these classes only rarely and ephemerally gained access to the ranked government offices.

The highest organ of the government was the State Council.* This was a policy organ having general powers of surveillance over all government offices and affairs. The State Council had seven members clearly divided into two groups. The top three, the High State Councillors, acted as a kind of presidium: the king often referred questions to them alone, and typically they acted independently of their colleagues in presenting views or proposals to the king. Long-term tenancy was the ideal and, to a large extent, the norm of appointments to High State Councillor position. To become a High State Councillor was one of the chief glories to which an official might aspire. Such an appointment, ordinarily, was the culmination of a lifetime of public service.

The four lower State Councillors, on the other hand, had little more than nominal importance. Most frequently, officials would alternate between Board Minister (see below) or comparable posts

---

*The Korean terms for the posts and offices of the government are in Appendix A.

and the lower rungs of the State Council; tenure was shorter than for the High State Councillors. Moreover, since policy matters were handled largely by the High State Councillors and since there were no administrative responsibilities, these posts tended to be regarded as dignified sinecures. On the other hand, nominations to fill vacancies among the High State Councillors almost always were made from among those who had served in the lower State Councillor positions.

In the early period of the dynasty, Merit Subjects predominated in the High State Councillor positions. Only three of twenty men who occupied such posts during the first three reigns, a period of twenty-six years, and again but three among thirty-five High State Councillors in the period from Tanjong through Sŏngjong, 1452-1494, were not Merit Subjects. In the intervening period, the thirty-four years of the reigns of Sejong and Munjong, the reverse situation obtained but this, no doubt, was largely because by that time most of the Merit Subjects enrolled earlier in the dynasty had passed from the scene. Similar reasoning probably explains why a majority of the High State Councillors under Yŏnsangun, Sŏngjong's successor, were not Merit Subjects.[10]

The chief administrative organs were the Six Boards. In brief, the Board of Personnel had charge of nominations for office, of certification of appointments, rank, and titles, of evaluation of the performance of office holders, of special procedures for recruiting personnel, and the like. The Board of Taxation was responsible for taking censuses and maintaining population registers, for making land surveys and keeping land registers, for collection of taxes and disbursement of government funds, and for administration of grain storehouse and transport systems. The Board of Rites handled problems of foreign relations, the administration of the school and examination systems, the licensing of Buddhist monks, and the conduct of a wide variety of state ceremonies. The Board of War was concerned with all matters pertaining to the military establishment, including personnel recruitment, supply, post roads, the beacon fire communications system, fortifications, weapons production, and special police and security problems. The Board of Punishments functioned more as judge and prison administrator than as public prosecutor; both civil and criminal cases fell within its purview. The Board of Works had charge of construction and repair of public buildings, bridges, and roads, of state mining and lumbering activities, and of the production of articles for state use by corps of artisans.

The activities of each board were directed by three officials of ministerial grade; the Board of War also had a Fourth Minister. In practice, however, responsibility for day to day operations tended to fall upon the young, lower-ranking Section Chiefs and Assistant Section Chiefs who supervised the clerical forces of the three or four functional units into which each Board was divided. This situation developed because the ministerial officials often were reassigned after a tour of duty of only two or three months, or even less.

In Sejo's reign (1455-1468) an important change occurred in administrative procedure. The early practice of the dynasty had been to make the operations of the Six Boards distinctly subject to the supervision of the State Council. That is, except for a few categories of highly urgent matters, the Six Boards were not authorized to present their business directly to the king but, rather, approached the throne through the State Council. This supervisory power of the State Council was called *sŏsa*. Upon complaints of arbitrary exercise of authority, T'aejong had stripped the State Council of this power, but it was restored some two decades later by Sejong. Moreover, because Tanjong, a mere boy, was unable personally to assume direction of the government, the general supervisory power of the State Council was reconfirmed at that time and, in fact, was defined in stronger terms.

There had to be a correlation, of course, between the power exercised by the State Council and that wielded by the king. Under a young or weak monarch, a preponderance of the power of decision might well rest with the High State Councillors, but a strong ruler would tend to seize the reins directly. Sejo, who had had an unparalleled opportunity as Chief State Councillor to assess the significance of the *sŏsa* power, abolished it shortly after assuming the throne. Accordingly, the Six Boards regained the privilege of direct access to the king on nearly all matters. The Six Boards retained this privilege—and in this sense the State Council remained enfeebled—for some sixty years, a period including all but the last three or four years covered by the present study. Under Chungjong, then, in 1516, the *sŏsa* power once more was restored to the State Council. But it seems that, at this late date, the reform was of little practical consequence.[11]

One may speculate that, in acting to enhance his royal authority at the expense of the State Council, Sejo may have dealt a serious blow to an important principle of sound administrative procedure. The right of direct access to the throne, after all, placed the Six Boards on an equal footing with the State Council. The seemingly equal rights of all the major organs of the government to present their views directly to the king and, more than that, the apparent equal rights in this regard of superior and subordinate within a single office are both conspicuous features of the period under study. Is it not possible that the winning of this privilege by the Six Boards opened the way for other organs to win it too? Some evidence will appear in later pages indicating that the right of a subordinate official publicly to offer views disapproved by his superior came to be acknowledged first in the early years of Sŏngjong. Certainly, at the least, the weakening of the supervisory power of the State Council was conducive to administrative chaos when the throne was occupied by a weak king.

The Royal Secretariat, as its name implies, processed all communications to and from the king. There were six royal secretaries, all of the same rank (Senior Third Rank). Each of the six had charge of matters concerning a particular one of the Six Boards. Because of their close proximity to the throne and because their duties acquainted them widely with the operations of the government, the officials of the Royal Secretariat came to have a policy role as well. Policy matters of lesser import, or procedural questions, often would be referred by the king directly to his royal secretaries. Two recorders in the Royal Secretariat acted, in effect, as historians of the day to day activities of the government, for the diaries they kept constituted one of the most important sources for the compilation of the *Sillok*.

The Office of the Inspector-General (OIG), on paper, was charged with criticizing public policy, scrutinizing the conduct of the officialdom, rectifying mores, redressing public wrongs, and preventing forgery and fraudulent misuse of public credentials. The Office of the Censor-General (OCG), on the other hand, was authorized to offer remonstrance to the king and to lodge complaints against office holders. This differentiation of functions, rather fine in theory, never was observed in practice. The two offices together took under surveillance all aspects of royal, official, and popular (principally yangban) conduct and mores. The OIG and OCG frequently presented their views jointly and, indeed, they came to be known by a single term inclusive of them both, *taegan,* which I have translated as Censorate.

There were six important posts in the OIG, ranging in rank from the Junior Second Rank of the Inspector-General to the Senior Fifth Rank of the two Fourth Inspectors. In addition, there was a large group of Bailiffs, for the OIG possessed certain police and judicial powers. The OCG was a slightly lower ranking office: the five Censors were headed by a Censor-General, who held Senior Third Rank. The positions of Inspector-General and Censor-General, being of high rank, were filled by experienced officials with a considerable record of public service behind them. Indeed, at critical junctures it was not unknown for a Sixth or Seventh State Councillor or a Board Minister to be reas-signed for a time as Inspector-General. The lower Censorate posts, however, most frequently were given to much younger men in the initial stages of their government careers. It was by no means un-common for those who had passed the final civil examination course only three or four years earlier to receive appointments as Fourth Censors or Fourth Inspectors. In fact, on occasion, preferment to Censorate position was won still more quickly than this.

One key function that the OIG and OCG exercised jointly was a limited kind of veto power over all appointments to civil and military offices below the Fourth Rank. In accordance with a procedure known as *sŏgyŏng,* a document bearing the name, lineage, and career data of each such appointee was submitted to the Censorate for endorsement, and if the Censorate officials failed to give their approval within fifty days, the appointment would be rescinded (see 1426.9.4, 1494.3.23).

There was another agency that often functioned, in fact, as a censoring organ. This was the Office of Special Counselors (OSC). A late addition to the office system, the OSC was established only in the ninth year of Sŏngjong (1478). Its prescribed duties were various: it was the repository for the government's holdings of books and thus served as a kind of state reference library; it under-took an assortment of specialized literary tasks, such as the composition of royal epitaphs and eulogies and the compilation of state-sponsored texts of many kinds; it served as a panel of advisers to the king on questions of policy or principle, calling to his attention, for example, the lessons of history or the precepts of orthodox Chinese writers.

There were seventeen primary duty posts in the OSC, the chief of which (Senior Third Rank) I have rendered as First Counselor and the lowest of which I have called Ninth Counselor (Senior Ninth Rank). Since twelve of these seventeen positions carried Senior Fifth Rank or less, it is obvious that a majority of the Special Counselors would be younger officials not long since embarked on their careers. Above the First Counselor were three positions filled concurrently by high officials whose primary duties lay elsewhere. The highest of these was always one of the High State Councillors, while the other two appear to have been chosen for their literary craftsmanship; none of the three exercised supervision over the activities of the Counselors.

The most significant feature of the OSC was that the entire roster of Counselors occupied, *ex officio,* positions in the Office of the Royal Lectures. The words employed in the National Code to define the sole function of this office might be rendered "to elucidate and discuss the conceptions" of Chinese and Korean classical texts.[12] In practice, however, the study of texts was a subsidiary activity at the sessions of the Royal Lectures. A session might begin with the reading and exposition of a specific text that had been selected for study, but it was a simple matter to relate the text under discussion to a topic of current significance, much as a Biblical passage is elaborated in a sermon. A Royal Lectures session, then, was tantamount to an extraordinary audience, at which the actual order of business was to debate the issues of the day. When this institution was functioning under optimum conditions, it was the major means through which the participating officials could offer remonstrance or present to the king their views on current policy questions.

The posts in the Office of the Royal Lectures were occupied by a broad spectrum of the officialdom. The three Directors of the office were always the High State Councillors, while six Deputy and Second Deputy Directors appear usually to have been chosen from among the other State Councillors and the Six Boards Ministers. The seven positions of Participant were filled by the Royal Secretaries and the OSC First Counselor, while the other Special Counselors served in the lower Royal Lectures posts. In addition, there was created the position of Special Participant, by which means officials whose duty posts were not privileged in this regard, or who did not hold duty posts at all, might be permitted to attend sessions of the Royal Lectures. Often these were Merit Subjects or leading military officials.

Ideally, Royal Lectures sessions were held three times each day, in the morning, at noon, and in the afternoon. Kings differed, of course, in their willingness to make themselves available so frequently. Sŏngjong and Chungjong, on the whole, faithfully convened these daily sessions, but Yŏnsangun attended more and more sporadically until, finally, he entirely abolished the office. Those who held concurrent positions in the Office of the Royal Lectures might attend all three daily sessions, and, in addition, the Censorate was authorized to participate in the morning and afternoon meetings.

This aspect of the Royal Lectures institution, the participation of the Censorate, doubtless was a major factor in the development of the Office of Special Counselors into an organ of remonstrance. Here on a single stage, which was used as a major forum for the offering of remonstrance, the OSC was brought frequently together with the two components of the Censorate. Possessed of a broad mandate to "advise" the king, it was inevitable that the OSC should present its views, solicited or not, on the questions raised by the censoring officials. Consequently, the officials of the OSC, although they did not normally initiate remonstrance, came to regard themselves as the arbiter of the Censorate's words and, in fact, the king often cast them in this role. On the whole, the OSC upheld the viewpoint of the Censorate, often endorsing its recommendations in still more strong and sweeping words than the Censorate had used. In time, this most vital function of the Office of Special Counselors was recognized by the creation of a single term *(samsa)* to designate collectively the OIG, OCG, and OSC; in my own usage, the terms "censoring organs" and "censoring bodies" are meant to subsume all three of these offices of remonstrance.

The State Tribunal was a judicial organ which concerned itself largely with crimes of serious moment committed by the yangban class. It could be activated only by the express command of the king and its function was to try the criminal cases he referred to it. In cases of major dimensions, such as purges or treason, the four Magistrates on the small permanent staff of the State Tribunal were supplemented by *ad hoc* Investigation Officers selected from among the highest ranks of officialdom. After conducting interrogations and completing the investigative process, they would don the ermine and recommend sentence to the king.

A few of the more important among the many other civil offices of the central government deserve brief mention. The Office of Royal Decrees was essentially a stenographic agency: its diarists recorded the discussions at the Royal Lectures and other exchanges between the king and his officials. The function of the Office of Diplomatic Correspondence was to draft, edit, calligraph, and record documents pertaining to Chosŏn's foreign intercourse. The Bureau of State Records served as a national archives and, in its aspect as the nucleus of the occasional Veritable Records Office, it was largely responsible for the compilation of the *Sillok*. The Bureau of Slave Administration maintained records on the slave population. The Crown Prince Tutorial Office undertook the education of the heir-apparent. The Royal House Administration had charge of issuing documents and maintaining records pertaining to the immediate royal family, and the Merit Awards Administration performed the same function for the Merit Subjects. There were also agencies which similarly acted in the interests of the clansmen of the king, the royal sons-in-law, and the Minor Merit Subjects. The Seoul Magistracy performed a multitude of duties connected with the administration of the capital area, and it possessed important judicial and police powers. There was also a Kaesŏng Magistracy, which, as in the case of Seoul, was independent of the provincial administration.

Local administration in Chosŏn was tied in closely with the central government apparatus. There were but two major levels of local government: the eight provinces and the county or similar units into which the provinces were divided. These provincial subdivisions differed in size and in the political status assigned to them, but none was administratively subordinate to another. Four, one at each major compass point, were designated by a term that I have rendered as Special Capital *(sogyŏng),* 4 as Special City *(taedohobu),* 20 as City *(mok,* translated Island in the case of Cheju), 44 as Town *(tohobu),* 82 as Great County *(kun),* 34 as County *(hyŏn,* governed by a *hyŏllyŏng),* and 141 as Small County *(hyŏn,* governed by a *hyŏn'gam)*.[13] The chief officers of these units, all of whom I have called Magistrates, were despatched from Seoul as were the provincial governors and a few other categories of officials having specialized functions. Among these latter were the army and navy commanders of each province and their principal subordinates.

For purposes of military administration the country was divided into five military commands. Each of these was responsible for garrisoning both a part of Seoul and a fixed provincial area. Overall responsibility was assumed by a small headquarters group in Seoul, the Five Military Commands Headquarters. The palace guards were under a separate command.

The highest ranking military agency was one which had no assigned duties, and this is why I have called it the Office of Ministers-without-Portfolio. Its table of organization provided sinecure positions for twenty-four officials of Senior Third Rank and above. Although these were military posts, a majority of the Ministers-without-Portfolio probably always were civil officials. The assignment of civil officials to military posts such as these was only a question of routine paperwork, and the Office of Ministers-without-Portfolio served as a convenient siding onto which an official might be honorably shunted. Men whose services in major civil duty posts were no longer wanted—for example, because of Censorate attack—frequently were eased out by this means.

The primacy of the civil official is a conspicuous feature of the office system of the Yi dynasty. This was largely due to the Confucian bias of the Yi, but it probably also reflected apprehensions stemming from the unfortunate experiences of Koryŏ, which had suffered through nearly a century of arbitrary rule by a succession of military strongmen. Certainly, the prestige and career opportunities of the civil official were markedly greater than those of his military colleague. Although military officials might legitimately aspire to such leading civil posts as those in the State Council and the Six Boards, not many succeeded in attaining them. Certain other offices were virtually or entirely closed to them—for example, the Royal Secretariat, the Censorate, and the Office of Special Counselors. On the other hand, nearly all of the important military posts were accessible to the civil officials. For instance, in the period of this study, there appears to have been an increasing incidence of appointment of civil officials as provincial army and navy commanders. The principle of civil primacy was institutionalized in the Board of War, which was a civil agency staffed most of the time by civil officials. The superior status of the civil official, to say nothing of his attitude of superiority, aroused considerable resentment among the military men, who on occasion gave vent to their feelings in acts of violence.

The most important method of recruitment of both civil and military officials was the government service examination *(kwagŏ)*. In brief summary, the candidate of the civil examinations, which were held regularly once in three years, was required to pass through two examination courses. The preliminary or lower course led to Literary Licentiate *(chinsa)* and Classics Licentiate *(saengwŏn)* degrees which, essentially, differed only in the emphasis of the examination questions. In the first stage of this course, seven hundred candidates were taken in examinations held locally and, in the second stage administered in Seoul, one hundred *chinsa* and one hundred *saengwŏn* degrees were awarded. The higher civil service examination course, for which licentiate degree holders among others were qualified, was conducted in three stages. In examinations held at the province level, 240 candidates were passed and next, at the Board of Rites in Seoul, about thirty-three were taken. These then proceeded to a third examination, held in the presence of the king, at which only the final ranking of the successful candidates was determined. Greater stress was placed on literary skill—on the ability to compose Chinese prose and poetry in a variety of stylized formats—in the higher examination course than on erudition in the Chinese Classics and other standard Chinese texts.

In addition to the regular triennial event, extraordinary examinations were held at other times under a variety of designations which are combined in the term "special examination" *(pyŏlsi)*. Normally, fewer candidates were accepted in these but, on the other hand, they were held with gradually increasing frequency as the dynasty grew older. In the two centuries from 1392 to the Hideyoshi invasion, nearly 4,200 men passed the higher civil examination, an average of 21 per year. But in the first sixty years of the dynasty, up to the reign of Tanjong, the yearly average was only about 15. Under Sejo the rate rose sharply to 26, probably representing a conscious attempt on his part to counteract the bad taste left by his usurpation. Then the rate dropped back to 18 under Sŏngjong but climbed again, to 21 and 24 respectively, in the reigns of Yŏnsangun and Chungjong. Again it fell slightly under Myŏngjong before soaring to 28 during the first twenty-five years of Sŏnjo.

Since the factor of the regular triennial examinations remained essentially constant, the accelerating number of successful candidates was in consequence of the special examinations. The average number who passed one of these examinations increased very little, holding fairly steady at around 15, but the special examinations came to be given more and more frequently. Whereas Sejong, for example, held only 7 special examinations in 32 years on the throne, Sejo averaged one in each year of his reign, and this rate was matched, or nearly so, under later kings.[14]

Military examinations were administered similarly to the civil, under the supervision of the Board of War. In a typical triennial examination, 28 candidates passed the final course. Special military examinations accompanied each special civil examination and, indeed, the numbers who passed often exceeded those who were successful in the counterpart civil examination.

One encounters occasional complaints of corrupt practices but, on the whole, in the early years of the dynasty the examination system appears to have been administered with admirable integrity. Evidence is not lacking, however, to indicate that a subtle form of favoritism sometimes was shown. For example, the sons of high officials and of Merit Subjects—and, on occasion, Merit Subjects themselves—seem to have been successful in the civil examinations in disproportionate numbers. No doubt this was still more the case with respect to the military examinations.

The government administered a school system as an adjunct of the examination system. The National Academy in Seoul was the highest preparatory school for the civil examination course. Its staff positions, of course, were an integral part of the office system. Although neither the supervisory nor the teaching posts in the National Academy were of particularly high rank, they carried considerable prestige, both because of the great importance attached to the educational process and because, being regarded as junior or apprentice members of the officialdom, the students constituted a political force of no mean potential. Enrollment in the National Academy was limited to 200 students, nearly all of whom held licentiate degrees. The National Academy was the site of the National Confucian Shrine, which honored the canonized elite among the Chinese and Korean Confucian sages.

In the provinces were the "local schools" *(hyanggyo)*, one in every sub-provincial administrative unit. The number of students admitted to these ranged from ninety down to thirty, depending upon the classification of the unit as a city, town, or county. Identical with the *hyanggyo* as training grounds for aspirants to a licentiate degree were the four colleges in Seoul, each of which had an authorized enrollment of 100.

The Military Training Administration provided schooling for military examination candidates. In addition, there were technical schools, each attached to an appropriate government organ, which trained those who sat for the various specialized examination courses. Among these were schools teaching foreign languages, medicine, astronomy, and law.

The examination system constituted the principal avenue to government position but not the only one. Chief among the alternate approaches was the "protection" route. This was a means of rewarding men who had rendered meritorious service to the state by giving office to their sons or other descendants. Merit Subjects were the most numerous beneficiaries of such rewards, followed by those related by marriage to the reigning line. There were others, too, such as men honored as Confucian sages or as officials of "perfect probity." Another recruiting procedure was aimed at availing the state of the services of "idle-literati" *(yuil chi sa),* those learned or virtuous Confucianists who had eschewed government careers. By and large, personnel recruited by either of these methods were relegated to peripheral posts of lower rank. A few might attain the middle reaches of the official hierarchy and a very few (in particular, kinsmen of a queen) might attain eminence. But, for most, to hold positions of any real importance in the government it was necessary to pass the civil or military examinations, especially the former.

Two years before he founded his dynasty, Yi Sŏng-gye arranged for a dramatic burning of the Koryŏ land registers and a sweeping reform of the corrupt land-holding system. His own regime, of course, adopted these reforms, the underlying principle of which was state ownership. On this basis, land was allocated to the royal house, to the organs of the central and local governments, to officialdom, and to the military establishment. The farmer-conscript was bound to the land by the stipulation that he might not alienate his tenant right, which, at the same time, was to be guaranteed against despoliation.

According to who held the right of tax collection, land under the Yi was divided into two basic categories. Taxes on public land *(kongjŏn)*—lands allocated, for example, for the maintenance of the palace and the agencies of the central and local administrations—were collected directly by the government. In the case of private land *(sajŏn),* the collection of taxes was entrusted to the royal clansmen, the individual officials, the Merit Subjects, and others, to whom the land had been assigned. These landholders would keep the bulk of the taxes themselves, passing on a small percentage to the central government.

Subsumed within the category of private land was a variety of specific types of land, designated in accordance with the use made of the land or the income from the land. Rank land *(kwajŏn)* yielded stipends to the members of the official class (including, of course, members of the royal clan) on the basis of their personal rank, regardless of whether they held office or not. Merit Subject land *(kongsinjŏn)* rewarded those enrolled on the several merit rosters. Special award land *(pyŏlsajŏn)* was given in instances of individual merit, such as that accruing from a successful embassy to China or from reporting a treason plot.

In original concept, these three types of land were to be entirely located in the capital district, that is, in Kyŏnggi province, for land throughout the rest of the country was earmarked as public land. However, there soon developed unexpectedly heavy drains on the land resources of Kyŏnggi. Merit Subject land had been recognized from the outset to be hereditary, and it had been awarded with both frequency and generosity. Moreover, although not hereditary in principle, grants of rank land and special award land were often accorded exceptional consideration and in this way tended to be removed from state control.

Consequently, already in the reign of T'aejong it had become necessary to divert land in the three southern provinces (Kyŏngsang, Chŏlla, Ch'ungch'ŏng) to use as rank land. This innovation, however, did not affect the root evil of alienation of land from state to private ownership, and so it proved to be of no avail. A few years later, under Sejo, the rank land concept was scrapped and was replaced by a post land *(chikchŏn)* system. As the term suggests, the beneficiaries of this plan were limited to actual office holders. Furthermore, rather than allow an official to receive his income in the form of taxes he himself collected, the government now acted as collector and paid the appropriate salary from the proceeds. The post land system was effective for a while, but from the time of Chungjong (1506-1544) once again a shortage developed in the amount of land available to the government for the payment of stipends to its officials.

Even from so brief a presentation it is evident, I think, that the early Yi dynasty was ripe for political conflict. Our attention has been drawn both to factors that might lie at the root of factional strife and to others that might determine the form such conflict would take. The system of land holding had been corrupted from the start. Land, the major form of wealth—almost the only form of wealth—had become increasingly concentrated in a few hands. Furthermore, these same hands, insofar as they belonged to Merit Subjects, had reached out to grasp the reins of political power. At the same time, however, the major instruments through which they might exercise political power had been seriously weakened.

Meanwhile, new aspirants to public office were being processed through the examination system in ever greater numbers. Their claims to preferment rested not alone on birthright but also on a different sort of merit principle, for they were the elite of a Confucian educational process. If economic affluence should prove unattainable, perhaps it would not matter to many of these men, who were of the third and fourth generations to be indoctrinated with Confucian morality. At any rate, whatever a young official's ambitions, he might best realize them through a career in public office, for this was the chief avenue to economic well-being, social prestige, and self-fulfillment. Moreover, the political system of the early Yi dynasty offered extraordinary media through which young and dedicated—or simply ambitious—officials might make a bid for power. The conflict resulting from such a bid for power is the central theme of the history of the fifty years from 1469 to 1519.

Chapter II

THE PURGE OF 1498

The twenty-five year reign of Sŏngjong (1469-1494) is most widely remembered for the great compilation and publication enterprises that the king zealously pushed forward. Such basic texts as the *Tongguk t'onggam* (General chronicle of Korea), *Tongguk yŏji sŭngnam* (Gazetteer of Korea), *Akhak kwebŏm* (Guide to the study of music), and *Tongmun sŏn* (Selections from Korean literature) belong to this period. Movable type was freshly cast in improved models, and a spate of literature was published in this way. The momentum supplied by the efforts of Sejong and Sejo was sustained in other spheres as well. The creation of the Office of Special Counselors and the Hall of Reading essentially brought to completion the political structuring of the new dynasty. Military expeditions to the northern frontier, in particular the effort led by Hŏ Chong in 1491, permanently solidified Korea's hold upon this troublesome area of the Korean peninsula.

Noteworthy as these achievements were, they give no hint of the political ferment for which Sŏngjong's reign is most remarkable. For in this quarter century there appeared a challenge to the system of government that had been established by the new dynasty, a system that, while claiming the sanction of Chinese Confucian doctrine, inevitably had been modified by the realities of practical administration, the Korean aristocratic tradition, and the hard facts of universal human frailty.

The vehicles of the challenge to the system were those organs of the central government entrusted with the power of remonstrance, that is, the Office of the Inspector-General, the Office of the Censor-General, and the Office of Special Counselors. The challenge was offered by the young, newly emerged literati who occupied a preponderance of the posts in these offices. Their challenge was directed at the older, experienced, higher echelons of the government, which then were peopled by a substantial carry-over of Sejo's right-hand men, by men closely related by marriage to the royal house, and by numerous others who owed their affluence to their somewhat fortuitous inclusion on one or more of the five state merit award lists which had been promulgated in the twenty years encompassing the reigns of Tanjong, Sejo, and Yejong, and the first years of Sŏngjong. Men of this background held all of the higher posts of government at the outset of Sŏngjong's reign. True, there were outstanding men of letters or scholars among them, but these too were first of all practical statesmen. They were accustomed to dominating government deliberations and having their advice stand or fall on its merits in the eyes of the king alone. They were now to find almost their every move challenged by their juniors, very often successfully, and their character and integrity frequently laid open to question. As a result, the concept of executive responsibility lost much of its validity, to be replaced by a kind of committee system of government in which the dominant voice was that of the censoring bodies.

Such a shift in the center of political authority could not have developed without the compliance, however unwitting, of the sovereign. Sŏngjong clearly subscribed to a broad definition of the function of remonstrance and exhibited a generous tolerance of the practice of it. It may be conjectured that his eminent predecessors on the Korean throne would not have countenanced the threat to sound administrative doctrine posed by the censoring power as it developed under Sŏngjong. In fact, his successor made first an oblique attack, then a massive frontal assault on the principle of remonstrance that Sŏngjong upheld and on the practices of remonstrance that Sŏngjong encouraged by his indulgence.

Sŏngjong's different orientation no doubt is ascribable in part to a different character, but the unusual set of circumstances surrounding his occupancy of the throne contain a more satisfactory explanation of his attitudes. Sŏngjong was but twelve years old when he succeeded his uncle, Yejong, who had reigned for little more than a year. Unlike his grandfather, Sejo, Sŏngjong did not owe his throne to his own enterprise or to that of his partisans. He was under no overriding obligation to any group or individual in the government. Accordingly he displayed an unusual degree of impartiality in his relationships with his officials and tended to bring an open mind to judgments of their character and ability.

More important still, Sŏngjong became the most thoroughly Confucian in outlook of all the Yi dynasty monarchs up to his day. This is perhaps surprising in view of the pronounced eclecticism displayed by Sejong and Sejo. To be sure, neither of them was lukewarm in his belief in Confucian precepts as the basis of good government. Nor were they lax in undertaking projects that stimulated learning and the literary arts, in particular those modeled after products of the Neo-Confucian influence in China. While Sŏngjong carried on this worthy tradition, he would devote no effort to enterprises (like Sejo's publication of Buddhist sutras) that could not be justified in terms of Confucian orthodoxy.

Finally, Sŏngjong was disposed to accept without question significant restraints upon his conduct and the exercise of his authority. While these restraints were inherent in the monarchic institution in Korea, they were subject to variation in degree and were not always tolerated by kings of different philosophy or experience. Sŏngjong, however, had been in the unique position of a boy sovereign. He had not awaited the succession through long years of idleness and pleasure seeking but, rather, had been impelled unexpectedly to the throne by his uncle's early death at the age of nineteen. Sŏngjong thus grew up as a king, under the regency of his grandmother. And in his formal education, Confucian in content and administered by Confucian scholar-officials, there must have been more than a normal sense of direction and urgency.

These factors combined to produce a favorable climate for the censoring organs to perform their functions on an enlarged scale. The sovereign's modest conception of kingship created a power vacuum that the censoring bodies rushed to fill. Since many of the protests of the censoring organs were based on Confucian premises and directed at non-Confucian targets, the sovereign generally was disposed to accept them. This particularly was the case with respect to Censorate views on the utilization of personnel.

Given these advantages, it was perhaps inevitable that the censoring organs should use them in a bid to become arbiters of the conduct of government affairs, and that such an attempt would encounter bitter opposition and engender bitter conflict. The history of the twenty year period preceding the Purge of 1498 is the story of this conflict; the Purge of 1498 is its first great denouement.

The 1478 Case: The Censorate Asserts Itself

In a footnote to the Purge of 1498 the *Sillok* historians conclude:

The more sophisticated sighed to themselves and said: In the 1478 criminal case the righteous attacked the evil clique; in the 1498 criminal case the evil clique brought down the righteous. In those twenty years one victory and one defeat, then chaos followed. What a pity! The administration of punishments by men of principle always errs on the side of magnanimity. The vengeful spirits of amoral men must be destroyed . . . If the men of principle had been able to apply the full measure of the law in 1478, then how could today's catastrophe have arisen? (1498.7.29 S)

The 1478 case *(musul chi ok),* which "the more sophisticated" observers pointed to as providing the proper perspective for appraising the Purge of 1498, is the first great instance of political strife in Sŏngjong's reign.[1] The detailed background of the case, involving charges of rape (or forced cohabitation) by one unimportant yangban against another, which charges apparently were prompted by the property interests at stake, need not concern us. The important point is that the First Royal Secretary at the time (mid-1477), Hyŏn Sŏk-kyu, was convinced of the error of the plaintiffs and concurred in the judgment of the State Tribunal that the defendant was guilty of no worse than fornication, or illegal marriage (the woman involved was a widow of the yangban class). The plaintiffs were charged with making false accusations. When his five subordinates in the Royal Secretariat memorialized asking that proceedings against the plaintiffs for false accusation be stopped,[2] Hyŏn Sŏk-kyu was vastly annoyed and, in a face to face session, castigated Sixth Royal Secretary Hong Kwi-dal for holding an erroneous view and especially for exceeding his authority in presenting his view to the king (1477.7.8 S, 7.9 S, 7.12 S, 7.17 S).

Hong Kwi-dal, refusing to back down, once again memorialized his view and was followed the next day by Second Royal Secretary Yi Kŭk-ki. Hyŏn Sŏk-kyu angrily counterattacked, whereupon Censor-General Son Pi-jang requested judicial proceedings against Hong Kwi-dal and the other Royal Secretaries on suspicion of taking bribes. Because of the arrogance of Hong Kwi-dal's deposition he was stripped of his office warrants, and the king then disposed of the other aspects of the case by approving sentences against both the plaintiffs and the accused couple (1477.7.8 S, 7.9 S, 7.12 S, 7.14 S, 7.16 S, 7.17 S).

But a new dimension already had been added to the case when Censor-General Son Pi-jang and his colleagues reported the rumor then afoot that Hyŏn Sŏk-kyu had humiliated Hong Kwi-dal by the use of undecorous language during the reprimand noted above. Hyŏn Sŏk-kyu denied this and the king accepted his word.[3] Sŏngjong then attempted to ascertain the source of the allegation of breach of etiquette against Hyŏn, and traced it to the Third Royal Secretary Im Sa-hong, who had claimed that he personally witnessed the scene (1477.7.17 S).

Hyŏn and Im, both married to granddaughters of a brother of Sejong and both men of formidable talent and repute, now confronted each other, the one accusing and the other denying. This called forth repeated Censorate requests that both Hyŏn and Im be punished for giving way to such unseemly altercation in the royal presence. Sŏngjong firmly refused to do this, but finally, in an attempt to break the deadlock, he resolved to transfer Im Sa-hong and two of the other Royal Secretaries to other posts of equal grade (1477.7.23 S, 7.24 S, 8.15 S, 8.16 S, 8.17 S).[4] Naturally this action was attacked (by officials in the Office of the Inspector-General and by Third Censor An Ch'im) as unfair, since it left Hyŏn alone among the disputants in his original post (1477.8.18 S, 8.19 S, 8.20 S). Moreover, an influential Merit Subject, Lord of Muryŏng Yu Cha-gwang, denounced Hyŏn for the crime of shaming a colleague (1477.8.23 S).

Under mounting pressure, the king finally transferred Hyŏn, but to the higher ranking post of Inspector-General. Then, when the Censorate objected, he named Hyŏn to the still higher position of Minister of Punishments (1477.8.26, 8.27, 8.29). But the Censorate refused to be cowed and presently Fourth Inspector Kim Ŏn-sin launched an extremely violent attack on Hyŏn, comparing him to Lu Ch'i and Wang An-shih[5] and calling him a genuinely amoral man. Yu Cha-gwang chimed in in similar vein. Sŏngjong then summoned the entire body of former State Councillors and incumbent high officials, all of whom concurred in the verdict that Hyŏn was not an amoral man. Accordingly the king jailed Kim Ŏn-sin and steadfastly ignored continuing Censorate demands that criminal charges be laid against Hyŏn Sŏk-kyu (1477.8.30, 9.5, 9.8).[6]

For some months the issue lay dormant. Neither of the chief protagonists had been hurt up to this point. Hyŏn Sŏk-kyu indeed had gained promotion. Im Sa-hong had been transferred without prejudice, from one Senior Third Rank post to another, and he continued to be named to posts of this level.[7] But within less than a year from the time of his wrangle with Hyŏn Sŏk-kyu, Im was banished to the provinces, charged with the crime of clique-forming, and his father was dismissed from office under charges of greed and corruption.

Im Sa-hong was married to a granddaughter of the second son of T'aejong, but this was not his only tie to the royal house. One son, Im Kwang-jae, was the husband of the daughter of Yejong, and another son, Im Sung-jae, was to be the consort of a daughter of Sŏngjong. Im was early famed for his literary talent and was especially noted for his ability in oral and documentary Chinese. After passing the civil examination in 1466 he had risen steadily in the official hierarchy.

Im Sa-hong's father, Im Wŏn-jun, was widely read, of prodigious memory, skilled in the literary arts, and thoroughly versed in medicine and geomancy. Successively serving under six monarchs beginning with Sejong, he was accorded especial favor by Sejo and Sŏngjong. In 1471 he was enrolled as one of Sŏngjong's Merit Subjects. In office he had already reached Sixth State Councillor.

Im Sa-hong's downfall was a direct consequence of a running battle with the censoring organs on the central issue of the proper role of remonstrance in the governmental process. The personal administration of Sŏngjong began only in his seventh year as sovereign, when the regency of his grandmother (Sejo's queen, Chŏnghŭi) was terminated (1476.1.13). As the monarch's wide tolerance of remonstrance became increasingly evident, the censoring organs became bolder and more extreme in the exercise of their power. In the year preceding his ouster there were a number of noteworthy instances where the censoring organs attacked prominent figures in the government and royal household and their way of life. It was in this connection that Im Sa-hong stepped forward as the leading advocate of an opposing school of thought.

In the latter part of 1477 Fourth Censor Kwŏn Kyŏng-u admonished the king against writing poetry, on the ground that his subjects might infer a royal predilection for the literary arts as opposed to the more vital pursuit of the study of the sages. The king accepted this view and called in the poems he had written by request for his elder brother (the Great Prince of Wŏlsan) and for Han Myŏng-hoe (a Prime Merit Subject of Sejo, the most exalted elder statesman of the time, and the father-in-law of both Yejong and Sŏngjong).[8] Both recipients had had the poems carved on hanging-boards for pavilions they had erected on the Han River and naturally prized the royal gifts very highly (1477.9.28).

At the same time Third Inspector Ku Cha-p'yŏng criticized the lavishness of the newly constructed residence of Princess Hyŏnsuk, Im Sa-hong's daughter-in-law (1477.9.29 S). Im, then Censor-General, and the Inspector-General Yi Sung-wŏn reprimanded the subordinate officials in the Censorate for memorializing their individual views in this and other recent instances. The resulting intra-Censorate conflict was resolved by the transfer of the entire Censorate roster to other posts (1477.10.1 S, 10.2 S).

At the beginning of 1478, Sŏngjong set in motion plans for special rites in honor of the aged, in the course of which he was to inquire of two elder statesmen concerning the way of good government. One of these specially designated elder statesmen was the famous scholar-official Chŏng In-ji, who was also a Prime Merit Subject (1478.1.22, 1.25, 1.27). But a Third Inspector, Pak Suk-tal, citing Chŏng's notorious concern with the accumulation of wealth and property, questioned the propriety of so honoring him. When other Censorate officials also criticized the choice of Chŏng In-ji, Sŏngjong abandoned his original design and contented himself with holding a state banquet in honor of all elderly officials (1478.2.20).

But even this occasion did not pass without incident. On the day the banquet was to be held, Fourth Inspector Yi Se-gwang and Fourth Censor Sŏng Tam-nyŏn asked that Kim Su-on not be permitted to enter the National Academy, the site of the banquet, on the ground that he was a believer in Buddhism. Kim Su-on was a Great Lord (a Sŏngjong Merit Subject) and a noted scholar, but he was a younger brother of a prominent monk, firmly believed in Buddhism, and was known once to have professed a desire to become a monk. The king concurred in the view of the Censorate officials and had Kim Su-on excluded from the banquet (1478.4.3 S).

Several other instances of remonstrance figure in the background of the 1478 Case. Although unrelated one to the other, they mostly concerned the private conduct of the king, of members of the royal family, or of the high officials. These activities of the Censorate naturally roused the ire of the high officials and others against whom they were directed, but it was the memorials of Yi Sim-wŏn and Nam Hyo-on that first drew sustained fire, and from Im Sa-hong in particular.

The royal clansman Yi Sim-wŏn, writing in response to the king's "appeal for counsel,"[9] discussed the distress of the people, asking that the extravagance of the high yangban class be curbed and that forced collection of private loans by powerful families be prohibited. He also intimated that Sejo's Merit Subjects should not be employed and urged that certain "idle literati" (he named Chŏng Yŏ-ch'ang, Chŏng Kŭg-in, Kang Ŭng-jŏng, and Kyŏng Yŏn) be given responsible positions in the government (1478.4.8 S, 4.24 S).

Soon after this a student, Nam Hyo-on, in response to the same appeal for counsel, memorialized an eight-point program, the main recommendation of which was the restoration of the tomb of Tanjong's mother. He went on to request that men noted for their filial conduct (such as Kyŏng Yŏn, Im Ok-san, and Ch'oe So-ha) be employed in the government (1478.4.15).

After reading Yi Sim-wŏn's memorial, First Royal Secretary Im Sa-hong ridiculed the author as an impractical dreamer, called him a stupid and irresponsible man, and asserted that the idle literati recommended by Yi were in no case worthy of employment. Im went on to argue that the king's recent overeagerness to accept remonstrance had resulted in Censorate abuse of its prerogatives, and he urged that the Censorate's words be heeded only after careful consideration. As Im put it, "Can it be proper to adopt invariably the views of the Censorate?" And he proceeded to defend two high military officials against the attacks which shortly before had been leveled against them due to their having memorialized the king on personnel questions (1478.4.9 S). When Nam Hyo-on's memorial appeared, Im asserted that it was an echo of Yi Sim-wŏn's words, and that these two and their ilk had formed a clique under the guise of promoting Neo-Confucianism. He alluded to several instances of factional strife in Chinese history and urged that this evil not be permitted to develop in Korea (1478.4.15).

Presently Im Sa-hong spoke out in a point by point refutation of recent Censorate charges. He minimized the importance of the series of natural calamities (asserting for example that human carelessness, not the wrath of Heaven, was responsible for an outbreak of fires in the capital), argued that a ban on wine ought to be lifted in the interest of proper performance of important ceremonies and banquets, held trivial and unenforceable further restrictions on house construction, and declared that the Censorate's advice on the king's poetry and archery would lead to deterioration of the civil and military arts (1478.4.21 S).

In reply, Sŏngjong upheld the Censorate on the questions of the natural calamities, the ban on wine, and the restrictions on construction, but recalled that he had not heeded the Censorate's remonstrance against an archery party. Later the same day, Im Sa-hong reiterated that the words of the Censorate should not always be heeded and said that when improper they should be rebuked. Furthermore, he offered his view that the exclusion of Kim Su-on from the banquet in honor of the aged had been improper, since other non-Confucianists (military officials) had been permitted to attend.[10] But again the king upheld the Censorate, specifically in the matter of Kim Su-on and generally by expressing his conviction that the exercise of the censoring function was a fine thing, which ought not be hobbled by reprimand (1478.4.21 S).

A few days later Im Sa-hong was violently attacked by OSC officials headed by First Counselor Yu Chin and Office of Royal Decrees personnel led by First Diarist P'yo Yŏn-mal. They began their lengthy memorial of denunciation with: "The words of Im Sa-hong are those of the evil men of yore; the king's injunctions in reply are those of the most sage and brilliant monarchs. We cannot praise the king enough; we cannot find words to express our indignation at Im Sa-hong." They went on to compare Im with the infamous Wang An-shih and to charge him with sophistry and deceit and with scheming to suppress the Censorate, thereby to "bring ruin to the state." They further castigated Im's father as evil, unorthodox, greedy, and corrupt. They concluded with a request that the king discharge Im Sa-hong and his father from their posts and banish them, thus to fulfill popular expectations, to answer the wrath of Heaven, and to provide a warning to evil and disloyal subjects (1478.4.27 S).

But this was too much for even the tolerant Sŏngjong. He instructed the Personnel Board to discharge from their posts the entire OSC and Office of Royal Decrees rosters, twenty-one officials, on the pretext that they had lacked the courage to bring to his attention their knowledge of the evil of Im Sa-hong and Im Wŏn-jun when the two were appointed to the posts they now held. At the same time, however, he took up the office warrants of Im Sa-hong, on the ground that Im's attacks on the Censorate had constituted a serious impediment to the free function of remonstrance. On the other hand, Sŏngjong refused to inquire into the charges against Im Wŏn-jun, and he turned down the resignation Im Wŏn-jun tendered (1478.4.28 S).

It was now that the *coup de grace* was administered to Im Sa-hong. Yi Sim-wŏn, the royal clansman whose memorial had been attacked by Im, urgently sought an interview with the king. Averring that as a close kinsman of Im Sa-hong he long and well knew Im's true character,[11] Yi personally endorsed the defamatory charges against Im and his father and added that Im had been behind the attacks on Hyŏn Sŏk-kyu the previous year, and thus was responsible for the political turmoil at that time (1478.4.29 S).[12]

Sŏngjong now was convinced of the guilt of Im Sa-hong. He restored to office the OSC and Office of Royal Decrees officials he had discharged for impeaching Im. Then, after interrogation by the king himself and judicial proceedings at the State Tribunal, Im Sa-hong, Yu Cha-gwang, Pak

Hyo-wŏn, and Kim Ŏn-sin were sentenced for forming a clique and causing turmoil in the government and presently were variously banished (1478.4.29, 5.6 to 5.8).[13]

In the course of his interview with the king, Yi Sim-wŏn also had leveled charges against Im Sa-hong's father, Im Wŏn-jun. In sum, Yi asserted that Im Wŏn-jun had tried to enlist his support in a royal clan succession dispute involving properties of great value, a share of which would be inherited by Im Sa-hong's wife. But Im Wŏn-jun and the hopeful legatee (Im Sa-hong's father-in-law, Yi Sim-wŏn's grandfather) both denied the allegation, and it was impossible to determine who was speaking the truth (1478.4.29 S). At the same time, Sŏngjong summoned the OSC and Office of Royal Decrees officials and asked them their basis for terming Im Wŏn-jun villainous and corrupt. Although the replies were inconclusive, the king discharged Im Wŏn-jun from his prinicpal post of Sixth State Councillor and relieved him of his Royal Lectures post as well (1478.4.29 S, 4.30 S, 5.1 S).

The 1478 Case even now did not come to rest, for the following months saw a number of counterattacks by Im Sa-hong's family and partisans. And when his own family sided with Im, Yi Sim-wŏn was undone. His great-grandfather asked that he be charged with crime, and a son of Sejong filled the king's ear with a detailed attack on Yi Sim-wŏn's stated views (1478.5.8 S). The initial result of this was a royal instruction against members of the royal house mingling and discussing government affairs with students of the National Academy (1478.5.15). But when Yi Sim-wŏn's grandfather charged that Yi had uttered impudent and disobedient words to himself, the king consulted with members of the royal family and the officialdom and then accepted charges of unfilial conduct against Yi Sim-wŏn and had him punished by loss of office warrants and banishment (1478.9.5).[14]

An investigation of the career of Im Sa-hong over the next twenty-five years reveals that he was never free of Censorate charge and condemnation. The Censorate protested when Sŏngjong released Im from banishment in 1480 (11.14 S, 11.15 S, 11.21 S, 11.22 S) and again objected when his office warrants were restored (1486.3.6).[15] In 1488 another incident involving Im Sa-hong occurred. Im's third son, Im Hŭi-jae, who was viewed by many as deficient in knowledge and ability, nevertheless passed the provincial examination. Since one of the examination officials was a relative, the situation quite naturally aroused suspicion and the OIG lost no time in making an issue of the matter (1488.9.4, 9.23 S, 9.28 S). Im Sa-hong shortly replied in his own defense, accusing the OIG of operating on the basis of the wildest surmise, without a shred of proof. Another son, Im Kwang-jae, seized the opportunity to revile the Censorate and to protest that his father had been framed in 1478. There ensued a succession of Censorate attacks against Im Sa-hong, but the king brushed them all aside (1488.10.2 S, 10.2).[16]

Sŏngjong had long wanted to reemploy Im Sa-hong, and the happenstance that Im Wŏn-jun had successfully given medical treatment to the queen mother now provided the pretext the king felt he needed (1488.11.29 S).[17] Accordingly, late in 1488 (11.15), Im Sa-hong was appointed to the military post of Fourth Deputy Commander of the Five Military Commands. The Censorate officials insistently protested, and were joined by the OSC First Counselor. Because of this furor the king sought the advice of the highest officials of the government. Two of these, Yun Ho and Hŏ Chong, are recorded as seeing no objection to the reemployment of Im Sa-hong, a stand which brought them in turn under Censorate attack. Then, when the State Councillors memorialized that "we have no certain knowledge as to whether or not Im Sa-hong really is an amoral man," and also voiced no objection to the appointment given Im, they were accused by the Censorate and OSC of truckling to the king and of sheltering a known man of evil. Subsequently the Censor-General, An Ho, went so far as to revile these high officials with the words that their defense of Im Sa-hong was tantamount to "pointing to a deer and calling it a horse." An Ho thus accused them of willfully deceiving the sovereign, and asked judicial proceedings against them. The king was greatly angered and only with difficulty refrained from taking punitive action against the censoring organs. And he steadfastly refused to heed their arguments against Im Sa-hong (1488.11.15, 11.29 S, 11.30 S, 12.1 S).

During the ensuing ten years Im Sa-hong received several further appointments, always to somewhat peripheral posts where his acknowledged talents in the Chinese language could be put to good use. Early in the reign of Yŏnsangun he was included on a routine rank promotion list. On such occasions, however, the censoring bodies spoke out strongly against him,[18] and it was only in the aftermath of the Purge of 1504 that he was able to attain truly distinguished government posts.

Censorate versus "Marriage Kin"

Despite its unique features, the case of Im Sa-hong by no means stood in isolation, for the "marriage kin" of the reigning line were a major target of Censorate activity in this period. Traditionally such men were often accorded unusual preferment—but the censoring bodies, especially during the later years of Sŏngjong, strongly challenged this type of favoritism. One such instance of serious and prolonged conflict involved Yun Ŭl-lo, elder brother of Sŏngjong's second queen, Chŏnghyŏn.

Yun Ŭl-lo was Second Minister of Personnel when charged by the Censorate with the crime of tax conversion (1490.4.27S).[19] Although the State Tribunal charged Yun only with complicity and pronounced a comparatively light sentence, the king lightened the punishment still further. The Censorate protested, asking the full penalty of the law. At first the king would not consent, citing Yun's close relationship to the palace, but presently he admitted the justice of the Censorate's case and ordered Yun punished as requested (1490.5.10 S, 5.11 S, 6.7 S, 6.12 S, 6.17 S, 6.19 S, 6.20 S).

Three years later, however, when Yun Ŭl-lo was appointed Second Magistrate of Seoul (1493.6.27), there was a renewed outcry from the censoring organs.[20] At the same time, the Censorate extended its fire to include Yun's younger brother, T'ang-no, and their father, Yun Ho.

This was because the king had seen fit to promote Yun T'ang-no to the third grade of official rank despite the fact that he had not served the prerequisite stint as a Local Magistrate. Sŏngjong's reply, defending his promotion of Yun T'ang-no, elicited only further argument from the Censorate. The king now became enraged and, saying that this trend toward picking fault with the actions of the sovereign must not be permitted to develop, was about to initiate punitive measures against the Censorate. But such high officials as Yi Kŭk-pae, No Sa-sin, and Hŏ Chong all admonished him and concurred in the Censorate's view on the Yun T'ang-no case. So Sŏngjong finally canceled Yun T'ang-no's promotion. These same officials, however, saw no objection to Yun Ŭl-lo's appointment, and for the time being the king was able to ignore further Censorate remonstrance on the matter (1493.7.12 S to 7.16 S, 7.18 S, 7.19 S).

Yet the issue of Yun Ŭl-lo's appointment did not die, and he was destined not to enjoy his new post for long. For some three more months the censoring organs continued to raise the question at every opportunity while Sŏngjong just as firmly refused to budge (1493.7.29 S, 7.30 S, 8.1, 8.4, 8.6, 8.7, 8.10, 8.11, 8.16, 8.21, 9.1, 9.5, 10.6, 10.23, 10.30). At last, however, when the furor showed no sign of subsiding, the king yielded and transferred Yun to a non-portfolio post (1493.10.30 S, 1494.2.15).

Yun Ŭl-lo came under attack again in the following year as a result of a property suit filed by his abandoned concubine. The case is very involved, and we can spare ourselves the details.[21] The king stoutly stood his ground, but it was with the din of daily Censorate outcries still ringing in his ears that Sŏngjong took ill and died (1494.12.8 S to 12.20 S, 12.24).

Others among the marriage kin also felt the sting of Censorate shafts in the last years of Sŏngjong's reign. The Censorate and OSC held improper the appointment of Pak Wŏn-jong (the younger brother of the wife of Sŏngjong's elder brother) as a Royal Secretary, on the grounds of his youth and inexperience and because he was a product of the military examination course (1492.8.7, 8.8).[22] Yun T'ang-no was charged with arrogance in failing to punish a servant of his who had insulted a State Council First Secretary (1493.9.2 S).[23] It was urged that appointments of Yi Ch'ŏl-gyŏn (son of an elder sister of Sejo's queen) to Fourth State Councillor, Han Kŏn (nephew of Sŏngjong's mother) to Second Minister of Works, and Yun T'an (the queen's uncle) to Governor of Ch'ungch'ŏng province be rescinded on various charges of ineptitude and unrectitude (1493.10.23, 10.29, 10.30, 11.3, 11.18).

This was part of a multi-pronged OIG indictment, the general themes of which were the over-weening arrogance of the houses of the marriage kin and the errors in use of personnel exhibited in recent appointments, especially of such marriage kin. It was on the heels of this memorial that Third State Councillor Hŏ Chong was moved to voice his personal concern over the baneful effect of remonstrance as practiced by the Censorate of his day. In Hŏ's view the Censorate by its choice of the weapon of vituperation and the target of the higher levels of officialdom was successfully assuming a role in governmental deliberations equal to that of the highest officials themselves. Hŏ

Chong concluded with the observation: "In the more than thirty years of Sejong's reign not even once were heard the designations of 'man of principle' or 'amoral man.' This phenomenon existed of old in the Sung dynasty; it is an extremely unlovely practice" (1493.11.3).

The Censorate continued its attacks on marriage kin under the new king. The appointment of Sin Su-gǔn (elder brother of Yǒnsangun's queen) as Second Royal Secretary (1495.5.11) was especial anathema because he was a holder of the military examination degree and because it was widely understood that the young king secretly consulted Sin before rendering decisions on important problems of the day (1495.1.7, 5.11, 5.25). Sin's further elevation to First Royal Secretary again drew immediate Censorate request for rescission (1497.6.14, 6.15, 6.28, 7.3). But Yǒnsangun paid no heed, and it was as First Royal Secretary that Sin Su-gǔn played a prominent part in the initial stages of the Purge of 1498.[24]

The Censorate versus High State Councillors

Perhaps the most significant effort of the censoring organs in the years preceding the Purges of 1498 and 1504 was directed not against the royal in-law families but against the highest officials in the land, and indeed against the sovereign himself. Instances of this already have been noted in connection with the affairs of Im Sa-hong, Yun Ǔl-lo, and others. This conflict between the censoring organs on the one hand and, principally, the State Council and palace on the other greatly increased in intensity during the late years of Sǒngjong and first years of his successor. The Yun P'il-sang and No Sa-sin cases provide the best illustrations of this struggle.

Yun P'il-sang, a kinsman of Sǒngjong's second queen (her father's cousin's son), passed the civil examination in 1450, and won military renown in the crushing of the Yi Si-ae rebellion (1467) and in the joint Ming Chinese-Chosǒn campaign to pacify the Chien-chou region (1479). He was both a Sejo-Pacification and a Sǒngjong Merit Subject. In 1478 he was named Third State Councillor, the next year rose to Second State Councillor, and in 1485 was appointed Chief State Councillor. It was thus after fifteen years as a High State Councillor, eight of them as the highest official in the land, that Yun P'il-sang was forced out of office by the attacks of the censoring organs. Although Yun had suffered indictment as early as 1485 (7.3, 7.6), on the basis of alleged commercial activities, demands that he be relieved of his post were dropped when the king failed to heed them. Serious and sustained efforts to oust Yun as Chief State Councillor arose, then, out of two great policy questions of 1491 and 1492.

The first of these was the Northern Expedition of 1491. In the first month of that year there occurred an unusually strong and destructive attack by a Yain tribe on the northern frontier. Sǒngjong, naturally, was incensed, and after consultation with the higher echelons of his officialdom he determined upon a full-scale expedition in reprisal, aimed at wiping out this threat to the security of Korea's northern borders. The plans agreed upon called for drawing the required troops from the three southern provinces and Kyǒnggi (1491.1.19, 4.11, 4.17, 4.19).

The decision to go to war was immediately attacked by all three censoring organs. The grounds adduced were in part practical, in part hypothetical, and in part philosophical. It was noted, for example, that the way of the sages in dealing with barbarians was to treat them like mosquitoes and horseflies—when they come chase them away, when they are away prepare to defend against them, but never go out to attack them. And it was asserted that the series of droughts and comet appearances in recent years clearly indicated that war was not in accord with the will of Heaven (1491.4.21 S). The king and his higher officials, however, rejected these arguments and pushed ahead with plans for a military campaign.

In their effort to stop the Northern Expedition the Censorate then claimed that Yun P'il-sang and others among the highest officials had come around to a posture of opposition to the campaign but were afraid to express this view to the king because of their original advocacy. When the king asked Yun P'il-sang and the others if this allegation were true, they all denied it, and so Sŏngjong discharged the entire Censorate on charges of deceit (1491.5.7 S to 5.9S). The new Censorate appointees, however, also spoke out in opposition to the Northern Expedition and went on to criticize the king for his action against the former Censorate. When their words were not heeded they resigned, setting off another round of changes in the composition of the Censorate (1491.6.5, 6.16).

Controversy flared still higher as a result of allegations by P'yo Yŏn-mal, who presently was named a Third Inspector (1491.6.17). P'yo memorialized that he had heard directly from Fifth State Councillor Ŏ Se-gyŏm that Yun P'il-sang had privately questioned the propriety of the Northern Expedition. Inquiring into the truth of this accusation, the king received replies admitting that Yun P'il-sang had expressed concern over the problems arising from the calling up of troops from the central and southern provinces but denying that Yun had said, or had been quoted as saying, that he now opposed the decision in favor of the expedition but did not feel he could say so publicly. And Yun himself denied that he had made such a statement. Thus, when former Second Inspector Ch'oe Kwan backed up P'yo Yŏn-mal's charge and firmly insisted that Ŏ Se-gyŏm's testimony was faulty, a disgusted Sŏngjong ordered Ch'oe Kwan tried by the State Tribunal and had P'yo Yŏn-mal await transfer to another post (1491.6.19 S to 6.21 S).[25] He then went ahead to carry out the Northern Expedition, which proved successful.

In the following year Yun P'il-sang again came into opposition with the censoring organs and suffered still more violent denunciation. The issue this time was legislation affecting Buddhist monks.

Although there were National Code provisions strictly governing the granting of licenses to monks,[26] these were very poorly enforced and there was a constantly growing number of unlicensed monks who sought to escape the obligations of taxation and corvee service. This problem had been faced before in the earlier years of Sŏngjong's reign (1477.i2.24 S), but apparently the measures instituted had proved ineffective or unenforceable. The Northern Expedition of 1491 tremendously aggravated this problem and focused attention anew upon it, for there was every reason to attempt to evade military and corvee service in connection with the war on the northern frontier.

These considerations, together with a deep-seated hostility toward all manifestations of Buddhism (which doubtless was the basic motivation), led the censoring organs to request that unlicensed monks be apprehended and that the protective clauses of the National Code be rescinded. These clauses were, in particular, those permitting the licensing of monks and the selection of monks by examination, and those prohibiting the searching of temple premises and the imprisonment of monks without express royal consent (1491.12.2, 12.7, 12.8, 1492.1.6, 1.16, 2.17). This request was repeated with special force because, just at that time, an office had been established to compile a supplement to the National Code (1491.10.17). Yun P'il-sang, No Sa-sin, and others among the highest officials, however, spoke out in opposition to rescinding these protective clauses, and Sŏngjong adopted their view (1492.1.16, 1.19 S).

Nevertheless, Sŏngjong did prove willing to suspend temporarily the monk license clause, in order to prevent further dwindling of the army's numbers (1492.2.3). Later in the year, in connection with prosecution of a public works program, Sŏngjong announced more stringent provisions directed at preventing men from becoming monks in order to evade state obligations and at making it difficult for monks assigned to corvee projects to flee and hide (1492.10.23 S). However, the two queen mothers (Yejong's queen Ansun and Sŏngjong's mother Sohye) handed down a document decrying the injurious consequences of the anti-monk enactments and pleading that they be rescinded. When Yun P'il-sang, No Sa-sin, Yun Ho, and others asserted that the king need not hesitate to follow the wishes of his mother and aunt in this matter, Sŏngjong not only rescinded the stringent measures of the previous month but also lifted the earlier suspension of the monk license law (1492.11.21).[27]

At this development, the censoring organs lashed out at the interference of the queen mothers in government affairs and also denounced, for toadying, the high officials who had urged acquiescence in their wishes. The OSC followed with the charge that the queen mothers had received coaching in the preparation of their arguments from ingratiating high officials. Officials of the Royal Secretariat and of the Office of Royal Decrees also joined in the protesting chorus (1492.11.21, 11.23 to 11.26, 11.28, 11.29, 12.2, 12.3). Yi Mok led a group of his fellow National Academy students in a vehement memorial in which the epithet "evil genius" was hurled at Yun P'il-sang. The angry king demanded of Yi Mok and his cohorts the basis for their insulting words, but in reply received still more audacious contumely. Sŏngjong then handed over Yi Mok and several other students to the State Tribunal (1492.12.4 S).

The usual voices were raised in instant and strong protest, and the Royal Secretariat as well asked that full sufferance be extended. The OSC officials asked that they too be imprisoned, for their views were no different from those expressed by Yi Mok, and several hundred other students of the National Academy and the Four Colleges entered a similar plea. Faced with continuing turmoil, Sŏngjong released Yi Mok and his fellow students and attempted to placate Yun P'il-sang in other ways, but he did not restore the anti-monk measures (1492.12.4, 12.5, 12.7, 12.8, 12.10, 12.14).[28]

Yun P'il-sang stayed on as Chief State Councillor for nearly one more year. But late in 1493 Inspector-General Hŏ Ch'im and his subordinates, taking advantage of the occurrence of unseasonable thunder, impeached Yun P'il-sang and several others (mainly marriage kinsmen or sons of high officials). The earlier charge of toadying was revived and it was requested that Yun and the others be removed from their posts and replaced by men of real talent (1493.10.23 S). Since coming under sustained attack by the censoring organs, Yun P'il-sang had repeatedly asked to resign (e.g., 1491.6.19, 1492.12.6) and now, at length, the king accepted his letter of resignation (1493.10.29).

The attacks on Chief State Councillor No Sa-sin in the early years of the reign of Yŏnsangun well epitomizes the conflict between the censoring organs and the highest figures in the government and the palace. No Sa-sin was a grandson both of No Kan, a Third State Councillor during the reign of Sejong, and of Sim On, Sejong's father-in-law and a Chief State Councillor. Passing the civil examination in 1453, he won rapid advancement under Sejo and later became both a Yejong and a Sŏngjong Merit Subject. In 1487 (9.28) he was named Third State Councillor and in 1492 (5.19) he became Second State Councillor. When Yun P'il-sang was attacked for supporting the protests of the two queen mothers against the anti-monk measures, No Sa-sin, who took an identical stand, also suffered indictment (1492.11.21, 12.3, 12.6, 12.10) and this may account for his not being elevated to Chief State Councillor in Yun P'il-sang's stead. However, because of age and ill health, the new appointee (Yi Kŭk-pae) did not take active part in the conduct of state affairs so that, in effect, No Sa-sin was at the head of officialdom. And when Yi Kŭk-pae resigned in 1495 (3.20), No Sa-sin was immediately named to replace him. It was shortly before this that No collided head on with the censoring bodies over the question of Buddhist funeral rites for the late King Sŏngjong, who had died at the end of 1494.

It had been the invariable custom of the Yi dynasty upon the death of a king or queen to carry out the Buddhistic rite of erecting "journey smoothing halls" *(suryuk chae),* [29] to speed the soul of the departed into the life after death. On the day after Sŏngjong's death, however, Minister of Rites Sŏng Hyŏn memorialized noting that no such thing was prescribed in the official Confucian rites text and that Sŏngjong had not believed in Buddhism. How should he deal with the problem? Yŏnsangun consulted the new queen mother (Sŏngjong's queen, Chŏnghyŏn) who declared that since Sŏngjong had left no testamentary instruction to the contrary and since, too, it had been performed for all his predecessors, this Buddhist rite should not now be discarded (1494.12.25).

The royal command to this effect, however, was questioned by the Censorate and OSC, who asked that it be rescinded. In reply Yŏnsangun defended his decision, but the indictments did not cease (1494.12.25). Ordered to compose the usual royal eulogies, the OSC officials were so occupied in presenting protests against the Buddhist rites that they neglected to prepare their compositions on time. When the king referred the matter to his highest officials, No Sa-sin replied that, in his view, the censoring organs were making a mountain out of a mole hill and that the king need not reply to any further remonstrance on the subject of the Buddhist rites. Accordingly, Yŏnsangun ordered the Royal Secretariat not to bring to his attention any more memorials protesting the journey smoothing halls (1494.12.28 S).[30]

This brought down on No Sa-sin the combined wrath of the Censorate, the OSC, and the National Academy students. The OSC and Censorate charged that No was obsequious, that he wanted to gag the Censorate and OSC so as to have his own opinions go unchallenged, and that he wanted to make himself the autocratic arbiter of the destinies of the State. He should be tried and severely punished. On the following day, Cho Yu-hyŏng led a large group of National Academy students in a scathing attack on Buddhism and on No Sa-sin for the grave error of his advice to the king on the rites issue (1495.1.1, 1.2).[31]

Upon completing the initial mourning rites, Yŏnsangun turned his attention to affairs of government and his first act was to imprison Cho Yu-hyŏng and 156 other students, whom he regarded as guilty of contempt of higher authority. Despite persistent Censorate and OSC attempts to secure generous treatment for the accused, and in spite of similar exertions on the part of the Royal Secretariat, Boards Ministers, and State Councillors as well, in the end Yŏnsangun banished three of the students and barred twenty-one others (headed by Cho Yu-hyŏng) from taking the civil examinations (1495.1.22, 1.22 S, 1.24 S, 1.27, 1.30 S).[32]

The ill will accruing to No Sa-sin for his role in these events (together with an accumulation of other grievances against him) prepared the ground for still more acrimonious conflict. Not long thereafter, after listing ten dangerous tendencies in the political and moral climate of the day, the Censorate launched a sweeping attack on No Sa-sin in which his support of the queen mother's wishes in the Buddhist rites controversy and his failure to succor the imprisoned students received prominent mention (1495.5.28 S).[33]

The stage was now set for the climactic final act in the drama of censoring organs versus Chief State Councillor No Sa-sin. As usual it was a rather unimportant issue out of which serious conflict developed. This was a criminal case involving Yun T'ang-no, a younger brother of Sŏngjong's second queen, Chŏnghyŏn. Earlier attacks against Yun T'ang-no, in 1493, have been briefly noted above. Now he became the object of judicial proceedings on the morals charge that he had cohabited with a *kisaeng* (professional female entertainer) during the period of national mourning for the late Sŏngjong. By claiming illness Yun succeeded in getting these proceedings stopped, but presently a Fourth Inspector, Cho Hyŏng, requested that they be resumed. High State Councillors No Sa-sin and Sin Sŭng-sŏn, however, had declared that since the *kisaeng* involved was one by whom he already had had children, Yun T'ang-no's conduct could not be construed as reprehensible. Accordingly, Yŏnsangun announced that he would pardon Yun (1495.5.24 S, 5.25 S, 6.6 S, 6.7 S, 6.12 S).

The Censorate, however, would not drop the matter, and when the king returned to the OIG a roster of criminal cases on which he had affixed the character "pardon" after Yun T'ang-no's name, the OIG took the unusual (if not unprecedented) step of refusing to accept the roster. Four times in all the roster was sent down to the OIG and four times it was refused. The king then relieved the entire Censorate and handed over its personnel to the State Tribunal, charging contumacy. The Censorate was released the next day, but not before No Sa-sin had gone on record in support of the king's action, which he termed "eminently fitting" (1495.6.15, 6.26, 6.28, 6.29 S, 6.30 S).

The new Censorate presented afresh the charges against Yun T'ang-no and backed its case with arguments convincing enough that the king discharged him from his post (1495.7.1 S, 7.3). The Censorate now held that this was not punishment enough and went on to attack No Sa-sin's "eminently fitting" statement as a betrayal of the prime duty of a High State Councillor to prevent the sovereign's lapse into error (1495.7.7 S). To this No Sa-sin feelingly replied as follows:

> Recently the Censorate, even in trivial matters, invariably has sought victory for itself, to this end furiously presenting indictments to the king, day after day and month upon month, stopping only after winning its point. The consequent evils have tended to undermine the authority of the king and this has long caused me great concern . . . [Hence it was that] when recently I received the royal instruction jailing the Censorate for contumacy, I regarded it as being truly the august judgment of an illustrious sovereign . . . What reason could there be for me to succor these criminals? (1495.7.7 S)

When the Censorate officials saw this memorial in which No Sa-sin had all but admitted that he favored some restraint of the censoring power, they immediately demanded that he be tried on the charge of attempting to gag the Censorate in order to further his own power-mad ambitions (1495.7.11 S, 7.12 S). The Censorate was strongly supported by the OSC, which cited one after another recent statement of No Sa-sin and sharply countered each of them, ending always with the query: "Are these not words to bring ruin to the State?" Concluding their attack with the declaration that No Sa-sin combined the evil genius of the infamous book-burning Li Ssu of the Ch'in and the sinister Li Lin-fu of the T'ang in a single character of the blackest villainy, they requested that he be distantly banished (1495.7.11 S).

Although this theme was reiterated with increasing vituperation, not only by the censoring organs but also by officials of the Office of Royal Decrees, Yŏnsangun took no action against his Chief State Councillor (1495.7.13, 7.18). Because of these violent denunciations No Sa-sin had gone into seclusion at his home, awaiting the royal judgment. Presently, when commanded to attend his post, he responded with a letter of resignation in which he summarized with great force and earnestness the case against the Censorate and OSC. This document is worth quoting at some length:

> The Confucian sages of yore have said: Political authority must not for even one day fail to reside in the administrative hierarchy, for if it does not reside in the administrative hierarchy then it resides in the Censorate, and if it does not reside in the Censorate then it resides in the palace. If political authority resides in the administrative hierarchy then there is good government; if it resides in the Censorate then there is turmoil; if it resides in the palace then there is [national] ruin . . .
>
> Lately the practices of the literati have daily grown in error. They regard the imputation of faults to others as forthrightness, calumniation of their superiors as lofty [virtue].

They do not take into consideration whether a matter is inconsequential or serious, great or small; rather do they merely hold their own words to be those of the Confucian sages, and at all costs strive to win their points. [Thus] do they arrogate to themselves an equal status with the sovereign. Day after day and week after week they continue their tumult. When they indict a man for crime and their memorialized request is not granted, they then invariably ferret out the man's past errors, like blowing apart the feathers of a bird to seek out the skin blotches underneath, only stopping when they have encompassed his downfall . . .

This dangerous practice is growing steadily more pervasive, while the mores of integrity and sincerity are daily deteriorating. When the Censorate speaks out, then the Office of Special Counselors follows suit, and, when the Office of Special Counselors has spoken, then the National Academy students follow up in turn — A sings and B harmonizes, together thus forming a chorus. They search for fault in faultlessness, manufacture a text of blank pages. Should someone differ with them, they instantly heap on abuse, reviling in every conceivable way. The high officials fear their tongues, and so do not dare adjudge right and wrong in their presence . . .

This practice never existed in olden times, did not exist even until the advent of the present dynasty. If this practice does not cease — if political authority gravitates to the Censorate, and the tongues of the highest officials are stilled — then how can one fail to be deeply distressed over the affairs of government? I have long grieved that the situation has come to this state. It is my view that this is not a condition which may be easily remedied by Your Majesty's subjects, but rather is an evil which can be eradicated only by the well-considered action of a sagacious ruler . . .

Now I have already reached the age of seventy and I have attained, moreover, the highest office in the land. The day of my death is not far off. What further ambitions could I have? What personal cravings for power could I aspire to satisfy? Yet . . . now, having been reviled in this way, with what brazen face might I continue to serve in the government? I humbly ask that the king in his grace consider my earnest entreaty — nothing would make me happier than that I be relieved of my post and punished for my crimes, thus to assuage the widespread and bitter feeling against me. (1495.7.19 S)

The king refused again to accept No Sa-sin's resignation but, in an attempt to quiet the furor, he ordered Yun T'ang-no banished in light degree (1495.7.19, 7.21). Nonetheless, the Censorate and OSC did not cease their indictments of No Sa-sin and presently, asserting that either they or he must go, laid aside their duties and resigned (1495.7.23, 7.25, 7.26). Yŏnsangun reiterated his faith in No Sa-sin and commanded the Censorate officials to resume the duties of their posts and, when still they failed to respond, he seized upon a convenient pretext to relieve the entire Censorate roster and institute judicial proceedings against them (1495.8.2, 8.8).[34] The king then made the offices of Inspector-General and Censor-General concurrent posts, naming to them officials incumbent in high positions. Under these he filled the Censorate posts, as usual, with young men not long emerged from the examination system (1495.8.9).

But this oblique attack on the problem also proved unsuccessful. The new Censorate held improper both the action taken against the old and the king's violation of the provisions of the National Code in naming, as the chief officers of the OIG and OCG, men who held other posts concurrently. The new Censorate, furthermore, continued the indictment of No Sa-sin (1495.8.11, 8.22, 9.3). In consequence, Yŏnsangun soon abandoned his concurrent office experiment and presently summoned the highest officials to discuss the question of No Sa-sin (1495.8.25, 9.8).

Now some among the highest officials had already taken the stand that, in endorsing the king's earlier action of jailing the Censorate (1495.6.28, when the Censorate refused to accept the king's pardon of Yun T'ang-no), No Sa-sin had gone too far, and that the king should heed the words of the Censorate (1495.7.15 S, 9.5 S). Yŏnsangun, however, felt that out of fear of incurring the wrath of the Censorate some officials at least had not and would not frankly speak their minds, and so he took special pains to urge that there be a free and outspoken expression of opinions (1495.9.8 S). But the consensus, voiced one feels with an air of regret, turned out to be that No Sa-sin should be relieved of his post. As Yun P'il-sang put it:

> The Censorate has continued its indictments week after week now for three months and still does not stop. When shall the government know peace? If No Sa-sin remains in office the situation will be extremely difficult. Why not transfer him and make him a Great Lord,[35] thus bringing tranquility to the government? (1495.9.8 S)

Consequently, Yŏnsangun relieved No Sa-sin as Chief State Councillor, giving him the title of Great Lord of Sŏnsŏng. The Censorate attacked this as far too mild a punishment but the king refused to heed their words (1495.9.15, 9.16).

These triumphs in the affairs of Yun P'il-sang and No Sa-sin, even though one concede them to be partial, did nothing to discourage the Censorate or to put a brake upon the exercise of the censoring function. Indeed, if anything, in the three years now remaining before the Purge of 1498 the censoring organs became still more promiscuous in their choice of targets, more intemperate in their choice of words, and more intractable in the assertion of their own righteousness. In consequence the political scene became even more turbulent. Let us look at highlights of this continuing conflict.

No Sa-sin came under attack once again in connection with the question of posthumous rites to honor Yŏnsangun's mother, who had been deposed (1479.6.2) and then executed (1482.8.16) by Sŏngjong on charges of excessive jealousy. The king had ordered the Board of Rites to draw up plans to honor the Deposed Lady Yun (as Yŏnsangun's mother is most commonly known) with certain posthumous rites (1496.5.15). But when the Rites Board pointed out that there was no precedent for the honors intended by the king, Yŏnsangun agreed to hear views on the question from a broad segment of officialdom (1496.6.3). Especially assembled for this purpose, the highest officials (with the sole exception of Yun P'il-sang) urged that the king be guided by his own feelings of filial piety. Furthermore, Seventh State Councillor Yun Hyo-son cited a statement by Sŏngjong lending explicit sanction to this view, whereupon No Sa-sin made the request that the Deposed Lady Yun be posthumously honored. Yŏnsangun concurred (1496.6.7).

The censoring organs, however, repeatedly attacked the king's decision as improper, and went on to request that Yun Hyo-son and No Sa-sin be charged with crime. But the king would not yield (1496.6.5, 6.7, 6.13, 6.29, 7.2).

Early in 1497, Second Censor Ch'oe Pu well illustrated one aspect of Censorate technique when he made a gratuitous attack on several of the high officials. Chief State Councillor Sin Sŭng-sŏn (Yŏnsangun's father-in-law) was criticized as weak and womanish, totally indecisive in handling affairs of state. Second State Councillor Ŏ Se-gyŏm was conceded to be a man of talent and learning yet one so unconscientious in performing the duties of his post as to have earned the sobriquet of "clock-watcher." Third State Councillor Han Ch'i-hyŏng, though a man of fine character, was said to be without learning. During his tenure of office he had been responsible for the only two measures initiated by the High State Councillors of the time; both these measures, however, were trivial in the extreme. Minister of Taxation Yi Se-jwa was excoriated for having thwarted the king's desire to decrease the land tax, Minister of Rites Pak An-sŏng for his abysmal ignorance of rites procedures, Second Minister of Personnel An Ch'im for appointing venal men from among his own kinsmen, and the Superintendent of the Royal Stables Administration, No Sa-sin, for securing promotions for his subordinates. These men, it was asserted, had abused the power of their positions. Ch'oe Pu concluded by asking that all those he had named be demoted and replaced by worthy men (1497.2.14 S).

The Censorate also found another opportunity to strike at No Sa-sin. The issue itself was quite trivial but it soon led to a heated exchange in the course of which No accused the Censorate of trying to cow others into silence, while the Censorate officials retorted that No was trying to gag them (1497.7.8 S, 7.14 S, 7.15 S). In the days that followed, the Censorate officials frequently made the expected demands that No Sa-sin be relieved of his post, tried, and punished, and urged further that he not again be permitted to participate in the Royal Lectures (1497.7.17 S, 7.18 S, 7.20 S). Fourth Censor Cho Sun unleashed the most violent denunciation of all, saying, in part:

> No Sa-sin . . . wants to cause the king not to heed the words of the Censorate, thus forcing reliance on his own words so that he may dare to realize his personal ambitions. In the phraseology of the *Spring and Autumn Annals,* No Sa-sin's crimes are so grave that, even if he were sentenced to death, it still would not suffice; we would want to eat his flesh. If this crime of his goes unpunished, then who among your subjects will speak out with forthrightness to the king? (1497.7.21 S)

This speech focused the king's wrath on Cho Sun, who was promptly jailed. Representations by the Censorate, the OSC and the Royal Secretariat failed to move Yŏnsangun, and presently Cho Sun was punished by discharge from his post (1497.7.22 S, 7.23 S). The Censorate continued to attack No Sa-sin, appending requests that Cho Sun be restored to office, but to no avail (1497.7.24, 7.28, 7.30, 8.4). Nor did the Censorate overlook Yu Cha-gwang, who had taken a stand with No Sa-sin against the Censorate a short while before (1497.7.15 S). It was asserted that on the basis of his past record (the *Sillok* makes clear that the reference is to the 1478 Case), Yu was most unfit to hold the position of a Special Participant, Office of the Royal Lectures (1497.7.30 S). The king, however, took no action against either No Sa-sin or Yu Cha-gwang.

In the year that now remained before the purge, there was no diminution of vigor in the practice of remonstrance; the censoring organs had not become remiss in their scrutiny of the affairs of government. Prominent among the problems with which they concerned themselves were many old familiar ones—the legal safeguards enjoyed by Buddhism,[36] Buddhist practices by and for the high born,[37] the favored treatment accorded marriage kin,[38] and the promiscuous and excessive bestowal of rewards.[39] Noteworthy among the new objects of Censorate displeasure were the king's efforts to enlarge the palace apparatus,[40] and his neglect of the pivotal institution of the Royal Lectures.[41]

But if there was no let up in the offering of remonstrance, there was evidence of change with regard to its acceptance. For it seems clear that the king's attitude toward the concept and practice of remonstrance was hardening. This may be inferred from Yŏnsangun's reluctance to yield to the pressures of the censoring bodies in this period, however strongly and insistently exerted. His displeasure with the course remonstrance was taking may be surmised, too, from pronouncements made by Yŏnsangun when particularly annoyed at Censorate pertinacity or presumptuousness.[42] And it may be seen unmistakably in Yŏnsangun's prosecution of the Purge of 1498.

The Purge Unfolds

The Purge of 1498 began to unfold when Yun P'il-sang, No Sa-sin, Third State Councillor Han Ch'i-hyŏng, and Yu Cha-gwang contrived to memorialize the king in private. Their statements on this occasion were not recorded but obviously contained serious accusations against Kim Il-son, a former Historian. State Tribunal officers already had been despatched to Kyŏngsang Province to arrest Kim (1498.7.1).[43]

For the next ten days the government in Seoul continued to function as usual, in apparent unawareness of the great storm about to break.[44] Then the king ordered the State Records Bureau to turn in to him all of Kim Il-son's history drafts. The Directors demurred, citing the long-standing precedent against a king's personal perusal of the drafts. A compromise soon was reached under which six paragraphs referring to events of previous reigns were extracted and sent in under seal. The king then ordered that portions referring to the royal family similarly be made available to him (1498.7.11).[45]

Kim Il-son now arrived under arrest and was summoned into the royal presence. Upon questioning, he readily admitted to writing up items in his drafts which reflected unfavorably on the personal conduct and political actions of Sejo, but he justified himself on the general ground that it was the traditional duty of the historian to set down all such matters. Perhaps most significantly, in view of later events, the king asked Kim Il-son what had been his thinking in once requesting that the tomb of Munjong's queen be restored.[46] Kim Il-son replied that, just as Sejo's ordering of rites in honor of the Koryŏ royal house of Wang was an act of praiseworthy royal virtue, so would be the honoring of Munjong's queen by the reestablishment of her tomb beside that of her husband (1498.7.12).

Kim Il-son had indicated that his source of information on two matters related to the personal conduct of Sejo was Hŏ Pan.[47] But when Hŏ Pan was questioned, he denied having passed along such information to Kim Il-son, suggesting that Kim's recent illness may have made him mentally confused. This Kim vehemently denied. The king, convinced that Hŏ Pan was lying, ordered him beaten but to no avail. At the same time, further interrogation of Kim Il-son was ordered (1498.7.12).

On this same day, a search of Kim Il-son's house turned up letters to him from Yi Mok and Kwŏn O-bok. The former expressed unreserved approval of Kim's history drafts and related the determination of the Second Deputy Director of the State Records Bureau, Yi Kŭk-ton, to prevent their inclusion in the *Sillok;* it closed with an injunction to burn the letter after reading it. The second letter deplored the hostility aroused by the recent censoring activities of Kim and his colleagues and displayed deep concern for Kim on this account (1498.7.12 S).[48]

At the command of the king, the State Tribunal officer who had taken Kim Il-son into custody reported what Kim had said en route. In sum, Kim had surmised that his arrest was due to his work as a historian and, in particular, to the enmity of Yi Kŭk-ton. Kim had recounted in his drafts some unflattering incidents involving Yi which Yi did not dare delete because of the inviolate character of the drafts for this most important of all state records. Yi Kuk-ton, Kim was alleged to have speculated, probably had sought a way out of his dilemma by spreading rumors of what Kim had written about the royal house (1498.7.12).

Before the day ended, Kim Il-son had undergone a paragraph by paragraph interrogation, handled personally by Yu Cha-gwang, on his motives in writing as he had and on his sources of information. Among the items on which he was questioned the most prominent were those in which he indicated his approbation of the high principles of the so-called Six Martyred Subjects [49] and those in which he recorded acts of greed, lust, and high-handedness on the part of Hakcho.[50] Yi Ch'ong and Pak Kyŏng, who had been mentioned by Kim as sources, and Yun Hyo-son and Sŏng Chung-ŏm, who had figured prominently in Yi Mok's letter to Kim Il-son, also were interrogated on this day. These all either flatly denied the words attributed to them or minimized them (1498.7.12).[51]

As the interrogation of Kim Il-son continued the king handed down a significant instruction to Yun P'il-sang and the other leading figures conducting the investigation in their roles as Magistrates of the State Tribunal. Included were these points which Yŏnsangun wanted put to the accused: "Having already requested the restoration of the tomb of Munjong's queen, you then, in writing of the traitorous officials [the Six Martyred Subjects], held them up as examples of fidelity to the death. Surely you must harbor subversive thoughts." Again: "The achievements and virtue of the Sejo reinvigoration now belong to the past and his descendants have succeeded one another unto this day. In view of the fact that you harbored subversive thoughts from the outset, why is it that you serve in my government?"(1498.7.13)

In answering the first point, Kim Il-son repeated his conviction that the Six Martyred Subjects were praiseworthy in remaining loyal to Tanjong, the king they originally had served. To the second question Kim replied: "Sejo was a heroic and magnificently gifted sovereign; he tranquilized the state and achieved a reinvigoration. Sŏngjong was a peerless ruler who preserved and added to his heritage. The present king has succeeded to these enterprises. Therefore I serve him"(1498.7.13).

In further response to interrogation, Kim gave his sources and attempted to justify his inclusion of several other items in his history drafts. For the first time he mentioned his teacher, the late Kim Chong-jik,[52] as a source. Also, for the first time mention was made of Kim Chong-jik's composition titled "Lament for the Rightful Emperor" (Cho Ŭi Che mun)—made famous by its role in this purge— to which Kim Il-son had given space in his drafts in connection with his praise of the Six Martyred Subjects (1498.7.13).

In consequence of a royal order Yi Mok's house too had been searched and a letter from Im Hŭi-jae found. The letter lamented that the growing ascendancy of reactionary forces in the court had driven into retirement a number of "good men" and had placed in jeopardy those who remained. By name were mentioned Chŏng Sŏk-kyŏn, Kang Paek-chin, Kang Hun, Kwŏn O-bok, and Kim Koeng-p'il. The letter went on to deplore the king's refusal to heed remonstrance. In closing, the writer urged Yi Mok to relinquish thoughts of continuing in government service and expressed his own desire to live out his years in retirement. The king, after ordering further interrogation of Im Hŭi-jae (whose deposition had been at variance with the tenor of his letter),[53] added: "Today the crowd of amoral men is forming a clique and is busily vilifying the highest officials, to an extent constituting a problem of grave national concern. We must severely punish and eradicate this trend" (1498.7.14).

At this point Yu Cha-gwang memorialized a detailed interpretation of Kim Chong-jik's "Lament for the Rightful Emperor" and asked that the author's crime of treason be punished in full accordance with the law. He also requested that Kim Chong-jik's published literary collection be burned, together with the blocks used in printing it. The king concurred and further ordered the interrogation of the editor of the collection, Cho Wi, and of its publisher Chŏng Sŏk-kyŏn (1498.7.15).[54]

Two days later Yŏnsangun handed down a decree in which he said:

Kim Chong-jik was a lowborn yangban from the hinterland. He passed the civil examination in Sejo's reign and in Sŏngjong's reign was promoted to a Royal Lectures post. Thus long in a position of proximity to the throne, he was able to reach the office of Minister of Punishments and receive the royal favor. When he retired due to illness, Sŏngjong extraordinarily ordered the provincial authorities to award him grain, to enable him to pass his remaining years [free from want].

Yet now his disciple Kim Il-son, in his history drafts, has falsely recorded events of Sejo's reign in improper words and has included his master's "Lament for the Rightful Emperor." Kim Chong-jik wrote this in the tenth month of 1457,[55] on the pretext of having had a dream. He compared Sejo to Ch'in Shih Huang Ti and Tanjong to I Ti . . . Kim Il-son approved of this text and held that it expressed loyal indignation.

Now it seems to me that Sejo, at a time of national crisis when the danger of a treasonous plot by villainous officials was on the verge of unfolding, killed the rebels and so pacified the state. And his descendants have succeeded to the throne even unto the present. Kim Chong-jik and his disciples have vilified the royal virtue and have even gone so far as to have Kim Il-son falsely write up history. Truly this secret harboring of disloyal thought spans three reigns. When we think of this, we cannot help feeling the chill hand of dread. Let all military and civil ranks third grade and above, and the Censorate and OSC officials, discuss the punishment and memorialize. (1498.7.17)

This was done. The highest officials asked that Kim Chong-jik be charged with high treason and that the punishment be fixed at beheading of the corpse. The participating Censorate officials, on the other hand, asked only that he be posthumously stripped of rank and title and that his posterity be disqualified from office. The king adopted the former view and, indeed, ordered judicial proceedings against the Censorate on the charge of shielding Kim Chong-jik (1498.7.17).[56]

The large body of Kim Chong-jik disciples now became the center of the king's attention. In consequence of Yun P'il-sang's assertion that Kim Chong-jik's poem "On Wine" (Sul chu si) was even more "extreme" than the "Lament for the Rightful Emperor," Yŏnsangun ordered all of Kim's disciples subjected to the judicial process (1498.7.17).[57] Asked to provide a list of Kim Chong-jik disciples, Kim Il-son responded with twenty-six names, a number that he admitted was incomplete (1498.7.17).[58] Then, when it was observed that Kim Chong-jik's "Lament" had been praised in Kwŏn Kyŏng-yu's history drafts as well, Yŏnsangun ordered that all of Kim's disciples be imprisoned (1498.7.17).[59]

The net had now been drawn, and only a few more days were needed to complete the case against the disciples of Kim Chong-jik and against those who had been implicated on tangential grounds. Presently Yun P'il-sang and his fellow State Tribunal investigation officers memorialized their recommendations. They asked that twenty-eight men be sentenced for crimes ranging on the whole from high treason to cliquism, their punishments to range from execution by dismemberment to discharge from office. In addition they suggested that two men, recently deceased, be posthumously divested of office warrants. The interrogation of another, it was noted, had not yet been conducted while still another had fled arrest. And they urged that the officials of the former Censorate be charged with cliquism because they had proposed too mild a sentence for Kim Chong-jik (1498.7.26).[60]

Yŏnsangun accepted these recommendations almost without change.[61] He ordered the five executions carried out immediately and fixed places of banishment for twenty-six others (including the former Censorate officials). At the same time, seven supervisory officials of the Veritable Records Office were discharged or demoted.[62] Yŏnsangun then ordered the drafting of a "moving" proclamation to the nation, reported the event to the ancestral shrines, accepted the congratulations of officialdom, and announced a general amnesty. Nor did he neglect to bestow handsome rewards on the Investigation Officers and on a score of others who had assisted in prosecution of the purge (1498.7.26, 7.27). Finally Yŏnsangun ordered the offensive history drafts burned (1498.7.28).[63]

But the purge had not yet run its full course. At the instance of Yu Cha-gwang and Yun P'il-sang, some ten or twenty men were ordered arrested and interrogated on charges tantamount to anti-social conduct. One group called itself the Seven Sages of the Bamboo Grove *(chungnim ch'irhyŏn)* and, allegedly, was wont to seek diversion in aimless strolls, drink, and mocking discourse. Another adopted the sobriquet of the Ten Disciples of Confucius *(sipch'ŏl)*. The names of those linked with these two groups do not all appear in the record nor is the disposition of the case entirely clear.[64] At least two men, however, were banished and enslaved (1498.8.10, 8.16, 8.20, 9.18).

A final purge case developed at the end of the year when a resident of Ch'ŏnan, in Ch'ungch'ŏngdo, reported that young students of the area had indignantly asserted that Kim Il-son, Kim Chong-jik, and so forth were innocent victims of the avarice and villainy of Yun P'il-sang and Yu Cha-gwang. After confessions had been extracted by torture, three of the accused were executed and perhaps nine banished or assigned to corvee. In addition, at least four others who had been mentioned in the students' depositions suffered banishment (1498.11.29 S, i11.6 S, i11.9 S, i11.11 S, i11.12 S, i11.14 S, i11.19).[65]

Analysis of the Purge

In a kind of postscript to their record of the purge events, the *Sillok* historians offer us the classical explanation for the Purge of 1498. They write:

> Yu Cha-gwang was an illegitimate son of the Special Capital Magistrate, Yu Kyu. In youth he was an idler but put himself forward as an armored soldier and was given a post by Sejo. In 1468, for his merit in reporting an incident [the plot of Nam I], he was enfeoffed as a Merit Subject and was enrolled in the First Rank of the officialdom. He regarded himself as an illustrious personage and always sought to effect the downfall of anyone who surpassed himself in talent and royal favor. Once when sojourning in Hamyang County, he wrote a poem and induced the County Magistrate to have it carved on a board and hung up for display. Later, when Kim Chong-jik became Magistrate of this county, he destroyed the board. Yu Cha-gwang ground his teeth in angry resentment.

> Kim Il-son had studied under Kim Chong-jik and, when Third Censor, had exerted himself to the utmost in remonstrating, heedless of the power or status of those he attacked. Once he denounced the existence of antagonism between Yi Kŭk-ton and Sŏng Chun, and Yi Kŭk-ton harbored a sizable grudge on this account. When Yi Kŭk-ton became a Director of the Veritable Records Office, he saw that Kim Il-son's history drafts exposed all of his

own evil acts and wrote up critically matters of Sejo's reign, whereupon he began to hatch a scheme with Yu Cha-gwang. Yu Cha-gwang then sought out No Sa-sin, Yun P'il-sang, and Han Ch'i-hyŏng and elicited their sympathetic support by reminding them of their indebtedness to Sejo. Presently No Sa-sin and the others took First Royal Secretary Sin Su-gŭn [brother of the queen] into their confidence and so presented their memorial. When Sin Su-gŭn first became a Royal Secretary, the Censorate and OSC had strongly attacked the appointment on the ground of his blood relationship to the palace, and he held a grudge on this account. Accordingly, Sin Su-gŭn chose to regard Yu Cha-gwang as acting out of loyalty to the state and lent the scheme his warm support . . .

To the end of preventing outsiders from learning what was going on, palace eunuch Kim Cha-wŏn was made to handle the documents [relating to the case]. Yu Cha-gwang personally took charge of the criminal proceedings. Presently he pointed to the "Lament for the Rightful Emperor" and to the poem "On Wine" in Kim Chong-jik's literary collection and criticized them. Now this was in revenge for the Hamyang incident. Yu Cha-gwang took advantage of the king's anger and tried to effect a wholesale purge. To Yun P'il-sang and others he said: "We must thoroughly investigate this cliquism, utterly root out the evil, and thus purify the government." His hearers all were silent but for No Sa-sin, who spoke up to say that the principle of freedom of remonstrance ought not be destroyed. Again, on the day when sentences were passed No Sa-sin alone held to a contrary view. Yu Cha-gwang's face clouded over and he rebuked No Sa-sin. And the king gave his consent to the body of opinion headed by Yu Cha-gwang.

From this time on, Yu Cha-gwang's authority was felt strongly in the capital and in the provinces. The more sophisticated sighed and said: "In the 1478 criminal case the righteous attacked the evil clique; in the 1498 criminal case the evil clique brought down the righteous." (1498.7.29)[66]

However strong the motives of personal revenge may have been, it does not follow that the charges against the victims of 1498 were entirely fabricated. Kim Chong-jik's "Lament" was no mere happenstance nor was its inclusion by Kim Il-son and others in their history drafts an act of innocence. The Korean king was then, as Korean kings continued to be, descended from Sejo, not from Tanjong. Two safe centuries were to pass before an Yi monarch, the eleventh generation descendant of Sejo, could overlook the rebuke to his ancestor implicit in the act of restoring Tanjong to full kingly status and dignity.

The charges against the other leading victims of 1498 also were related to the single theme of treason to the still fresh memory of Sejo and thus, by extension, disloyalty to the reigning monarch. In some cases, it is true, the connection was tenuous, the only visible link being through disciple status. Yet in a majority of instances the record reveals that the individual actions or words of a purge victim formed the basis of the charges preferred against him. It is probable that the absence of such a record in still other instances is the result of oversight. The inclusion of Yi Ŭi-mu on the purge roster may be more significant than it appears at first glance, for he seems to have been implicated solely on the ground of having urged the restoration of the tomb of Tanjong's mother.

But, in fact, were Kim Chong-jik, Kim Il-son, or any of the others traitors, disloyal to the sovereign they served? Of course they were not. These were neither ignorant nor unreasonable men and they perfectly well understood that Sejo's usurpation, however regrettable or reprehensible on moral grounds, was a political reality. Moreover, the same creed that made them honor Tanjong would require them to render service to Yŏnsangun. Their beliefs would allow them to retire into rusticity, abandoning the traditional career of public service, but once having made the decision to serve they could not serve with less than full fidelity. Had not Kim Chong-jik and others among the victims of 1498 served Sŏngjong with unquestioned loyalty?

A charge of treason, then, may be justified but only insofar as it is based on evidence of a condemnatory attitude toward the Sejo usurpation. The attempt to validate the charge in terms of Yŏnsangun's reign rings false. Neither the ruling monarch nor his high officials were in any danger from advocacy of the rehabilitation of Tanjong. This moral wrong of forty years in the past had no intrinsic connection with the political realities of 1498. An explanation of the purge must be sought elsewhere.

It seems clear that, at bottom, the Purge of 1498 was a reaction against the enlarged role in the processes of government claimed by the organs of remonstrance. It was initiated, apparently, by a small group of responsible administrative officials and high policy advisers and it won the eager support of the king. The purge was not directly aimed, however, at either the concept or the institutions of remonstrance. Rather it was an oblique attack, levelled against Kim Chong-jik and his disciples as symbols of the menace of the rapid growth of the censoring power.

What was the nature of the threat posed by the censoring bodies? Most vitally, it was a threat to the constitution of the state. The activities of the censoring bodies challenged both the king, in the exercise of his sovereign power, and the high officials, in the authority and dignity of their offices. On the personal level, the strictures of the censoring bodies had limited the king's freedom of personal conduct, and had endangered the careers of individual high officials. Insomuch as personal resentments were motivating forces in the purge, they were of this origin.

The architects of the Purge of 1498, then, had both reasons of state and personal reasons for taking action to restrict the exercise of the function of remonstrance. Yet the object of the purge was not the censoring organs but Kim Chong-jik and his disciples. How is this to be explained? Is it possible to regard the excesses of remonstrance that developed under Sŏngjong as simply a manifestation in another sphere of the moralism of Kim Chong-jik? Is, for example, the desire to "eat the flesh" of No Sa-sin derived from admiration for the loyalty to the death of the Six Martyred Subjects?

There are obvious difficulties in the way of making such an equation. Although in outlook and in operational techniques they were wonderfully consistent, in personnel composition the Censorate and OSC underwent constant change. However large the body of Kim Chong-jik disciples, by no means all of them enjoyed government careers and some of those who served never occupied positions in the censoring bodies. At any given time, the proportion of Kim Chong-jik disciples among the officials of the Censorate and OSC could not have been more than fractional.

Moreover, even in the classical explanation of the purge it is conceded, in effect, that the motivations of one of those who joined in preparing the purge had no connection with the Kim Chong-jik group. Yu Cha-gwang, the story goes, was impelled by personal rancor toward Kim Chong-jik, while Yi Kŭk-ton held a grudge against Kim Il-son. These two, then, enlisted the support of other highly-placed men on the basis of the outrage to the memory of Sejo they found in the writings of the two Kims. Sin Sŭ-gun, however, "lent the scheme his warm support" because of the enmity he felt toward the Censorate due to its opposition to his initial appointment to the Royal Secretariat. But this Censorate was not composed of Kim Chong-jik disciples—in fact, perhaps not even one can be found among them. The same is true of the Censorate that protested Sin Su-gŭn's promotion to First Royal Secretary.

Nevertheless, there was good reason why Yu Cha-gwang and Yi Kŭk-ton might equate Kim Chong-jik and his disciples with abuse of the censoring power, and why Sin Su-gŭn might make the same equation in reverse. Identification was possible in the sense that both sought to impose restraints upon the discretionary exercise of sovereign and executive power. Men of the Kim Chong-jik persuasion rested their case on the moral sanctions of orthodox Confucianism, while the censoring bodies sought to act as institutional checkreins. Moreover, among the most vocal of the occupants of censoring stations in the twenty years preceding the Purge of 1498 were some acknowledged Kim Chong-jik disciples. P'yo Yŏn-mal and Ch'oe Pu come readily to mind as prominent victims of the Purge of 1498 who also were leading architects of the new edifice of remonstrance. And the new concept of remonstrance most often adduced moral grounds rooted in Confucian doctrine.

Another important basis may be postulated for identifying Kim Chong-jik with the excesses of the censoring organs. A cliche of the time, "contempt for constituted authority," described a fault that could be imputed both to the censoring bodies and to the Kim Chong-jik group. Veiled criticism of the Sejo usurpation and outspoken opposition to the will of the reigning monarch, admiration for the Six Martyred Subjects and vituperative denunciation of incumbent State Councillors—such attitudes show this common characteristic. All were attitudes that might well be construed as seditious; certainly they were subversive of the established order.

It does not seem unlikely that such considerations as these were present in the thinking of Yu Cha-gwang and Yun P'il-sang. Indications of this were remarked upon earlier in the discussion of this chapter, as were signposts pointing to a similar train of thought on the part of Yŏnsangun. The record available to us seems to show that only No Sa-sin differentiated the two objects of anathema—or, at any rate, thought it wise to spare one for the sake of a larger concern. He was willing to punish the body of Kim Chong-jik disciples on the basis of the disrespect they had shown for Sejo, but he did not want the purge to "ramify"—that is, he was unwilling to condemn the practices employed by the censoring bodies so dramatically against himself.

If the real concern of the purgers was to redress the political imbalance that had developed in favor of the censoring organs, then why did they rest content with attacking an imperfect symbol? I can make no clear suggestion. If legal niceties were to be observed—and the history of this period of the Yi dynasty shows that compulsions always existed in this direction—Kim Chong-jik could not well be linked with the excesses of the censoring organs. He had remained aloof from the day to day performances of the great political spectacle of his time and his name nowhere appears in connection with the campaigns of the censoring organs described in the preceding pages. Perhaps not only No Sa-sin but others as well among the high officials would have opposed such an extension of the purge. Perhaps Yŏnsangun, young and not long on the throne, was unsure of himself.

Whatever the case, coming events would prove that the Purge of 1498 constituted a warning to those charged with the power of remonstrance. And because the warning went unheeded, the events of 1498 gave but a mild foretaste of what the practitioners of the expanded concept of remonstrance would suffer in the ensuing Purge of 1504.

Chapter III

THE PURGE OF 1504

If the Purge of 1498 was indeed intended as a warning to the censoring bodies it was not a resounding success. The record of the six year interval between it and the Purge of 1504 indicates clearly that, while the Censorate and Office of Special Counselors may have been sobered by the events of 1498, they were by no means cowed. To be sure, there were fewer instances of long sustained attack, and there does not seem to have been a level of vituperation approaching that of the pre-1498 period. On the other hand, from the positions prepared by their predecessors, the censoring bodies continued to fire away at familiar targets—Yu Cha-gwang, Im Sa-hong, the marriage kin, Buddhism, border policy. Furthermore, the censoring officials of these years did not hesitate to venture onto more dangerous ground.

The official and personal conduct of the sovereign was a basic concern of the censoring organs. From the outset of his reign Yŏnsangun had been prone to elicit remonstrance with uncommon frequency but, at the same time, he had shown little disposition to welcome or even tolerate its utterance. Both these trends now grew more pronounced. Just as the censoring officials, joined often by the State Councillors, viewed with increasing alarm the aberrations of their ruler, so Yŏnsangun made clear his increasing hostility toward the censoring function as a valid concept of the art of government and toward its practice in his day, in particular as its exercise impinged upon constituted high authority. But, needless to say, to bar the censoring bodies from acting in this vital arena would be to emasculate them beyond recognition, almost to deprive them of their reason for existence.

Yŏnsangun understood this only too well, and when the censoring organs failed to adjust themselves to his ever-shrinking specifications, he proceeded ruthlessly to exterminate them. Then, his sickened mind slipping into paranoia (surely not an unreasonable diagnosis), he perceived that the pernicious attitude of contempt of higher authority had spread to other segments of officialdom and to members of his palace staff, indeed to all strata of the society, and he never lacked a pretext to apply his brutal methods of correction. Corrective measures they were in his eyes, but history knows them as the massive Purge of 1504.

Remonstrance: The Continuing Issue

It is significant that Yu Cha-gwang, who came to be regarded as the arch villain of the Purge of 1498, remained a prime target of the censoring bodies in the years 1498-1504. While the purge was still in progress it is recorded that the OIG decided to protest the promotions awarded Yu Cha-gwang and one of his sons (and a palace eunuch as well) for merit in prosecuting the purge. On this occasion, however, Fourth Inspector Chŏng In-in, who had been designated to present the memorial, was too frightened to carry out the assignment (1498.7.29).

At the beginning of 1499, the Censorate asked that charges be preferred against Yu Cha-gwang for misdeeds committed while on a mission to Hamgyŏngdo. In the main, Yu was accused of forcing local government offices to provide sea food delicacies, which he then despatched to the king's table by government transportation (1499.1.10). When the king paid no heed the OSC seconded the Censorate's charges, and Fourth Censor Yun Ŭn-bo reiterated the case against Yu. The king's response was to castigate the Censorate and OSC for their irresponsible and extreme words and to order that Yun Ŭn-bo be beaten and demoted (1499.1.17, 1.18).[1] When the Censorate denounced this action, at the same time repeating the charges against Yu, the king answered with a formal pardon of Yu Cha-gwang, on the grounds that his motives were not open to question and that he was entitled to special consideration as a Merit Subject (1499.2.1, 2.18). Continued Censorate indictments, however, led Yŏnsangun to refer the question to his highest officials. Finding among these some (including his father-in-law Sin Sŭng-sŏn) who upheld the view of the Censorate, Yŏnsangun in the end removed Yu Cha-gwang from his posts of Special Participant, Office of the Royal Lectures, and Commander of the Five Military Commands Headquarters (1499.2.23).

Some two years later Yu Cha-gwang again was appointed Commander of the Five Military Commands Headquarters (1501.8.14). The Censorate immediately attacked the appointment and asked that Yu be removed (1501.8.20). When the indictment went unheeded it was repeated, salted with old charges against Yu culled from the writings of the late State Councillor and long-time OSC Director, Sŏ Kŏ-jŏng.[2] Yu spoke out in his own defense and was supported by Second State Councillor Sŏng Chun, who in turn was attacked by the Censorate. The king then had the record searched for clarification of the anti-Yu allegations (1501.8.29, 9.16, 9.27). Meanwhile, when the Censorate again attacked him, Yu asserted that their attempt to fabricate crime charges on the basis of the false accusations in Sŏ Kŏ-jŏng's book, and thus to force his dismissal, proved that they were members of the Kim Chong-jik–Kim Il-son clique (1501.9.29, 10.7, 10.11). When the whole question was referred to the highest officials, the High State Councillors interpreted the result of the research into the record as vindicating Yu Cha-gwang (1501.10.12).

Nevertheless, the Censorate continued to press the assault, finally summing up the case in a statement of the "five great crimes" of Yu Cha-gwang. These ranged from the accusation that Yu had willfully deceived the king (in his refutation of the allegations of Sŏ Kŏ-jŏng) to charges that Yu not only had insulted but also had attempted to intimidate and destroy the Censorate by his recent insinuations. Included, too, was a reference to Yu's complicity in the 1478 Case (1501.10.22). Still failing to achieve their end the Censorate officials sought to resign; although rebuffed, they abandoned their posts anyway and did not comply with a royal command to resume their duties (1501.10.29, 11.6, 11.10).

At this point Yŏnsangun again referred the matter to the State Council and heard this response from Third State Councillor Yi Kŭk-kyun: "Yu Cha-gwang is guilty of no particular crime, so there certainly is no reason why he should be punished . . . Although the Censorate officials would like to [cease memorializing and] withdraw, yet . . . they are under pressure from the OSC and are unable to stop of their own volition" (1501.11.11 S, 11.12 S).

This statement naturally subjected Yi Kŭk-kyun to Censorate displeasure and it also brought the OSC into the fray with an attack on Yu Cha-gwang and the State Council. Yŏnsangun reacted swiftly, ordering the OSC officials imprisoned and judicial proceedings instituted against them (1501.11.16). But, perhaps because of Censorate representations, the OSC officials were let off lightly, most of them merely being transferred to other posts (1501.11.17, 11.23). Thus came to an end another series of attacks against Yu Cha-gwang, but this time he emerged the victor.

There appears to be only one other instance of Censorate hostility to Yu Cha-gwang during these inter-purge years. A very brief affair, it occurred when one of Yu's sons was appointed a Copyist in the Bureau of State Records. This was criticized on the ground that appointees to such posts should be men of faultless family background; but when the king paid no heed the matter was dropped (1503.1.2).

Im Sa-hong, too, continued to be anathema to the censoring bodies, which took exception to nearly every personnel action involving him. They objected to Im being raised in rank (the Censorate resigned over this issue, but without effect, 1499.4.29, 5.3), to the appointment of this "villain" to a ceremonial military post (1500.9.18), and to the enfeoffing of this "amoral man" as a Lord (for he was the heir of his father, a Merit Subject; 1503.2.30). The king heeded none of these indictments, but it should also be noted that Im Sa-hong continued to be relegated to minor or peripheral posts.

During this period the censoring bodies again had ample opportunity to protest the favoritism shown to marriage kin, for Yŏnsangun was assiduous in giving appointments and promotions to such men and in otherwise singling them out for preferred treatment. None of these cases merits detailed discussion, although on occasion the king took punitive action against the Censorate and OSC officials concerned (e.g., 1502.9.23, 10.4). It may be noted that Yun T'ang-no, Sin Su-gŭn and his two brothers, and Pak Wŏn-jong were especially frequent objects of attack.[3] Yŏnsangun rarely heeded remonstrance in these cases, and when he did almost invariably it was where reasons had been adduced in addition to that of relationship by marriage to the royal house.

The censoring bodies were assiduous, as always, in upholding Confucianist mores and in denouncing behavior based on other patterns of belief. Although there is no evidence to indicate that the king himself was a Buddhist devotee,[4] nevertheless, apparently in harmony with the wishes of the women around him (especially the queen mothers), he supported or tolerated a number of circumstances favorable to Buddhist temples, monks, or believers. To name a few of these to which the Censorate objected: the printing of sutras,[5] the rash of small Buddhist shrines set up outside the city gates to cater to women of the palace,[6] and the burden imposed on the local populace by the transport of salt bestowed on certain Kangwŏndo temples.[7] Protests also were voiced against shamanistic practices which, in one case at least, involved the palace.[8] And the censoring organs were able to point to numerous instances of departure from the strict requirements of the Confucian code, such as the shortening of the mourning period,[9] the king's excessive performance of rites for his mother,[10] and a royal command to compose poems on the topic of two accomplished *kisaeng.*[11]

The single great debate of the inter-purge years was on the question of frontier or defense policy. Here, as was the case in Sŏngjong's reign, the censoring bodies steadfastly opposed aggressive measures against Chosŏn's troublesome neighbors in the north. Indeed, it may not be too much to say that they opposed minimum measures of preparedness. Arrayed on the other side, again as before, were the king and much less firmly the State Councillors and other high officials. In the end, perhaps in part because the provocation was less great and certainly due in part to vacillation and schism in the ranks of the State Councillors, the views of the censoring organs were allowed largely to prevail.

It all began with two raids across the Hamgyŏng Namdo border by small bands of mounted tribesmen (1499.4.3, 5.9), after which the king decided on a punitive expedition and initiated planning toward this end (1499.5.9, 5.12). The first objections came from the OSC, which argued that aggressive military action was not the proper approach to the barbarian problem and pointed out the strain put on the national economy by a succession of lean years (1499.5.12, 5.21). Further protests from the censoring organs were such that the king retreated to the extent of submitting the question for general discussion. A consensus favored strengthening defenses and awaiting further provocation before resorting to sterner measures (1499.5.28, 5.29, 6.7).

Presently, however, a further incident nearby in P'yŏngando (1499.6.17) led the king to solicit views on punitive action in this direction. The recommendation of certain State Councillors and leading military men, which the king adopted, was to conduct a thorough reconnaissance of the enemy and terrain and an assessment of the army's state of preparedness before coming to a final decision (1499.6.27). Accordingly, preparations went forward on the assumption that there would be an expedition the following year (1499.6.28, 7.2, 7.11, 7.12, 7.24). But after two more violations of the border, a Royal Secretary requested that a punitive expedition be launched that same year. From elder statesman Yun P'il-sang on down, however, all but one of the high officials consulted held that no military action should be undertaken other than a major expedition in the following year. The single exception was Third State Councillor Sŏng Chun,[12] who advocated a small-scale attack in the current year to be followed by a major assault the next. The king at first adopted Sŏng's view but due to the resulting furor he reversed himself and accepted the recommendation of Yun P'il-sang and the others (1499.7.20, 7.23, 7.28).

Although two more incidents occurred in the next two months, the high officials refused to approve military reprisals. Then, after three months during which discussion of border policy focused on defensive measures and on stratagems of tricking the enemy into complacency preparatory to launching a surprise attack, the plans for a western expedition were dropped. The Censorate and OSC had remained steadfast in opposition, and now Second State Councillor Han Ch'i-hyŏng and Third State Councillor Sŏng Chun himself also urged in the strongest terms that it be canceled. These latter based their argument, in the main, on the pitiful condition of army food stores, the result of a succession of lean years. In consequence, Yŏnsangun had no choice but to abandon the enterprise (1499.9.10, 9.22, 10.12, 10.23, 12.24, 1500.1.9, 1.12, 1.21 S, 1.22 S).[13]

A second phase of the debate on border policy revolved around the question of constructing—actually reconstructing—a long wall all the way across northern P'yŏngando and Hamgyŏngdo. The Board of War presented a detailed plan immediately prior to the decision to cancel the western expedition and its feasibility was ordered studied (1500.1.20). Apparently a decision had not as yet been reached on the question when the Censorate cautioned against it. The king consulted his Office of Fortifications[14] and was told that it had to be done; accordingly, Yŏngsangun ignored repeated Censorate protests (1500.6.25). Presently, in a further discussion of the question, the State Councillors and leading military men alike asked that the plan be carried out in spite of inevitable minor evils. The Censorate, however, countered with the assertion that the attendant evils would be great, not minor, and the king therefore had the matter discussed once more. The result this time was a decision to wait until the following spring to begin the work (1500.7.14, 7.18). The record reveals that a few days later, the State Councillors still held to their original view in favor of the project, while other high level advisors now agreed with the Censorate's arguments for abandoning it (1500.7.28). But Yŏnsangun noted at the end of a Censorate memorial that a hundred such documents would not make him change his mind, and he did not answer the next Censorate communication on the subject (1500.8.4, 8.13).

Nevertheless, Yŏnsangun eventually did change his mind. The following year, on the basis of good local harvest prospects, he ordered a P'yŏngando section of the wall constructed in the coming fall and there were no objections voiced (1501.5.25). But a month later, in the course of a discussion of the feasibility of going ahead with the long-wall project, the OSC and Censorate assailed Second State Councillor Sŏng Chun and Third State Councillor Yi Kŭk-kyun for supporting the plan in the face of an opposing consensus. Sŏng and Yi retorted that they were thoroughly conversant with frontier affairs, which the OSC was not, and added: "That the Office of Special Counselors should engage in remonstrance—in the past there was not this practice. Yet nowadays, when an issue is met, the OSC is quicker still to speak than the Censorate" (1501.6.30 S). The king then rejected once again the arguments against the long-wall project (1501.6.30, 7.5). Presently, however, a new discussion of the matter revealed a split among the high officials, with one group suggesting that, instead of making a special effort involving utilization of troops from the southern provinces, the construction work might be accomplished gradually by local and nearby military manpower. The king's decision at this time is not recorded but, in the absence of further mention of the long-wall project for at least three years, it seems fair to assume that he now, or shortly, gave up the idea (1501.8.7 S).

In these between-purge years the censoring bodies not only opposed the royal will in a number of questions of state policy; they also often spoke out in criticism of the personal conduct of the king. Remonstrance on this subject became increasingly frequent, and increasingly pertinent, as

Yǒnsangun more and more neglected his duties in favor of hedonistic pursuits. As an indication of the range of problems of this sort to which the censoring bodies addressed themselves, one might cite the keeping of hunting dogs and falcons inside the palace,[15] and the eviction of hundreds of families from the vicinity of the palace walls, done largely to prevent observation of the king's wanton frolics in the palace gardens.[16]

Indeed, Yǒnsangun's chief occupations at this time appear to have been hunting and partying, both of which entailed significant increases in palace expenditures and were responsible as well for a score of other evils great and small. Accordingly, in addition to trying to halt a variety of royal actions on moral grounds, the censoring bodies time and again called for a reduction in unessential palace expenditures[17] and enjoined the king to devote more attention to affairs of state, in particular to attend the Royal Lectures with greater regularity.[18] Yǒnsangun paid little heed, and when he deigned to answer at all it was nearly always in the negative or in feeble self-justification.[19]

The State Councillors and other high officials often echoed the pleas of the censoring bodies for royal restraint in the spheres of palace expenditures and personal conduct. These themes are by far the most prominent in the record of high official concern during these years.

Particularly disturbing to the State Councillors were the king's ever increasing efforts to flesh out the palace purse and palace staff, as well as the private purses and staffs of favored royal kinsmen, at the expense of the resources of the government proper. As early as 1499 we find the entire State Council enjoining the king to return a considerable number of slaves previously detached from various government offices, while at the same time they urged cessation of imports of luxury goods from Ming China, of lavish royal disbursements, and of independent action by the burgeoning Palace Supply Office in matters of slaves and taxes (1499.3.27). Other memorials attacked such evils as the transfer of fishing rights from the jurisdiction of local governments to that of the Palace Supply Office (1501.5.6), the award of irrigated crop lands to a princess (1501.6.18, 1502.5.2), and the usurpation of government firewood lands by members of the royal clan (1501.8.11). At one point the High State Councillors presented the king a detailed accounting of extraordinary expenditures made over a period of one year, including substantial human and material resources diverted from normal utilization by various government agencies, and urged that economies be effected (1502.1.28; see also 1502.10.12).

The burden of the State Council's dissatisfaction with the activities and conduct of Yǒnsangun is well summed up in a single memorial of the High State Councillors, in which they cited ten "evils of the day." These were, in summary: (1) the king's persistent failure to attend the Royal Lectures; (2) the granting of firewood lands to princes and princesses; (3) the king's disporting in the palace park in the company of eunuchs, to the exclusion of contacts with the officialdom; (4) the great backlog of unattended official business; (5) the inability to reach the king in an emergency, due to his proceeding too deeply into the palace park; (6) the incessant construction activities in the palace park; (7) the demands for the procurement of fast horses for palace use; (8) the overlong detention on palace tasks of painters and artisans of all kinds; (9) the unrestrained level of expenditures; and (10) the exorbitant demands for tribute tax goods from Kyŏnggi province. Yŏnsangun's reply forbade further grants of firewood lands but gave rather lame justification, if any, for other practices (1502.3.25 S).

In their firm and frequent posture on the subject of royal prodigality, the State Councillors no doubt drew strength from the knowledge that they were not without support within the palace itself. It is recorded that the queen mother, Insu (Tŏkchong's queen and Sŏngjong's mother), secretly adjured her kinsman, Chief State Councillor Han Ch'i-hyŏng, in these words: "If the king's conduct continues like this, unmended, and you, the foremost minister in the land, cannot set aright [the ship of state] by putting forth the fullest measure of your effort, then with what [brazen] face will you encounter the shades of our royal ancestors in the world beyond?" (1502.6.28 S). And it is added that the State Councillors thenceforth remonstrated still more frequently (1502.6.28). The king, however, was seldom disposed to listen. His attitude toward criticism of any aspect of his conduct was succinctly expressed in this reply to one State Council plea for economy: "The expenditures of the Palace Supply Office, etc., are entirely unavoidable; one may speak of economizing, but how can one fail to expend what must be expended?" (1501.8.9 S). In other words, the king was to be the sole judge of the propriety of the king's actions.

As concerned as they were at these aspects of the king's personal and official conduct, the high officials were at one with Yŏnsangun in condemning the developing pattern of Censorate and other lower-level attacks on their persons and authority. Toward the end of 1503 the infuriated Chief State Councillor, Sŏng Chun, had occasion to memorialize as follows:

The habit of contempt of higher authority is characteristic of our dynasty. The young men band together in friendly association and develop deleterious habits. After 1498 these habits somewhat subsided but now they have begun to wax again. I occupy the Chief State Councillor position, [but even so] have suffered truly many insults. I now ask to resign. (1503.9.8 S)

The king was in full sympathy with the plaint of his chief minister, since this habit of "contempt of higher authority" was the aspect of the political and moral fabric of his time over which Yŏnsangun professed the greatest concern. This concern is more readily seen in the events of the Purge of 1504, but it is amply demonstrated, too, by the record of the inter-purge years. A closer examination of the king's thinking, including the component of his views on the function of remonstrance, will lay bare the great theme of the second purge and will lead directly into the incident that touched it off.

At the beginning of 1499, in what may be construed in part as a shaft aimed at the concept of remonstrance itself, Yŏnsangun sent the following message to the State Council:

The ordinances of the government must of necessity be consistent; they must not be subject to random change. Nowadays one observes that men severally hold firmly to their own opinions . . . unhesitatingly offering their views and putting forward a multitude of irresponsible proposals. Though a matter of state policy has been decided, still they do not know to stop [debating it]. Is this not tantamount to a government without mores, wherein authority flows forth from many founts? Moreover, even the various [lower level] agencies of government contend with each other, bent on winning [acceptance of a parochial point of view], A saying aye and B nay, each presenting its own case in memorials, so that a decree of the morning is changed in the evening . . . [In consequence] the civil administrators know not what to enforce, and the people know not what to obey. If this evil persists, law in the end will be reduced to turmoil. Let all ranks of the official-dom clearly apprehend my will, so to ensure that this injurious practice is not perpetuated. (1499.1.25 S)

At the height of the attack by the censoring organs on Yu Cha-gwang in late 1501, Yŏnsangun found fault with the censoring function as then practiced, in these words: "The Censorate and the Office of Special Counselors each have their respective duties. Yet nowadays, whenever the Censorate memorializes, the OSC follows up and speaks out on the same matter. Now, these bodies do not censure the actions of their own colleagues, but invariably attack all matters related to the high officials. Is this not an unseemly practice?" (1501.10.26 S).

Just three months prior to the start of the Purge of 1504, an OIG Bailiff took steps to effect the arrest of a boy orderly from the palace on a petty breach of etiquette charge (1503.12.22 S). Yŏnsangun responded by arresting and discharging the Bailiff, and when a Third Inspector protested that the king had meted out an extra-legal punishment, Yŏnsangun replied: "I took this action be-cause [the Bailiff's act] displayed contempt of higher authority. And the OIG's censoring of my action likewise is such an act of contempt" (1503.12.26 S).

The Purge Begins

The Purge of 1504 began with an incident essentially trivial but which fitted perfectly the theme of "contempt of higher authority." Yŏnsangun had ordered a granddaughter of the Kyŏnggi Governor, Hong Kwi-dal, sent in to the royal harem. The girl's father, however, failed to comply, asserting that his daughter was ill. Then, when the king initiated criminal proceedings against his son, Hong Kwi-dal explained that he was responsible for his son's refusal and he added: "If the girl were not really ill, how could I dare hesitate [to have her sent in]? Though Your Majesty has ordered her sent in imme-diately, it simply is not possible" (1504.3.11 S).

Angered, Yŏnsangun took up Hong Kwi-dal's office warrants and banished him to Hamgyŏngdo, issuing this explanation: "On the whole, today's high officials have the habit of contempt of consti-tuted authority. If this is not severely punished, the younger officialdom will take it as their model. Hong Kwi-dal's utterance of disrespectful words is due simply to the fact that Yi Se-jwa was not sternly punished [for his crime of *lèse majesté*]" (1504.3.11)[20]

The Yi Se-jwa affair had occurred half a year earlier. Then Minister of Rites, Yi had accidentally spilled wine on the royal robes in the course of a state banquet. At first he and three of his sons merely had been removed from their posts, but presently he was banished in mild degree to Chŏlla and almost immediately transferred in harsher degree to Hamgyŏngdo. At the same time the Censorate officials, who had failed to indict this crime of *lèse majesté*, were removed, demoted, and barred until further notice from holding Censorate or OSC positions (1503.9.15, 9.20 S, 9.21 S).[21]

Yi Se-jwa had been released at the beginning of 1504 (1.11) by special royal command, but with the Hong Kwi-dal incident he was banished again (1504.3.11). This was followed immediately by banishment in mild degree of the incumbent Censorate officials, as punishment for not having protested Yi Se-jwa's release from banishment (1504.3.12 S).[22] This action was accompanied by a proclamation to the nation:

The distinction between sovereign and subject must not fail to be kept strict; the habit of contempt of higher authority must not fail to be reformed. The mounting evils of today stem from the developing mores of arrogancy . . . Among the high officials too there has been the crime of disrespect. The Censorate without fail should have impeached [Yi Se-jwa and Hong Kwi-dal] but, conscious of their entrenched position and fearing their power, did not speak forth. [Yet] when someone is seen to be alone and defenseless, then the Censorate invariably attacks violently and unceasingly. When the Censorate should speak out, it does not; and when it should not, it speaks out strongly. Not only the Censorate, but the highest officials as well did not dare censure. Such conduct on the part of the present high officials and Censorate . . . serves to set the sovereign apart in helpless isolation. This habit must not be permitted to develop. Let capital and provinces be clearly warned that I will thoroughly root out this pernicious trend. (1504.3.13 S)

The king next ordered beaten and banished all those who had held Censorate office subsequent to Yi Se-jwa's unfortunate slip of the hand, and in addition he punished the OSC officials of the same period by forty strokes commuted to a fine (1504.3.14). When Yŏnsangun declared his intention to punish the OSC officials as well, he remarked: "The OSC at bottom is not a locus of anti-personnel remonstrance, yet at times it has indicted personnel, saying: Standing in such close attendance upon the king, we do not dare remain silent. Neverthless, there was nary an OSC official who indicted Yi Se-jwa" (1504.3.14 S).

Responding to cue, the newly appointed Censorate asserted that Hong Kwi-dal and Yi Se-jwa had been dealt with too leniently and requested penalties of death and far-banishment respectively (1504.3.14). Presently they were brought back from the road to banishment and beaten, and before long both were executed (1504.3.16, 3.30, 6.16).[23] Meanwhile, many others were being engulfed in the personal tragedies of Hong and Yi. Sons of both were first removed from certain of their posts, then one son of each was beaten and banished, and shortly all the sons and sons-in-law of Yi Se-jwa were beaten and banished afar (1504.3.16, 3.17, 3.19). At the same time, the State Tribunal was ordered to ascertain those who had visited Yi Se-jwa upon his prior release from banishment and the first victims of this investigation were the Fourth State Councillor, No Kong-p'il, and the Minister of

Rites, Kim Ŭng-gi, who were divested of office warrants and banished in mild degree (1504.3.17).[24] Substantially the same penalty was meted out to two newly appointed Censorate officials who had protested against the punishment of the entirety of former Censorate and OSC personnel in the Yi Se-jwa case (1504.3.18).

At this point in the initial stage of the purge there occurred the following exchange between the king and his Royal Secretariat. The king's statement was a naked challenge:

Recently those among the higher and lower levels of the officialdom who have been sentenced to crimes have been extremely many. The government doubtless regards this as tyranny. Of yore it was said: To make others stand in awe is to command their obedience. Today's officialdom looks upon their sovereign as so much loose straw. Hence this turn of events. (1504.3.23 S)

The reply of the Royal Secretaries, however predictable, was all that Yŏnsangun could have hoped for: "The higher and lower officials have themselves fashioned their crimes. Who would dare say this is tyranny?" (1504.3.23 S).

Now began one well remarked facet of the Purge of 1504—the punishment of those living and dead who were connected in some way with the deposition and execution of Yŏnsangun's mother. Already the king, with his own hands it is said, had beaten to death two concubines of Sŏngjong whom he held responsible for his mother's fate and had had their corpses torn asunder, salted, and cast out into the open. The two sons of one of them, his own half-brothers, he had ordered beaten and banished (1504.3.20).[25]

Yet, despite this solid indication of Yŏnsangun's strong feeling on the subject and the warning contained in the exchange of messages with the Royal Secretariat, there still were those who opposed Yŏnsangun's desire to bestow further posthumous honors upon his mother and to curtail mourning rites for the two concubines. As might be expected, nine of the ten high officials whose views are recorded fully approved the king's intentions, while the tenth objected only to the abbreviated rites for the concubines. The OSC and Censorate personnel, on the other hand, opposed additional honors for Lady Yun on the ground that all permissible rites had been performed, and also (the Censorate with somewhat more force) held improper the rites curtailment proposal. This act of temerity— perhaps courage is more apt—resulted in the rod and banishment for the OSC and Censorate officials and a fine and banishment in mild degree for the dissident high official (1504.3.23).[26]

The king's next step was to have the official records searched for the names of those high officials who had participated in the events surrounding the deposition and death of his mother (1504.3.24, 4.1). On the basis of the information obtained, Yŏnsangun ordered Yi P'a's corpse beheaded, his property confiscated, and his posterity banned from public office.[27] Five other deceased high officials of the time were to be reburied as commoners and their sons banished,[28] and Yun P'il-sang, who had continued to play an active role in the government after his removal as Chief State Councillor under Censorate attack in 1493, was to lose his office warrants and his property and be banished together with his sons (1504.4.18, 4.19).[29]

Far from satisfied, Yŏnsangun ordered the records searched again for high official participants and then broadened his instruction to include the Censorate personnel as well as the Rites Board, Royal Secretariat, and various miscellaneous officials of the time. Punishments ranging from dismissal from office to banishment were pronounced on sixteen men, living and dead (1504.4.21, 4.23, i4.5, i4.13, i4.16).

In the meantime, numerous others were suffering for a variety of offenses. Second State Councillor Yi Kŭk-kyun was banished in mild degree because of his attempts to succor Yi Se-jwa (his nephew), No Kong-p'il, Kim Ŭng-gi, and certain of the relations of the royal concubines (1504.3.28). Six weeks later he was sentenced to death, on which occasion the only ground cited was his attitude in the Yi Se-jwa case (1504.i4.11,i4.12).[30] A disrespectful palace eunuch was executed (1504.3.30). Three female slaves were beheaded for talking about happenings at the palace, and their parents and brothers were assigned to duty at the remotest government outposts (1504.4.1). Several others were severely beaten and sent to duty on the border for a similar offense (1504.4.3). Two officials were banished afar for sitting with their backs to the royal presence during the regular triennial military examination (1504.4.10). For uttering disrespectful words three named but unidentified persons, perhaps palace attendants, were executed by dismemberment (1504.4.25 S). Two female palace attendants were banished in harsh degree (and later executed) for jealousy and disobedience (1504.4.25, 6.8, 6.20). Two palace eunuchs were assigned to corvee because they were believers in Buddhism and had commingled with monks (1504.i4.8 S).[31] A eunuch was beheaded and gibbeted for taking too light a view of Yi Kŭk-kyun's crimes (1504.i4.10).[32] Former OSC and Censorate officials Yi Yu-nyŏng and Pyŏn Hyŏng-nyang were sentenced to death for making allegedly groundless and personally motivated charges of immoral conduct against two members of a prominent yangban clan (1504.i4.11).[33]

No sooner had Yŏnsangun finished wreaking his initial revenge on those connected with the misfortunes of his mother than he turned his attention to those who had criticized his personal or official conduct or that of his palace staff, or who had spoken in some other context construable as impinging upon the dignity and authority of the sovereign status. Quite naturally, former Censorate and OSC officials comprised the bulk of such offenders. Indeed, the king presently ordered the records searched for all those among the Censorate and highest officials who had questioned the propriety of his conduct or who had been contemptuous of higher authority (1504.5.8 S).

To one Sim Sun-mun, who once as a Third Inspector had criticized the breadth of the royal robes, goes the distinction of being the first victim of this phase of the purge. Initially he was only beaten and banished, but later he was beheaded (1504.i4.25, 11.27 S, 12.5 S). Immediately following this, charges of crime were leveled posthumously against former Chief State Councillor Han Ch'i-hyŏng, for taking exception to such royal actions as erecting a palisade around the palace precincts (as a defense against prying eyes) and for urging economy, and against former Second

State Councillor Ŏ Se-gyŏm, for criticizing palace expenditures (1504.i4.26). Then five former Censorate officials were sentenced for having spoken out on trivial palace matters. Four of these were condemned to death and their sons to banishment and slavery, while the fifth escaped with the rod and banishment (1504.i4.27, 5.12).

Again, four more former Censorate officials were held accountable for once questioning the propriety of the riding of horses by palace eunuchs (1504.i4.28, 5.1). At the same time, former Chief State Councillor Sŏng Chun, banished less than a month before because of his role in the deposition of the king's mother, was noted as having spoken out on the same subject. The combined weight of these two charges led to a sentence of death by strangling for Sŏng Chun and appropriate punishment of his two sons, a grandson, and others among his clansmen (1504.i4.28, i4.29, 5.4, 5.15).[34]

If those who had not served in recent years as State Councillors or Censorate officials were congratulating themselves on their immunity from the king's wrath, they were premature. No matter what position a man had held in the official hierarchy, chance might at any time turn Yŏnsangun's attention toward a matter with which he had been connected. In one case, Yŏnsangun reached back into the late years of his father's reign for grounds on which to base the execution of former Censor-General Yi Tŏk-sung. Yi had been banished by Sŏngjong for "conjecturing about palace matters." Yŏnsangun now beheaded him (1504.5.22). Suspecting in another instance that officials of the Royal Stables Administration had informed Yi Kŭk-kyun about the racing of horses in the palace grounds, the king divested of office warrants and banished four such functionaries. Two others, however, a brother-in-law and a maternal uncle of Yŏnsangun, were especially excepted from this disposition of the case (1504.5.15, 6.7 S). Again, a former roster of Royal Secretariat officials was punished for criticizing the tardy response of a palace eunuch whom they had summoned to convey a communication to the king. Yŏnsangun now regarded this as an act of contempt of the sovereign dignity (1504.5.18, 5.19 S).

A more unfortunate victim at this time was Chŏng In-in, who was ordered beheaded for his crime of flouting the royal authority. There were three specifications to the charge against Chŏng: that once, when he was an OSC Third Counselor and received with his colleagues a command to compose a single poem, he alone had presented two poems (1502.11.29); that formerly he had feigned illness in an attempt to evade an appointment as Magistrate of Cheju Island (1503.5.22, 6.9; on this occasion he had been beaten and assigned to corvee); that he once had spoken out in opposition to the transfer of certain lands from a government to a palace agency (1504.5.4, 5.21).[35]

In a case of a different type, two minor functionaries and a Classics Licentiate were executed by dismemberment. Their crime was that they had gone picnicking at a time of national mourning for Yŏnsangun's recently deceased grandmother (1504.6.1).

At this time, some three months after he had initiated the blood bath, Yŏnsangun issued a brief but remarkably candid statement appraising his actions and aims:

These days [many] criminals are being sentenced to severe punishments and without doubt the country is shocked at this . . . But the corruption of mores is such that benevolent rule is powerless to effect reformation. What we have been doing recently comes close to being tyranny, but how is it possible to rectify mores otherwise? (1504.6.2 S)

To this the Royal Secretariat replied:

Who could be shocked after reading the royal pronouncements detailing the charges against these criminals? In our view, already mores have greatly changed and among your subjects high and low none is not transformed — all are serving you with proper reverence. (1504.6.2 S)

The Royal Secretariat's suggestion, perhaps only a wan hope, that the king might consider his end already attained met with no success. For Yŏnsangun rejoined that only after ten years or so could one tell whether mores really had changed and he proceeded to give every indication of continuing his corrective measures indefinitely.

It was at this time that the *Sillok* historians, in an aside, captured something of the atmosphere behind the scenes and gave a glimpse of Yŏnsangun's psychology and of the awful predicament of the official class, who often could not save themselves or their associates without dooming others:

At the time, the king desired to close off the channels of remonstrance and so dug up affairs of the past, without fail inquired who had been the prime advocates, and meted out death sentences. As a means to save themselves, those under interrogation implicated those already dead. Although the king was well aware of this still he wanted to brandish his authority. So, without inquiring into the degree of guilt, in every case he had the coffins of the accused opened and their corpses mutilated, and in some instances he further had their property confiscated and the wives and children enslaved. The wails of the innocently wronged rose on high but the State Tribunal officials, though they were aware of the unsubstantiated nature of the charges, remained silent, on the ground that they could not endure killing the living. (1504.6.6 S)

Punishing the Remonstrators

Purge cases in this pattern dominated the third quarter of 1504. For a fortnight, Yŏnsangun moved against what he perceived to have been improper remonstrance, criticisms most frequently by the censoring officials questioning his exercise of the royal authority and the activities of his palace staff. For such crimes as having objected to royal archery practice in the palace park, to promotion of a distantly related royal relative, to the rising level of palace expenditures, and to the frequency and destructiveness of royal hunts, at least fifty former members of the censoring organs were severely punished.[36] Then almost two months passed before the parade of purge cases concerned with the punishment of improper remonstrance resumed. In response to a royal command, the records had been searched to identify the participants in eight such instances. When Yŏnsangun saw the resulting list, containing more than forty names, he deplored this fresh evidence that the official ranks had been filled so largely with amoral men and then ordered that the prime advocate of each remonstrance be determined (1504.8.8 S).

The first to suffer as the purge now gathered fresh momentum was a former Fourth Inspector, alleged by his colleagues to have been behind an OIG criticism of the razing of dwellings which neighbored on the residence of a royal concubine; his corpse was beheaded and his property confiscated (1504.8.5 S, 8.8 S, 8.10 S). Next, a former Fourth Censor was beaten and banished for having questioned the need for flowered mats in the palace (1504.8.8 S, 9.1 S), while a number of former Censorate officials who had participated in protests against the transfer of fishing grounds in the Haeju area to the Palace Supply Office were sent into banishment (1504.8.8 S, 8.10 S, 8.27 S, 9.1 S, 9.18 S).[37] In another case, the current Third Royal Secretary, Kang Ching, was accused by former colleagues of responsibility for Censorate contentions that, since offerings of game already had been made at the royal ancestral shrine, there was no valid reason for staging still another formal hunt. Despite Kang's protestations that he had been misinterpreted, he was lashed, banished afar, and enslaved, while more than a dozen others who had gone on record with similar views were sentenced to beating or banishment or both (1504.8.8 S, 8.10 S, 8.14 S, 8.26 S, 8.27 S, 9.1 S, 9.18 S, 9.19 S, 9.24 S, 9.30 S). In the fifth of these eight instances of improper remonstrance, former First Royal Secretary Sin Yong-gae was fined and divested of office warrants for his view that "the people's grapes ought not be gathered for presentation [to the palace]" (1504.8.8 S, 8.20 S). But the record offers no firm evidence that the guilty were punished in the three other cases under investigation at this time.[38]

The next great wave of belated punishments of officials who, it now developed, had abused the censoring function, once again took as its theme the manifold injustices suffered by the deposed Lady Yun. Participants in five separate instances of opposition to the posthumous honors Yŏnsangun wished to accord his mother were determined by a search of the records and, in many cases, sentenced to banishment or worse. Fifteen purge victims in this category were those OSC and Censorate officials already in banishment for their objections to the additional rites proposed by the king at the very outset of the purge. Other victims came from among the Censorate officials of the early years of Yŏnsangun's reign who had opposed the king's desire to rebury his mother and honor her ritually. Former Third Inspector Kang Hyŏng, who had argued that Yŏnsangun must not contravene the expressed injunctions of his father, was sentenced to execution by dismemberment and confiscation of his property (1504.9.26 S, 9.28 S, 10.1 S, 10.4 S). Another Third Inspector of the period, Yi Su-gong, was beheaded because of his views on an aspect of the reburial question (1504. 9.26 S, 10.27 S, 10.28 S). But a dozen more former Censorate officials, who were reported to Yŏnsangun as prominent participants in the discussions of these questions, evidently were not punished.[39]

Yŏnsangun occupied himself during the last weeks of the purge year with the prosecution of still another cluster of improper remonstrance cases. Two of these are of some special interest. Severe posthumous punishment was dealt to two deceased former Censorate officials, beating and banishment to three former Royal Secretaries, and milder penalties to several additional former

Censors for their objections to a promotion in rank the king once had awarded a son of Im Sa-hong (1504.10.11 S, 11.9 S, 12.16 S, 12.19 S, 12.20 S, 12.22 S, 12.23 S). Because they all had urged restoration of the tomb of Tanjong's mother, Nam Hyo-on, Kim Il-son, Yi Chu, and Han Hun suffered fresh or further posthumous punishments (1504.9.30 S, 10.1 S, 10.18 S, 11.9 S, 11.13 S).[40] And in other cases, several former Censorate officials were given comparatively mild sentences for their roles in remonstrance relating, in general, to the palace apparatus and the conduct of palace affairs. (1504.11.9 S, 1505. 1.4 S, 1.6 S, 1.8 S).

Again in the first month of 1505, and more notably in the second month, Yŏnsangun undertook to inquire into a wide variety of instances of abusive exercise of the power of remonstrance and to punish those who had participated. Most of those involved, of course, were former Censorate officials, and in their choice of subjects for remonstrance they were guilty, on the whole, of what Yŏnsangun termed "angling for repute." By this he meant that those offering remonstrance had been less concerned with the principle or issue at stake than with winning the plaudits of their contemporaries or of posterity. In Yŏnsangun's view, the sovereign dignity was inviolate and the sovereign authority beyond delimitation. This concept was at the very foundation of the social order, and yet members of officialdom consciously, even frivolously, had questioned the propriety of the monarch's personal conduct and of his dictates in respect to the administration of palace and government affairs. At this time of "rectification of mores" these crimes could not, and did not, go unpunished.[41]

The Roster of Other Offenders

At the same time that he was punishing this long list of officials guilty of improper remonstrance, Yŏnsangun did not neglect to attend to many more who had behaved offensively in a variety of other ways. One interesting, if difficult to fathom, category of such offenders consisted of those of extraordinary repute as paragons of loyalty, filial piety, or fidelity. The outstanding instance of this type was the beheading and gibbeting of a P'yŏngando man, then over seventy, who was widely known for his filial character (1504.9.6).[42] In an explanatory aside to the record of this event, the *Sillok* historians remark: "At this time [the king] termed loyal subjects, filial sons, faithful wives, and chaste maidens 'suspiciously non-conformist figures,' and executed them all" (1504.9.24 S). The language employed here would appear to be misleading, for there seems to be but one other purge case which might be placed under this heading. And this, the execution of former Second Counselor Chŏng Sŏng-gŭn and former First Tutor of the Crown Prince Tutorial Office Cho Chi-sŏ, is complicated by the presence of other factors.[43]

There are other miscellaneous purge cases deserving brief mention. Cho Sun, who had been discharged as Fourth Censor in 1497 (7.21) for his violent denunciation of No Sa-sin, now suffered further punishment on this account.[44] A former Copyist in the State Records Bureau suffered for having once requested that Recorders of the daily logs of government affairs be permitted to be present at deliberations of personnel nominations.[45] The royal clansman Yi Sim-wǒn, famed for his exposé of Im Sa-hong in 1478, was executed, his property confiscated, his brothers banished, and a second son beheaded (1504.9.27 S, 10.1S, 10.22 S).[46]

Another major theme of the Purge of 1504, one for which it is widely remarked, is the wholesale execution of the surviving victims of 1498 and the posthumous indignities heaped upon those already deceased. It was hard on the heels of his first move against Yi Sim-wǒn that Yǒnsangun voiced his well remembered condemnation of the men of 1498, in these words:

> With regard to the history drafts affair of 1498, those cliquists are mostly in banishment in the provinces. The High State Councillors of the time were all of the villainous crowd and employed personal bias [in their handling of the case.[47] Consequently] there lived [some] who should have died, and, on the contrary, [some] who died should have lived. Yet of what use is it to let this crowd exist? Have them all brought under arrest. (1504.9.26 S)

Yǒnsangun then decreed that Sǒng Chung-ǒm and Kang Kyǒm were to be executed by dismemberment and Kang Paek-chin and Kim Koeng-p'il beheaded, the property of all four to be confiscated, their wives enslaved, and their sons and brothers beaten and evicted from the capital. Yi Wǒn and Ch'oe Pu were to be beaten, banished, and enslaved (1504.9.26 S).[48]

But even before this, a number of 1498 victims had been made to suffer again for their old crimes or on other counts of the sort common to many 1504 purge cases. Quite early in the purge, Yi Chu had been beheaded and gibbeted, charged with having once requested provision of an assembly room for Censorate use when on business at the palace (1504.i4.26 S, 5.22 S).[49] Royal clansman Yi Ch'ong had incurred the same penalty; his crime, consorting with members of officialdom, was no more than a succinct restatement of the 1498 case against him (1504.5.30). A one-time Royal Secretary, Hong Sik, was beheaded at the same time, accused of having "divulged matters of the palace" (1504.5.30).

Then, soon after announcing his determination to exterminate the "clique of 1498," Yǒnsangun also thought to further punish the Censorate officials of the time who had argued that high treason was too extreme a charge to lay against Kim Chong-jik. Accordingly, he ordered them beaten, divested of office warrants, and enslaved (1504.10.14 S). There then ensued mutilation of the corpses of Hǒ Pan, who had been beheaded in 1498, and of Cho Wi, P'yo Yǒn-mal, and Chǒng Yǒ-ch'ang, all of whom had died in banishment or enroute to banishment (1504.10.24 S). At the same time occurred the most intriguing of all these re-purge cases, the execution by dismemberment of Im Hǔi-jae, a son of the putative arch villain of 1504, Im Sa-hong (1504. 10.23 S, 10.24 S, 10.28 S).[50]

Thus, in general, those who had been banished in 1498 were executed in 1504, some on the basis of charges pre-dating 1498, and others simply because they belonged to the "1498 clique."[51] A 1498 victim of simple capital punishment, or one who had died in the meantime, suffered further posthumous penalties.[52] On the other hand, those involved peripherally in 1498, or to an extent meriting punishment less harsh than banishment, were not re-purged in 1504 unless by reason of unrelated additional offenses.

The King's Institutional Changes

Essentially, now, the purge was over. In the year and some months remaining to him, Yŏnsangun no more called to mind past instances of improper remonstrance, he no more sought revenge for the death of his mother, nor did he impose new penalties upon the victims of 1498. It might be suggested, of course, that the king had exhausted available stocks of candidates for purge action in these categories, and doubtless this was a factor in the abatement of the purge. But a more likely reason is that Yŏnsangun could now conclude that he had made his point.

The essence of this point was that the government could only function properly and effectively if its lines of authority were firmly drawn, separating the functions of each component agency, passing through the channels of the Six Boards and State Council, and all converging in the sovereign at the top. The sovereign's discretionary power should be unlimited and his actions should be beyond cavil or reproach.

Yŏnsangun stressed this point in ways other than by mere terror. Even when most busied by the purge, he found time to begin a campaign against those institutions and practices which apotheosized the outlaw mores of "contempt of higher authority." He stopped convening sessions of the Royal Lectures, citing physical indisposition and the pressure of the purge events (1504.i4.23). Subsequently, he eliminated the post of Special Participant (1504.12.27) and changed the title of the Office of Royal Lectures itself, rejecting the hallowed connotation of exposition of the Classics in favor of a term that implied a more mechanical reading of texts (1505.1.4). And in the end he entirely abolished the Office (1506.5.1).

The censoring organs fared little better. Yŏnsangun first laid down rules of procedure requiring all Censorate memorials to carry notation as to who had proposed each point and who had concurred in raising it (1504.6.7). His next step was to abolish the posts of Fourth Inspector and Fourth Censor, create an additional post of Third Censor, and order that the Censorate positions thenceforth be filled by officials of at least the Third Rank (1504.12.26 S). Eventually he abolished the Office of the Censor-General (1506.4.25), having already stripped the Censorate of its so-called *sŏgyŏng* power, that of limited veto over lower level appointments (1505.1.13). Meanwhile, the third censoring organ, the Office of Special Counselors, had also been abolished (1504.12.27, 1505.1.13, 7.7).

The established practices of other government organs were curtailed so as to make the monarch immune from criticism. The Royal Secretariat was reminded that its only function was to process communications; it was not to "discuss matters" (1504.6.15). Historians were ordered to record nothing but personnel and other routine administrative matters; they were not, as was traditional, to compose history drafts which they would keep in their homes until called in for *Sillok* compilation (1506.4.20; see also 1506.8.14). The position of Copyist in the Bureau of State Records was abolished (1505.1.15) and other steps were taken to restrict the scope of the basic source materials for future *Sillok* (1505.7.9).

Not content with all but excising the concept of remonstrance as institutionalized in the government, Yŏnsangun went to extreme, indeed paranoiac, lengths to insure freedom from private censure as well. He issued a number of decrees aimed at keeping knowledge of happenings within the palace from being circulated outside, especially to the ears of officialdom.[53] Another series of royal commands was designed to prevent private discussion of public business. In this direction, Yŏnsangun finally went so far as to ban visiting among any and all government personnel (1506.2.17), and he followed this up with a prohibition against government officials visiting anyone but their parents, brothers, and sisters (1506.4.25). It seemed a good idea, as well, to bar men fond of wine from posts in the Six Boards, Censorate, or OSC (1504.6.12). The king also thought it prudent, apparently, to announce penalties for those who divulged Korean internal affairs while on embassies to China (1505.4.18). Discussion among students, too, was forbidden (1504.5.18, 12.26).[54] These measures were accompanied by others which conduced to a bearing of greater subservience and respect toward the king on the part of the officials and others (see 1504.i4.6, i4.27, 5.7, 6.1, 7.13, 9.10, 1505.6.30, 1506.3.1).

While thus debilitating key agencies of the government and cowing its officers into silent impotence, Yŏnsangun moved to strengthen the palace apparatus and increase the economic resources at its disposal. To the Palace Supply Office was restored the privilege of direct communication with the throne, which had been an important issue in the purge (1504.5.9). After first assigning government personnel to handle the busy work load of that office (1505.1.16), Yŏnsangun upped its status to that of an organ of the government, manned at the top, in the usual fashion, with hierarchic yangban officials (1505.8.4, 9.14).

To fill his depleted coffers, the king turned to the most conspicuous concentration of private wealth and ordered that all lands and slaves awarded to Merit Subjects, beginning with the very first list of T'aejo, be repossessed (1504.5.7, 5.8).[55] Slaves and other properties confiscated from the purge victims were mostly turned over to the Palace Supply Office (1504.5.9, 6.2). Numbers of monks and nuns were returned to lay status and impressed into service in the palace (1506.3.23).

The palace had need of new sources of income, for in addition to the more run-of-the-monarch extravagances, Yŏnsangun had embarked on a project with almost inexhaustible potential for dissipating the resources of the state: the creation of a kind of royal hunting preserve, a huge extension of the palace park. Starting with the grounds contiguous to the palace, Yŏnsangun first went eastward, out beyond East Gate, before concentrating on expansion to the west. Since entrance to the area was forbidden to all but the king and his guests, it was necessary to erect a palisade around it and to patrol its boundaries. It was necessary, further, to raze many existing structures and to build new ones to meet the king's purposes. Yŏnsangun's private preserve consumed great quantities of time and treasure, and in the end it extended some 20 miles westward, more than halfway to Inch'ŏn.[56]

Yŏnsangun's End and His Legacy

In the light of his terrible misrule and his wholesale alienation of his subjects,[57] in particular the members of the official class, it is surprising that an effort to remove Yŏnsangun from the throne did not come sooner. But, at last, toward the end of 1506, that effort came. The coup was headed, in the main, by men who had continued to serve Yŏnsangun in high office, little affected by the purge. They acted after hearing of the escape from banishment of certain of the king's victims, who were rumored to be raising forces in the provinces against the tyrant.[58] Enlisting the support of key military men and of other officers of the government, the plotters deployed their troops in front of the gate to the palace grounds. Quickly deserted by his guards and by the rest of his palace staff, Yŏnsangun was easily compelled to yield up the badges of royal office. Then, bearing the consent decree of the queen mother, the procession moved on to the residence of Yŏnsangun's only legitimate half-brother and persuaded him to accept the throne (1506.9.2). The new monarch, King Chungjong, sent Yŏnsangun into banishment (1506.9.2), where he soon died (1506.11.6). It had been an all but bloodless coup.[59]

The nature of the Purge of 1504 is clear. Perhaps it was largely incidental to his autocratic inclinations, but Yŏnsangun had made a remarkably perceptive analysis of the political ills of his society and times. Unfortunately for his purpose, and for Chosŏn, the corrective measures he applied were overlaid with too much self-indulgence, too much petty tyranny, and too terrible a cruelty. His efforts failed; but worse than that — the manner of his attempt hallowed the very evils he had sought to eliminate. The political legacy of Yŏnsangun, then, was far-reaching in effect, for in truth, he bequeathed another purge.

Chapter IV

THE PURGE OF 1519

Yŏnsangun's years of misrule left a legacy that powerfully affected the shape of events in the early years of his successor. Indeed, the direction of the main political currents from Chungjong's accession in 1506 to the climactic Purge of 1519 was determined by the fact of Yŏnsangun's tyranny and the manner in which his tyranny was overthrown. Thus the key to the nature of the third Literati Purge is to be sought in the events surrounding the first two.

What were the significant codicils of this legacy of Yŏnsangun? Above all must be noted the character of the force that toppled him. The coup was initiated and officered, on the whole, by men high in the official hierarchy, men in positions of close proximity to the throne. The more important of the followers of these men presumably were bound to them by ties of blood or friendship. Obviously no one who played an active part in the deposition coup could have suffered serious injury at the hands of Yŏnsangun, for the king's victims were dead or banished from the capital.

The inescapable corollary to the nature of the coup that deposed Yŏnsangun was that, at the outset of his reign, King Chungjong had to accommodate three rather distinct forces in his government, among which there were ample grounds for distrust or enmity. There was the group that held high office at the end of Yŏnsangun's reign, the men who engineered the coup. Many of these had advanced at an abnormal rate due to the decimation of officials, and they now were to receive further rewards for their roles in enthroning Chungjong. At the same time, because of its record of acquiescence in the evil acts of Yŏnsangun, this group was vulnerable to attack.

A second group, an amorphous one, was composed of men who escaped punishment in the purge years and yet did not participate in the overthrow of Yŏnsangun. Some of these had been in provincial posts during the critical years; some had been taken away from the central government scene by other causes; some had emerged from the examination system too late to be involved in the purge events and were still in minor posts at the beginning of Chungjong's reign. The plight of many of this group was that the smooth resumption or progression of their official careers tended to be blocked by the weightier claims to higher office of the other two forces in the government.

Finally there were the survivors among the purge victims, including the kinsmen who had been associated in their guilt, who now were free to return to the political stage. In apparent recognition of their sufferings in the cause of good Confucian government, a number of these were summoned back at a level higher than that held when purged. On the other hand, this group frequently found the route to prominent government position barred by the incumbency of fortune's favorites, the men who had enthroned Chungjong. In other words, added to the physical suffering and the loss of two to eight years of seniority due to the purge was the galling circumstance that men who profited from the purges (if they had not actively cooperated in them) were in positions of authority above them.

A second important feature of the Yŏnsangun legacy was the unconventional aspect of the passage of the throne to Chungjong. The fact that deposition of a reigning monarch was by no means a rare occurrence in Korean or Chinese dynastic annals did not lessen its significance for the position of the new ruler. Chungjong inevitably was to some extent the creature of those who raised him to the throne. Since Chungjong was not in the regular line of succession, until the moment of the successful coup he had no following of men of influence loyal to his person. Quite the contrary. The fact that Chungjong was a half-brother of Yŏnsangun had meant a high degree of isolation from the residual points of political power. Moreover, Chungjong at first did not even have behind him a body of "marriage-kin" whose interests coincided with his own, for his consort was a niece of Yŏnsangun's queen, and her once powerful father (former Second State Councillor Sin Su-gŭn) and uncles had been killed in the deposition coup.

The implication for Chungjong in his unusual position was that he must act to buttress his insecure underpinnings. This he sought to do by amply rewarding the men to whom he owed his throne and by seeking to inculcate a sterner code of loyalty to the sovereign, the code rooted in Neo-Confucian concepts. For others the implication was that a sovereign enthroned by a coup could be dethroned the same way. Perhaps it is a law of the monarchic system that one departure from the normal pattern of succession breeds new attempts to duplicate the phenomenon. Chungjong, at any rate, encountered a number of treasonous plots, the unusual frequency and nature of which must have profoundly influenced his thinking and actions.

A third vital feature of the Yŏnsangun legacy was the enhancement of general esteem for the objects of Yŏnsangun's abomination. It is difficult to document this, yet surely this was a natural reaction. If the evil of Yŏnsangun were universally acknowledged, then only a brave discriminating few would hold that the targets of his tyranny were less than good. Despite the anomalies thus created, the deposers of such a tyrant could not but justify their action in the most sweeping terms. The Confucian philosophy of government demanded no less and practical politics, too, required that such a coup seek the broadest possible support among the power elite. Thus the rehabilitation of the victims of the purges of 1498 and 1504 was an inevitable byproduct of Chungjong's enthronement, and with this rehabilitation went an aura of martyrdom ample enough to envelop also the principles on which these victims stood. This goes far to explain the accelerated acceptance of Neo-Confucianism as the ideal basis for personal and political conduct, as well as the greatly increased tolerance of the censoring function, both of which are marked phenomena of the early years of Chungjong's reign. It will be useful to bear in mind these aspects of the legacy of Yŏnsangun while reviewing the events from Chungjong's accession to the Purge of 1519.

Excessive Rewards to Merit Subjects

The most striking feature of the political scene in these years once again was the clash between the censoring bodies on the one hand and the State Council (frequently backed by other high-ranking elements) on the other. The larger questions at issue in this running battle were closely linked to the nature of the political settlement that followed the enthronement of Chungjong. By 1519, to be sure, the composition of the rival forces had undergone considerable change. Most significantly, the victims of 1519, on the whole, were younger men whose first appearance in the arena of the central government postdated 1506. But they were a product of the times and the issues they faced and the positions they took were in large measure inherited. Moreover, the favorable climate in which they operated also was an inheritance. Exploiting to the utmost this naturally advantageous situation, the 1519 purge victims pushed too far too fast and, after alienating all the other concentrations of political power, at length lost the favor of the king. Ironically, then, King Chungjong, symbol of the vindication of the principle of untrammeled operation of the censoring function, in 1519 lent his ultimate authority to crush still another group of men for abusive exercise of this power.

Almost the first act of the new regime was to reward those who had participated in the deposition and enthronement coup. Promotions in rank were given forthwith to the three principal leaders of the coup, Pak Wŏn-jong, Sŏng Hŭi-an and Yu Sun-jŏng (1506. 9.3).[1] This was immediately followed by the creation of one hundred seventeen "Tranquilize the State Merit Subjects" *(chŏngguk kongsin),* who were divided into four classes of merit and rewarded proportionately with land, slaves and titles of enfeoffment (1506.9.8).[2] In addition, a large number of Minor Merit Subjects, over two hundred at the least, was created. These appear to have been rewarded principally by promotions in rank.[3]

It is important to consider briefly the composition of these groups of Merit Subjects. Little more than a month before he was deposed, Yŏnsangun had held a special ceremony celebrating the loyalty to the throne of his highest ranking officials. On this occasion a "Respect Vows [of Loyalty] Text" *(kyŏngsŏmun)* containing the names of twenty-three high officials was formally deposited in the Veritable Records Archives *(sillokkak).*[4] All but the three of these who were killed in the deposition coup were shortly to be enrolled as Chungjong Merit Subjects.[5] Some few others who held responsible government posts at or near the end of Yŏnsangun's reign also are to be found on the merit list. The list further contained a considerable number who held minor civil or military posts, a dozen or so close kin of leading Merit Subjects, a handful of members of the royal house, three or four close kin of Sŏngjong's queen, and six palace eunuchs.[6]

Very little information is available on the make-up of the Minor Merit Subject group. A good portion were low-ranking military men. Some were close kin of the more prominent Merit Subjects. Others had no connection with the enthronement but were included because of their relationships to Chungjong in the years prior to 1506. Only a very few appear to have been, or were to become, men of stature in the government.

The creation of the Chungjong Merit Subjects drew immediate criticism from the Office of the Censor-General which memorialized as follows:

In determining merit, the great ministers who initiated the coup, the high officials who raised the king to the throne, and the various military commanders who lent their support to the movement of course should be heavily rewarded. But there are some sons and younger brothers who were enrolled because of their fathers or older brothers, and there are enrolled some who did nothing but come in the evening and participate in the congratulation ceremonies. All these are without merit, yet they too have been enrolled as if they had done great deeds. This is extremely intolerable. Let the high officials who initiated the coup be questioned again and let those of the greatest merit be enrolled; as for the rest, let them be assigned to the category of Minor Merit Subjects. (1506.9.9 S)

The king, however, following the advice of his State Councillors and principal Merit Subjects, did not consent, and the censoring bodies for the time being did not press the issue (1506.9.9).

It was a different story with regard to the rewards bestowed upon the Minor Merit Subjects. From the outset the Censorate attacked as excessive the promotions in rank given members of this group and ultimately, after a sporadic battle extending over two years, was able to wring substantial concessions to its point of view from the king.[7]

Meanwhile, the Censorate had renewed the charge of "unreasonable excess" against the enrollment of the Merit Subjects, and with some success. This time it was asked that the land, slaves and body servants given to "those without merit" be reduced by half and that the awards thus recovered be assigned to state use. At the same time, it was requested that promotions to Senior Third Rank and above granted to Merit Subjects be cancelled (1507.11.30).[8] Chungjong at first refused, but before long he felt compelled to go a good way toward meeting the former request and a little later gave in also to the latter.[9] At this point the issue appears to have been dropped.

Retribution and Redress

The very first concern of the new reign had been to punish the "evildoers" of Yŏnsangun's reign. For the most part these turned out to be members of the non-yangban classes — harem favorites, powerful eunuchs, royal physicians, and other palace minions.[10] Not many members of the official class suffered serious inconvenience as a result of their actions or conduct during the preceding reign. With the exception of the handful killed in the course of the coup,[11] there appear to have been no executions, and there is recorded but one instance of banishment in the immediate aftermath.[12] The reasons for this seem clear. In the first place, those few high officials against whom personal blame might be assessed for their roles in 1498 were by now deceased. (The fate of the one glaring exception, the agile Yu Cha-gwang, will be treated presently.) And it was recognized by all that 1504 was the doing of Yŏnsangun himself; the only officials who had abetted him significantly already had been disposed of in the course of the coup. Secondly, as already noted, those of Yŏnsangun's officials who survived and thrived to the end of his reign were the very men who set Chungjong upon the throne.

This is not to say that the question of collaboration was of little importance in the political history of the period. While retribution against members of the official class was not a matter of high government policy,[13] it was very much a concern of the censoring organs. Especially in the year following Chungjong's accession but also frequently thereafter, the Censorate and OSC sought to prefer charges of crime on the basis, generally, of "toadying" to Yŏnsangun or having occupied the position of a "special favorite." Some of these efforts of the censoring bodies met with success, although perhaps just as often they did not. Quite logically there were a number of Merit Subjects among those attacked in this way, and the king was most reluctant to take action against them. When such a figure was discharged or relieved of his post, it normally was not long before he was permitted to return to the political scene.[14]

It must be stressed, however, that at this time but more especially in later years, the charge of toadying to Yŏnsangun appears to have been used by the censoring bodies for its nuisance value rather than with the thought of just retribution for acknowledged crimes. In other words, the charge became but one more weapon to be trotted out when Censorate purposes required defamation of character. Herein lies the significance of the question of collaboration.[15]

The case of Yu Cha-gwang does not fit this pattern, for his leading role in bringing about and prosecuting the purge of 1498 was writ large in the record and in the public consciousness. More-over, when once his downfall had been encompassed, he was able to make no further comeback.

It is easy to imagine that Yu Cha-gwang must have felt his position under Chungjong to be insecure. He was a living anomaly, the embodiment of a fundamental contradiction in the character of the new regime—namely that the enthronement of Chungjong constituted a symbolic rejection of the force that placed him on the throne. Perhaps it is surprising that attempts to bring Yu down did not follow hard on the heels of the deposition coup, but it must be borne in mind that his own role in the coup won him fourth position on the Merit Subject roster, just behind the Three Great Generals. Still Yu's day of reckoning was not long in coming.

Fittingly, it was the Censorate that sped Yu Cha-gwang to his downfall. Seizing upon his criticism that their indictment of two Local Magistrates "was not meet," the Censorate accused Yu of "personal motivation" (1507.4.12).[16] In the days that followed the Censorate broadened its assault to include a recitation of Yu's crimes and a demand that he be deleted from the merit rosters and executed. When Chungjong did not consent the Censorate resigned, and the OSC, Office of Royal Decrees, Office of Diplomatic Correspondence, Royal Secretariat, and students of the National Academy all joined in the outcry against Yu. At length, then, the king summoned his State Councillors for discussion, removed Yu from all merit lists, and banished him in light degree. Presently, further Censorate demands resulted in a more severe degree of banishment (1507.4.23), and Yu was still in banishment when he died (1512.6.15).[17]

There are two other noteworthy instances of retribution against villains of 1498. The first was the posthumous revocation of the office warrants of Yi Kŭk-ton on the ground of his role in divulging the contents of Kim Il-son's history drafts. In order to get under way the compilation of the *Sillok* for Yŏnsangun's reign, a routine order was issued requiring that privately held history drafts be turned in. But "everyone regarded the 1498 affair as a warning and no drafts were submitted," so a law was promulgated providing the death penalty for anyone who divulged the contents of a history draft (1507.6.17). Then an inquiry was conducted to determine the source of the leak in 1498 (1507.6.28, 7.15, 7.18, 11.22), and the blame was fixed on Yi Kŭk-ton.[18] In the second such case, the same punishment befell Yi Sŭng-gŏn, who as Governor of P'yŏngan in 1498 had reported the defamatory poem written on a post station wall by purge victim Yi Chong-jun, who was then executed (1518.4.8).[19]

The obverse of the coin of retribution is redress. The great majority of the victims of 1504 were quickly rehabilitated by an order calling for "requalification for public office of all those who suffered crime charges from 1504 on because of remonstrance" (1506.9.5). This was followed by special awards to the houses of the two martyrs to filial piety, Chŏng Sŏng-gŭn and Yi Cha-hwa, and restoration to the loyal, filial and chaste of honors which had been revoked by Yŏnsangun (1506.9.19).[20] Subsequent actions redressed other wrongs done certain 1504 victims.[21]

Steps to rehabilitate those who had suffered in 1498, though taken more hesitantly, were perhaps more sweeping in character. After a month on the throne Chungjong issued an order to "release the living among those charged with crime in 1498 and posthumously bestow office and rank upon the dead and requalify their posterity for public office" (1506.10.7). Moreover, although office and rank were not to be posthumously conferred upon Kim Il-son, Kwŏn O-bok and Kwŏn Kyŏng-yu "on the ground that they had written matters concerning Sejo in their history drafts" (1506.10.7, 11.12 S), this qualification may shortly have been removed.[22]

One further aspect of the Chungjong political settlement must be mentioned briefly, the putting aside of Chungjong's first consort. The day after the promulgation of the merit roster, to make a cynical juxtaposition of dates, the leading Merit Subjects and other high officials approached the king in this wise:

"First getting rid of Sin Su-gŭn when we initiated this affair was for the sake of achieving our great purpose. Now the daughter of Sin Su-gŭn is in the palace, but if she should be formally invested as queen, then men's minds will be dangerously suspicious and there will be repercussions affecting the state. We ask, therefore, that you override your personal feelings and send her outside the palace."

The king replied: "What you have memorialized is, of course, correct. Yet how can I thus discard my faithful and blameless wife?"

In response all memorialized: "We too have already given this every consideration; but what of the larger interest of the state? We ask that a clearcut decision be made without delay."

The king then answered: "In the face of weighty reasons of state, how can I take account of my personal feelings?" And following the consensus of the government, the king sent his consort out of the palace. (1506.9.9 S)

No protest was voiced at this time, but some years later this action was called into question and a violent controversy ensued.

The Censorate Flexes its Muscles

Two features stand out in the topography of the first years of Chungjong's reign. One of these is the now familiar conflict between the censoring bodies and the higher strata of the officialdom, in particular the High State Councillors, and the second is the matter of plots against the throne. Aspects of the first issue already have been brought out in the discussion of the issues of merit enrollment and collaboration. The two most extreme instances of this type of conflict in this period should be examined. While admittedly not typical of the never ending stream of lighter Censorate assaults on their favorite target, the higher officialdom, these instances by their nature as exercises in sustained warfare will all the more reward careful observation.

Early in 1508, while the debate on the issue of excessive rewards to Merit Subjects was still in process, Sŏng Hŭi-an, one of the Three Great Generals (see above at note 1), spoke out in criticism of the Censorate's methods. Charging that the Censorate scrutinized the qualifications of office holders on the basis of untruths or of past misdeeds, Sŏng asked that the king take this into consideration in making his judgments. The Censorate officials then tendered their resignations and, when these were not accepted, asked that Sŏng be prosecuted for the "crime of repressing the Censorate." Chungjong refused (1508.3.1).[23]

Presently the Censorate tried again. In accordance with a Censorate memorial, fourteen men had been stricken from the roster of those deemed qualified for appointment to OSC posts. Sŏng was able to get them re-enrolled, but only to have the Censorate once more charge "repression" (1508.4.1). When Chungjong, at the instance of Sŏng, Chief State Councillor Yu Sun, and Third State Councillor Yu Sun-jŏng, failed to revoke the contested rank promotions of Minor Merit Subjects, the Censorate accused Sŏng of "irresponsible flaunting of power" and Yu Sun of abetting him. Rebuffed again by the king, the Censorate resigned and, while Chungjong took no action against Sŏng, he did feel compelled, as we have seen, to revoke some of the rank promotions (1508.5.23).[24]

Some three years later the Censorate and Sŏng Hui-an, now Third State Councillor, locked horns once again. In response to an appeal for counsel the Censorate had requested that three State Councillors, all Prime Merit Subjects *(wŏnhun)*, be removed from their posts, asserting that Second State Councillor Yu Sun-jŏng devoted himself solely to amassing wealth and that Sixth State Councillor Hong Kyŏng-ju and Seventh State Councillor Sin Yun-mu lacked public confidence (1511.10.11). In the course of the ensuing debate the Censorate charged that Sŏng had remarked that "literati mores are contemptuous of constituted authority." However, when Sŏng convincingly denied the allegation, the king handed down the Censorate personnel to the State Tribunal and in the end transferred the Inspector-General and Censor-General to inactive duty and demoted all the rest (1511.10.21, 11.1).

Thus Sŏng Hŭi-an emerged a clear victor, by no means an inconsiderable feat. Perhaps he owed a measure of his success to his relative immunity from charges of collaboration during Yŏnsangun's reign, for Yŏnsangun had demoted him to a lowly military post where he remained throughout much of the critical period 1504-06.[25] At any rate, Sŏng now quickly rose through Second State Councillor (1512.10.7) to the highest office in the land (1513.4.2), in which post he soon died (1513.7.27).

Sŏng Hŭi-an was succeeded at the helm of the government by Song Chil, a Merit Subject whose career in public office went back some thirty-five years.[26] But, unlike Sŏng, he was not able to withstand the sustained pressure of the censoring bodies and was relieved after serving less than a year as Chief State Councillor.

The attack on Song Chil appears to have had no connection with any specific question at issue but rather was based on his lapses in personal and official decorum. The assault was launched by the OCG, which memorialized that four high officials headed by Song Chil were unfit for their posts. When pressed for specifications the OCG was joined by the OIG in alleging that Song had personally supervised the building of a new house while in mourning for his father, that he had taken unlawful possession of lands in P'yŏngando, and that he had accepted bribes (1514.2.22).

When the king rejected the memorials they offered repeatedly over a period of two months, the Censorate officials resigned. This caused the Royal Secretariat to urge Chungjong to quickly heed the Censorate's arguments, but he again refused (1514.4.17). After an absence from their posts of more than a month had failed to budge the king, the Censorate officials returned to their desks, only to be attacked by the OSC for "resuming their duties without due cause." Whereupon the king relieved the Censorate and appointed a new one (1514.5.28, 6.4).

The new Censorate, however, not only continued the indictment of Song Chil and the others, but went on to demand that the former Censorate be punished for abandoning their efforts "without due cause" (1514.6.8). There then developed a split within the Censorate as to whether the original Censorate officials had been right or wrong to return to their posts, and this required the king once more to appoint a new group of Censors and Inspectors (1514.6.18, 6.19). At this point Chungjong relieved the other three high officials under attack, all of whom had repeatedly tendered resignations, but refused to accept the resignation proffered by Song Chil (1514.6.23).

This second new Censorate also kept faith with its predecessor, asking again that Song Chil be relieved and that the original Censorate personnel be discharged from their posts. The king at first consented to the latter request but was persuaded to countermand his discharge order by the Second and Third State Councillors (1514.6.23). Presently, however, the Censorate succeeded in obtaining the transfer to inactive duty of the original Censorate (1514.7.15) and then, at last, the king succumbed to the demand that Song Chil be removed from the office of Chief State Councillor

(1514.7.16). From this time until his death in 1520 (1.6), Song Chil did not again hold a portfolio post.

Plots Against the Throne

A second remarkable feature of the political landscape in the years 1506-1515 is the number and nature of plots, actual or alleged, against the throne. The more significant of these are intimately related to the activities of the censoring bodies with regard to the Chungjong Merit Subjects. Before turning to these, however, we must not neglect to treat a conspiracy brought to light at the very outset of Chungjong's reign, a conspiracy directed not at the king but at three of his high officials. This affair has a special interest and perhaps significance, deriving from the identity of those connected with it.

Early in 1507 Third Minister of Works Yu Sung-jo went to the Royal Secretariat and reported that Pak Kyŏng, an illegitimate son of a prominent yangban family, and Kim Kong-jŏ,[27] a palace physician (and also illegitimate), were plotting to assassinate Pak Wŏn-jong, Yu Cha-gwang, and No Kong-p'il.[28] An identical report was made independently by Nam Kon, Sim Chŏng and Kim Kŭk-sŏng.[29] Use of a hot iron soon wrung confessions from Pak and Kim, revealing the details of the conspiracy to have been the following:

To begin with, Pak and Kim had plotted this affair with the brothers Yi Chang-gil, Yi Chang-sŏng and Yi Chang-bae, and with National Academy student Cho Kwang-bo.[30] They had also spoken to National Academy students Mun Sŏ-gu, Cho Kwang-jwa, Cho Kwang-jo and Kim Sik, saying:[31]

"The law of seniority ought not be applied and the civil examinations ought not be conducted. Illegitimate sons should be permitted access to the higher posts and members of the royal house should be qualified for employment in ministerial posts in the Six Boards. Pak Wŏn-jong keeps in his household many of Yŏnsangun's female palace attendants . . .[32] Yu Cha-gwang in 1498 killed the sage and good and he collaborated with Im Sa-hong in perpetrating evil; yet still today he moves without restraint. Beyond doubt these two are about to create [further] turmoil. Furthermore, No Kong-p'il is very intimate with Yu Cha-gwang and is an obstacle to good government. If we get rid of these three and make the Great Lord of Haep'yŏng, Chŏng Mi-su,[33] Chief State Councillor, then we can see good government."

Although both Pak Kyŏng and Kim Kong-jŏ were of the lowly order of illegitimate sons, Pak was renowned for calligraphy and Kim for medicine, and they frequented the houses of the highest ministers, of the officialdom, and of the royal clansmen. They had spoken of the affair to Yu Sung-jo and to such others as OSC Director Kim Kam, Inspector-General Yi Kye-maeng[34] and royal clansmen . . . [Yi] Pok-su and . . . [Yi] Kŭm-san, but had been rebuffed by all. Thus it was that they had not yet been able to set the conspiracy in motion. At this point, then, Yu Sung-jo and the others reported it. (1507.il.25)

Disposition of the case did not take long. Pak Kyŏng and Kim Kong-jŏ were beheaded, their property confiscated, and their wives and children enslaved. Yi Chang-gil, Yu Sung-jo, Yi Kye-maeng, Kim Kam, Chŏng Mi-su, and Yi Kŭm-san were banished.[35] The students and Yi Pok-su were released. The interrogation officers and the informers were rewarded (1507.il.25).[36]

The Pak Kyŏng - Kim Kong-jŏ conspiracy, at the least, heightens our appreciation of the charged political atmosphere of the time. But it has been suggested by a modern student of the period that the affair contains a deeper meaning. He writes:

Now Nam Kon and Sim Chŏng from the beginning had been designated as amoral men by the 1519 group,[37] and the basic reason for this was that they had secretly reported the plot of Pak Kyŏng and Kim Kong-jŏ. . . . It is not known whether Cho Kwang-jo, [Kim Sik,] etc., agreed [to join the conspirators], but what should be well noted is that Cho Kwang-jo was implicated by them and that those who reported the plot were Nam Kon and Sim Chŏng. Thus it may be said that the antagonism between Cho Kwang-jo and Kim Sik on the one hand and Nam Kon and Sim Chŏng on the other dated already from this time.[38]

This would seem to be a rather extreme interpretation, for in the years preceding the Purge of 1519 ample reasons emerged to explain the hostility between Cho Kwang-jo and his opponents. This is true particularly in the case of Nam Kon, who often took a public stand in opposition to the men of 1519 on the great issues of the day. Yet it may well be true that memories of the Pak Kyŏng affair served to further widen a natural rift.

Later in 1507 another plot was reported, this time aimed at the throne itself. It was alleged that a former Headmaster of the National Academy, Yi Kwa, resentful over his exclusion from the roster of Merit Subjects, was plotting to depose Chungjong and elevate in his stead his half-brother Yi Ton. Yi Kwa and his fellow conspirators were counting principally on the support of Palace Guardsmen who were also unhappy over not being enrolled for merit. In the ensuing investigation confessions were forced from three of the accused and finally also from Yi Kwa, who was promptly executed (1507.8.26, 8.27, 8.28, 8.29).[39]

The background of the Yi Kwa plot is of obvious significance. A victim of 1504, Yi Kwa at the very end of Yŏnsangun's reign joined others who had been banished to Chŏlla, notably Yu Pin and Kim Chun-son,[40] in an effort to raise troops to depose Yŏnsangun and seat Chungjong on the throne. But the Seoul-centered coup, moving more quickly (though only, it is said, after hearing of the manifesto issued by the Chŏlla group),[41] forestalled this attempt (1506.9.2). In consideration of their efforts in his behalf, however, Chungjong later enrolled these three men as Merit Subjects Fourth Class and two others who abetted them as First Class in the minor category. But when this action was sharply denounced by the Censorate, the king downgraded all five, thereby reducing Yi Kwa and his cohorts to the status of Minor Merit Subjects (1507.6.17). Shortly after this, ninety Palace Guardsmen were enrolled in the Third Class of Minor Merit Subjects (1507.7.21).[42]

The aftermath of the Yi Kwa affair is also of some importance. Likening the case to the plot of Nam I in the reign of Yejong, the king wanted to create the Yi Kwa Plot Merit Subjects (chŏngnan *kongsin).* In this desire he was opposed violently by the Censorate and also by the State Councillors, who asked that only the informer's merit be recognized.[43] But Chungjong insisted and twenty-two men were enrolled in three classes of merit, while a number of others were rewarded in lesser ways (1507.9.2, 9.6, 9.19, 9.20). The partial success of the Censorate in getting reduced the awards given to these and to the Chungjong Merit Subjects has already been noted. Ultimately, with the single exception of the informer, this entire merit roster was expunged.[44]

In the years 1508 and 1509 two more alleged plots aganist the throne were uncovered, but neither was of major dimension. Then, after four years free of conspiracy against the throne, there occurred in 1513 the alleged plot of two Prime Merit Subjects, Pak Yŏng-mun and Sin Yun-mu. Reference already has been made to the early Censorate indictments of Pak and Sin,[45] who continued to suffer Censorate attempts to remove them from whatever positions they might attain.[46] Their 1513 plot was reported by a State Council slave, whose accusation has been summarized as follows:

> Full of rancor against the civil officials because they had been impeached and removed
> from their Board Minister positions, Pak Yŏng-mun and Sin Yun-mu, at Sin's house on
> the night of the thirteenth, compacted secretly to initiate a coup on the occasion of the
> royal hunt on the sixteenth of this month and elevate to the throne . . . [Chungjong's
> half-brother Yi] Chŏn. They then intended to kill the Second and Third State
> Councillors, make Hong Kyŏng-ju Chief State Councillor and themselves Second and
> Third State Councillors respectively, and appoint Min Hoe-bal Minister of War,[47]
> thereby transferring political authority to the military officials. (1513.10.22)

The investigation of the Pak-Sin affair was conducted with dispatch—when the rod was applied, both readily confessed and were executed. They had implicated no one else in their statements, so sentences were additionally adjudged only against their close kin (1513.10.22, 10.24).[48]

The period 1506-1515, then, was one of frequent and often bitter political conflict. This conflict was characterized in particular by the recurrent attacks of the censoring bodies against the High State Councillors and the Chungjong Merit Subjects and by numerous plots against the throne, which represented an extreme form of reaction to these attacks. Into the center of the political stage then stepped Cho Kwang-jo, who in the short span of four years set the stage for purge.

The Emergence of Cho Kwang-jo

Cho Kwang-jo was born in Seoul in 1482 of the Hanyang (Seoul) Cho clan. Although his immediate forbears were men of no great distinction, some of his more distant ancestors had played vital roles in the establishment of the dynasty. His great-great-grandfather, Cho On, was enrolled as a Merit Subject on three occasions, by T'aejo, Chŏngjong, and T'aejong. Cho On's half brother, Cho Yŏn, born of a sister of Yi T'aejo, as a youth served the founder in a military capacity and eventually rose to Third State Councillor under Sejong. That the line suffered temporary eclipse at this point seems to have been due in part to the alignment of some of its members on the side of the unfortunate Tanjong. Cho Kwang-jo's grandfather, Cho Ch'ung-son, for example, was banished to the northern border by Sejo and there died.

When Cho was sixteen, in 1498, his father took up a minor appointment in P'yŏngando. There Cho became a disciple of Kim Koeng-p'il, who had just been banished to the same area. Thus Cho came to be in the direct line of Neo-Confucian orthodoxy in Korea, for Kim Koeng-p'il was the foremost disciple of Kim Chong-jik. And it is said, however apocryphally, that Cho immersed himself completely in the study of the Classics and in particular the Chu Hsi texts, intentionally neglecting the literary training so essential in the Korean civil examination system.

The association of Cho's name with the Pak Kyŏng plot of 1507 has been noted (see above at note 38). At this time Cho was studying and teaching in Seoul, having married (1499) and mourned his father (1500) and teacher (1504). In 1510 he took a first in the Literary Licentiate examination and in the following year was included in a selection by the Board of Rites and National Academy of students meriting preferment into the lower government posts, but the employment order of the Board of Personnel was caused to be suspended (1511.4.11). The same year Cho went into mourning for his mother, and it was not until 1515 that he began his official career.

In mid-1515 the National Academy made a selection from among its students of those most "learned in the Classics and cultivated in character." Acting upon this recommendation, the Board of Personnel, then headed by An Tang, requested that Cho, Kim Sik, and Pak Hun (two close friends and later colleagues of Cho) be extraordinarily employed at the Junior Sixth Rank level (1515.6.8). Thus named to his first post, in the Paper Manufactory, Cho soon passed the civil examination as the number two man (1515.8.22) and was appointed Librarian in the National Academy (1515.8.29). Within three months he received appointment as a Fourth Censor (1515.11.20) and immediately stirred into flames the embers of the greatest controversy of that day.

In the four years remaining to him, Cho Kwang-jo achieved a phenomenal, perhaps unprecedented, advancement in public office. This can be better appreciated by a simple listing of the principal stages in his official career:

Date	Post	Rank
1515.8.22	Passed civil exam. holding	Senior Sixth Rank
8.29	National Academy Librarian	" " "
11.20	Fourth Censor	" " "
1516.3.6	Junior Sixth Counselor of OSC	Junior Sixth Rank
3.28	Sixth Counselor	Senior Sixth Rank
1517.2.3	Junior Fifth Counselor	Junior Fifth Rank
7.28	Fourth Counselor	Senior Fourth Rank
8.22	Third Counselor	Junior Third Rank
i12.13	Second Counselor	Senior Third Rank
1518.1.15	First Counselor	" " "
5.2	Sixth Royal Secretary	" " "
5.5	First Counselor	" " "

7.11	Assistant Director of the National Academy (concurrent)	Junior Second Rank
11.21	Inspector-General	”　　　”　　　”
1519.3.15	First Counselor	Senior Third Rank
5.16	Inspector-General	Junior Second Rank
8.10	Special Mentor of the Crown Prince (concurrent)	”　　　”　　　”
11.15	Purged	

Cho Kwang-jo's rapid rise in office testifies to the high esteem in which Chungjong held him and indicates that Cho was in a position to exert great influence upon the king. The magnitude and direction of Cho's influence will be clearly seen in the discussion below of the great issues in which he played so leading a part. But before turning to these, a consideration of Cho's role in two of the lesser debates of the day provides a preliminary assessment of his stature.

When Cho was OSC First Counselor in mid-1518, Fourth Inspector Kim Sik and Third Censor Yu Yong-gŭn memorialized asking that the Sogyŏksŏ be abolished (1518.6.21). This was a government agency that supervised the performance of Taoistic rites on such occasions as the illness of the king or of his immediate family. In previous years its abolition had been requested by all levels of officialdom but Chungjong had steadfastly refused to give his consent, and he now refused again.[49] Presently, however, the entire Censorate and the OSC as well began to wage a persistent campaign against this non-Confucianist institution. Again rebuffed, the Censorate officials resorted to the tactic of resigning their posts. This brought the High State Councillors, the Ministers of the Six Boards, Cho Kwang-jo, and various other officials to their support, but the king would not budge and, indeed, proceeded to appoint a new Censorate. The new appointees, of course, fully backed their predecessors and, failing to move the king, also resigned (1518.7.27, 8.22, 8.30, 9.1, 9.2).

At this point,

> The OSC, Office of Royal Decrees, Seoul Magistracy, the Ministers, Second Ministers, and Third Ministers of the Six Boards, and royal clansman . . . [Yi] Ch'ong all argued [for the abolition of the Sogyŏksŏ], and the students of the National Academy stood in a heavy rain outside the palace and urged [the same]. The king did not consent. With nightfall all retired except for Cho Kwang-jo and two or three colleagues, who argued the matter throughout the night. And finally the king had no choice but to abolish it. (1518.9.2)[50]

At the very same time, the government faced a growing menace of unrest among the Yain on the Hamgyŏngdo frontier. Accordingly, with the unanimous support of his High State Councillors and chief military advisors, the king determined to mount a surprise assault against a particularly persistent border violator who had been causing trouble for years. The reasoning of all was that if this Yain leader went unpunished, then other tribal groups along the border would be encouraged to emulate his depredations. So troops and supplies were started on their way and a commander of the expedition was named. The day of the commander's departure came and the highest officials of the government were gathered around the king for the formal send-off ceremony. But in the midst of the proceedings First Counselor Cho Kwang-jo appeared and asked the king for permission to speak. Granted this privilege, Cho advanced and argued that the plan for a surprise attack was dishonorable, that it "grossly violates the proper ethic of the sovereign in defending against the barbarian," and that it would bring disgrace upon the country and injure the nation's prestige. Chungjong then, over the vehement and sarcastic objections of his high officials, called off the expedition (1518.8.3, 8.16).[51]

Cho Kwang-jo, a mere Third Rank official, with one word was able to sway the king and choke off the discussion of this vital issue. Men all looked askance.[52]

"Both Right Both Wrong"

The incident which first brought Cho Kwang-jo into the limelight was the long and acrimonious controversy which had its origin in a proposal to restore to the king's side his first consort, the ousted daughter of Sin Su-gŭn. The way had just been opened for such a request by the death of Queen Changgyŏng in giving birth to a first son, the later King Injong (1515.2.25, 3.2). Before a successor queen had been decided upon, the king had occasion to issue an appeal for counsel. It was in response to this that Kim Chŏng and Pak Sang, both then serving as Local Magistrates in Chŏlla province, made their startling proposal.[53]

The essence of the Kim-Pak argument was that, in putting aside the blameless Lady Sin, the king had committed the most grievous sort of breach of moral rectitude. He had been coerced into doing this, they went on, by the Three Great Generals who, having killed the father, thought only of protecting themselves from possible retribution by the daughter. The acknowledged merit of their services to the throne could not obscure the monstrousness of their crime. They should be posthumously stripped of all offices and titles and Lady Sin restored to her rightful position (1515.8.8 S).[54]

While Chungjong was not at all pleased with this memorial, his original intention was to take no action against its authors, for their words were clothed in the (theoretically) inviolate garb of a response to an appeal for counsel. Censor-General Yi Haeng and Inspector-General Kwŏn Min-su, however, asserting that Kim and Pak had voiced malicious views in a matter of vital concern to the state, persuaded their Censorate colleagues to join in demanding the arrest of the pair and a judicial inquiry into the real motives behind their proposal (1515.8.8).[55] Yi Haeng's line of reasoning in taking this position is explained by the *Sillok* historians in the following terms:

Yi Haeng had in mind that, in spite of the death of [Queen] Changgyŏng after giving birth to an heir and the consequent vacancy at the king's side, the foundation of the state long had been secure. But if Lady Sin were restored and an argument arose on the question of precedence, then Lady Sin would be preferred over Changgyŏng.[56] This might well shake the foundation of the state . . . [Moreover] Yi Haeng said:

Changgyŏng has died and Pak Sang and Kim Chŏng have asked that Lady
Sin be made queen. But Lady Sin is the issue of Sin Su-gŭn, and if she should
attain a position of influence it is impossible to guarantee that she will not seek
revenge for her father. Then inevitably the government would be overtaken by
disaster. Yŏnsangun exacted revenge for [his mother] Lady Yun, gravely
imperiling the existence of the state. We must not embark again on so disastrous
a course. (1515.8.11 S)

Upon hearing the views of the Censorate, Chungjong summoned the State Councillors and
Board Ministers for discussion. These all were emphatic in condemning the "reckless irresponsibility"
and "blatant error" of the words of Kim and Pak and in asserting that, under normal cirumstances,
there would be no alternative to pressing charges of crime against them. At the same time, however,
they acknowledged that to prosecute in the case of a response to an appeal for counsel would be to
"exceed the bounds of propriety" or to "place restrictions on the freedeom of remonstrance."
Accordingly, they recommended only that the fallacy of the Kim-Pak position be made widely
known (1515.8.8, 8.11 S, 8.12 S).

This time, however, Chungjong showed not the slightest hesitation in accepting the counsel of
the Censorate over the united opposition of his higher ranking officials. He pointed out that Kim and
Pak had had ample opportunity, during previous tours of duty in censoring posts, to present their
views on this subject about which they felt so strongly. He went on to speculate that they would
wish to restore Lady Sin even if Changgyŏng were not dead. He then ordered Kim and Pak imprisoned
and interrogated and, brushing aside further protests, presently sentenced them to banishment
(1515.8.8, 8.23 S).[57]

Here the matter might have rested but for the coincidental appearance on the scene of Cho
Kwang-jo. It will be recalled that Cho passed the civil examination at just this time (actually one day
before sentence was passed on Kim and Pak) and before long was appointed a Fourth Censor.
Immediately upon taking up this post, Cho attacked his Censorate colleagues[58] for having asked
prosecution of Kim and Pak in disregard of the principle of freedom of remonstrance, thus leading
the king into unrighteousness. Chungjong turned down his request that the Censorate be discharged
but, when Cho persisted and the High State Councillors gave him their qualified support, the king
agreed to transfer the officials in question (1515.11.22).

Cho's approach was a fresh one, a fact which the king soon was to point out, for in all the
objections voiced to preferring charges of crime against Kim and Pak, both before and after sentence
had been passed, there was not one word of denunciation of the error of the Censorate in insisting
on punishment of the pair.[59] Cho, then, had put his finger on a striking anomaly. It had been the
Censorate, the zealous and resourceful guardian of the principle of freedom of remonstrance, that
had pressed for action in violation of that principle. And it had been the State Council, so often
accused by the Censorate of trying to place restraints upon the freedom of remonstrance, that had
led a preponderance of officialdom in upholding that freedom. Censor-General Yi Haeng had

persuaded his colleagues to make a serious tactical error and Cho was quick to take advantage of it. In consequence, the course of the controversy over the Kim-Pak memorial was radically altered, with profound repercussions on the history of the period.

The task of the new Censorate was to determine not the propriety of the Kim-Pak memorial but the propriety of the former Censorate's actions on the memorial. This they were unable to do with unanimity. Of those who expressed themselves, five held Cho to be correct in his criticism and two believed that he was not.[60] It was upon hearing these views that the king made known his opinion that:

> Cho Kwang-jo's upholding of the principle of remonstrance may be said to be proper, but at the time there were none who held the Censorate wrong for asking crime charges against Pak Sang and Kim Chŏng. How is it then that [Cho Kwang-jo] now attacks [the former Censorate and seeks its] removal? This to me is rather disquieting. (1515.11.27 S)

This left those Censorate officials who had upheld Cho with no alternative but to resign (1515.11.27).

In this moment of growing schism the Office of Special Counselors, under the leadership of Second Counselor Kim Al-lo, put forward the ingenious if futile face-saving formula which has become known in history as the "both right both wrong theory." The OSC officials said, in summary:

> The words of Kim Chŏng and Pak Sang were grossly in error, but on the ground that charging them with crime would constitute a restriction of the principle of remonstrance, from the very outset we asked that crime not be charged. However, the former Censorate asked that crime be charged solely out of concern for the larger interest of the state, and for this reason neither did we hold them to be wrong. Hence, although it is right that . . . [those present Censorate officials] speak out now on behalf of the principle of remonstrance, for them to hold the former Censorate to be wrong is wrong. And it is right that . . . [the minority of the present Censorate] should hold the former Censorate to be right, but for them to hold Cho Kwang-jo to be wrong is wrong. (1515.11.27)

Chungjong's immediate reaction was to name another new Censorate, and when these officials split between Censors who backed Cho Kwang-jo's view and Inspectors who advocated the both right both wrong theory, the king appointed still another (1515.12.3, 12.6).[61] Now, apparently, it was no longer required that the Censorate officials choose sides on the finer points of the dispute; instead, there began to appear requests that Kim and Pak be released (1516.1.5, 1.14, 3.8). Before long, the timely occurrence of natural disasters gave the king an excuse to do just this, and by the end of the year they had also been requalified for government employment (1516.5.8, 11.13).[62]

But this was far from the last echo of the affair of the Kim-Pak memorial; there was no turning back the clock. Already Yi Haeng, now OSC First Counselor (1515.12.6), had discovered that he had become anathema to many of his colleagues and so, pleading illness, had resigned (1516.10.12). Although it was not long before he was brought back into the government, he was not permitted to remain in peace.[63]

It was Yi Haeng's appointment to the highest Censorate post, that of Inspector-General, that brought matters to a head. His subordinates in the OIG and the OCG officials as well, with Fourth Inspector Yi Ch'ŏng and Fourth Censor Chŏng Ŭng in the lead, jointly requested that he be transferred and that the promotion in rank that accompanied his appointment be revoked. The justification they offered was vague, merely that Yi Haeng was unfit for the post and that in thought and deed he was a man of cunning deceit who, left in such a vital post, would do grave injury to the state (1517.8.27 S). The king then faced the dilemma of either transferring Yi or else all of the other Censorate officials, and he chose to do the former (1517.8.27 S, 8.28).

Help, however, was on its way. First on the scene was Chief State Councillor Chŏng Kwang-p'il, with a lukewarm endorsement of Yi Haeng's character (1517.8.28 S). Then Second State Councillor Sin Yong-gae, recalling that he had always regretted the slow pace of Yi's preferment in public office, asserted flatly that the allegations of his detractors were in error (1517.9.12 S). And soon battle was joined in earnest.

Unseasonable thunder had been heard and had been interpreted by certain Censorate officials as resulting from disharmony and strife in the government. By this was meant, we are told, the recent consistent opposition of the highest officials to the views presented by the censoring bodies. The challenge was quickly and forcibly taken up by the Fourth State Councillor, Kim Chŏn, in these words:

> When the High State Councillors and the Censorate work together in a spirit of give and take, then the affairs of the state will proceed smoothly and the government too will be in harmony. Today, however, this is not the case. When the Censorate discusses a matter and the views of the highest officials are slightly different, then the Censorate officials never fail to point to the difference and condemn it. From ages past the avocation of the sage and princely man has been the ethical service of his lord, and it was when he did not live up to this standard that his services were dispensed with. But how can it be proper to take one's own viewpoint as the standard and censure those who do not conform to it? . . .
>
> Men all are saddened by the ousting of Yi Haeng. How is it that such a man is dismissed on so tenuous a ground? Of late there have been many views aired which have startled men's minds . . . and now there has ensued the impeachment and ousting of Yi Haeng. That he, a man who in former days was recommended by many of the high officials, should now come to this end gives rise to utter astonishment. (1517.10.8 S)

This was immediately followed by the fuller and still more telling indictment of the Magistrate of Suwŏn, Yi Sŏng-ŏn:[64]

> Yi Haeng is a man of the very highest caliber, of surpassing ability and scholarship, truly a talent rare in any age. In the reign of Yŏnsangun, even under cruel torture he unswervingly upheld his own high principles, thus winning the respect of all of his contemporaries. After Your Majesty came to the throne not a few of your highest officials and counselors recommended him to you, yet not once was he favored with unusual preferment. This your subjects all deplored.

So recently, when Yi Haeng was extraordinarily appointed Inspector-General, the government and society at large all felt individually favored by the royal grace and congratulated the nation upon finding a man of such parts. But now he has been driven away again. With one word he has been removed from his post and with a second his rank has been reduced. He has been discarded like a dead decaying rat, with no effort to distinguish whether he is a man of evil or of rectitude. Can this be a happy portent for the government?

The men of today act in too great haste; in their desire to eliminate the evils of the present they take no heed of the harmful consequences of their actions for the future. Wishing to re-create in a single stroke the land of Yao and Shun, they call those who agree with them good and those who differ with them evil men. When they discuss a matter and there is someone with a divergent view or a different approach, then they claim that he is obstructing the expression of the public consensus or that he is a man of unscrupulous bent. Thus, first quickly sowing seeds of doubt and uncertainty, in the end they attack an opponent on the basis of some vague and undemonstrable allegation of evil, making it impossible for him to raise his head again. In consequence, men all have drawn back in trepidation and do not say openly what is in their minds . . .

Both when something is discussed and when something is carried into effect it is always done on the basis of private caucus; political authority has entirely come to reside therein. Alas! If political authority reposed but in the Censorate it would be sufficient to cause turmoil. How much more so when it resides in private caucus!

In discussing an issue Yi Haeng does not tailor his views to what others want to hear. Because of this he ran afoul of the prevailing climate of opinion and in the end acquired a name for evil. When recently he was downgraded, many of the officialdom . . . beat their breasts and gave vent even to tears, but not one man moved staunchly to his defense. If Yi Haeng truly is a man who would do grave injury to the state then let him be punished for this crime. And punish me too for the crime of deceit. (1517.10.10)[65]

The Censorate, of course, took violent exception to Yi Sŏng-ŏn's remarks. Asserting that he had confused right and wrong and driven a wedge into the ranks of the government, they asked that he be severely punished. The king held, however, that by their memorial on disharmony in the government the Censorate had proven themselves to be the divisive force, and with the unanimous backing of his highest officials, he removed the Censorate officials, restored Yi Haeng's rank promotion and appointed him Third Minister of Taxation (1517.10.10, 10.19, 10.20).[66]

The new Censorate officials, in the old tradition, were not loath to pick up the fallen gauntlet. They refused to obey a royal command to officiate at an examination, they attacked the high officials who had endorsed the transfer of their predecessors, they forced the removal of new appointees to Censorate posts whose views would be opposed to their own, [67] and they incessantly demanded that the king rescind Yi Haeng's appointment, banish Yi Sŏng-ŏn, and publicly acknowledge his own error of transferring the former Censorate. Meanwhile, the OSC stood shoulder to shoulder with the Censorate in its struggle and, indeed, at times criticized the Censorate for timidity in pressing the attack. Support came too from an unusual quarter; four royal clansmen memorialized the facts of Yi Sŏng-ŏn's "villainy" and requested an opportunity to speak personally on the subject to the king (1517.10.20, 10.23, 10.26, 10.27, 10.30, 11.18, 11.21, 11.22).[68]

There was no clear-cut final act to this drama: Yi Haeng backed off slowly to the wings while the other performers busied themselves with the next production. In the two years remaining before the purge, Yi Haeng continued to receive appointments at the same level as heretofore, but he either formally resigned them or neglected them and retired to his country home (1518.1.5, 1.12, 2.8, 7.19, 1519.2.18, 2.29). Yi Sŏng-ŏn, on the other hand, while not banished as the censoring bodies had demanded, was discharged from his post and is not heard from again for several years.[69] Needless to say, Chungjong did not accede to the demand that he openly admit the error of his transfer of the Censorate. Nevertheless, the censoring bodies had suffered no real setback. Their headlong rush against Yi Haeng had been turned aside short of its objective, but there were many other targets and no momentum had been lost. It still took courage to stand in their way.

The Canonization of Chŏng Mong-ju

Just before initiating their final campaign against Yi Haeng the censoring bodies had raised the question of the canonization of Chŏng Mong-ju, who is known as the father of Korean Neo-Confucianism. A leading political figure in the last years of Koryŏ, Chŏng Mong-ju at first had been closely associated with Yi T'aejo but was murdered by Yi partisans when he opposed the movement to set up a new dynasty. Although he made no direct contribution to the elaboration of the Neo-Confucianist philosophy in Korea, he was renowned in his age for his understanding of the interpretations of the Chu Hsi school, for his revitalization of the mourning system, and for the impetus he gave Chinese studies by the creation of a new system of schools. And in the circumstances of his death he had epitomized the cardinal Confucianist virtue of undeviating loyalty to one's lord.

The desire to install Chŏng Mong-ju in the National Confucian Shrine is not difficult to appreciate. A steady growth of interest among the yangban class in scholarship, i.e., in Chinese studies, was not only a response to a vital tenet of Yi state policy but was also a by-product of the conditions of relative stability and peace brought into being by the new dynasty. At the same time, the focus of Chinese studies in Korea came increasingly to be on the Neo-Confucianist texts. This was but a reflection of the dominant trend in contemporaneous Ming China and had for the moment no philosophical implications. The impact of the Chu Hsi school on the Koreans of this age lay in the re-direction of attention to the ancient texts and the re-interpretation of the society they pictured as one of glorious perfection. The metaphysical or speculative underpinnings of Chu Hsi's thought were just beginning to receive attention; what mattered more was his prescription for the ills of the individual and society.

The Neo-Confucianists took an unreservedly optimistic view of the perfectibility of human conduct and of man-made institutions and regarded the cultivation of moral character as the key to the achievement of such perfection. The texts of such a school would provide an ideal point of reference for those who wished to criticize the existing order of things, either out of altruistic concern or because they could not share in the ordering as it was or aspired to share more fully in it. At the same time, however, acknowledgement of the authoritative character of such texts would only complicate the task of the responsible administrator, a fallible ego dealing with others like him.

Now the events of the reign of Yŏnsangun, who came about as close as any historical figure to demonstrating the incurable evil of human character, could not but have a sobering effect on the minds of his contemporaries. While reflection on these events failed to uncover structural faults in the institutional fabric, it certainly revealed serious flaws in the cultivation of moral character. Fortunately there was a doctrine ready at hand to apply to the correction of these flaws and no lack of acknowledged practitioners. Cho Kwang-jo, while outstanding, was but one of many. This group believed passionately in the doctrine they espoused and in its efficacy as a solution to the ills of their society. They were interested, accordingly, both in honoring eminent exponents of their beliefs and in achieving more widespread recognition of the worth of their creed. The canonization of Chŏng Mong-ju, carrying with it the prestige of official sanction, would be in accord with both these aims.

But at the same time there were political considerations of an immediate and practical character involved. Cho Kwang-jo and his group also believed passionately in the unitary character of their relationship to Neo-Confucian doctrine; they alone could diagnose and prescribe, and the patient might protest in vain that he was suffering, if at all, from some other ailment. Moreover, being a potent force in the government, the Cho group stood to gain politically from the general prestige and implied official sanction of their views that canonization of Chŏng Mong-ju would bring. The import would be the greater for those like Cho who could trace their scholastic lineage directly back to Chŏng. Opponents of canonization, on the other hand, while they could and did find no fault with many a lesser measure proposed for the purpose of stimulating Neo-Confucianism — for they had no quarrel with the doctrine in the abstract — might well balk at such a tacit endorsement of the program of its leading contemporary exponents. Meanwhile the final arbiter of the issue, the king, already had displayed a desire to see a stiffening of the moral fiber of his subjects, especially in the matter of loyalty to their sovereign, and he also had made plain his belief in the efficacy and worth of the study of Neo-Confucian texts.

The canonization of Chŏng Mong-ju was first discussed as early as 1510 (10.18).[70] The initial reaction of the High State Councillors of that time seems to have been prompted only by their conservative instincts. Their opinion was that such a decision should not be made lightly, since in the long years from the founding of the dynasty canonization never before had been considered (1510.10.19 S). Asked to further deliberate the matter after examining the evidence of Chŏng's merit, they gave this recommendation:

Chŏng Mong-ju's great fidelity to the principles of loyalty and filial piety, an inspiration to later ages, together with his achievements with respect to Neo-Confucianism, assuredly qualify him for canonization in the National Confucian Shrine. But if the sages among men all should attain canonization, then this act would be little more than an empty honor. (1510.12.21 S)[71]

Consequently the king refused consent and the issue was not pressed. Another request four years later, made by Kim Ku, a leading member of the 1519 group, was apparently not even discussed (1514.11.12 S).

The 1517 campaign to install Chŏng Mong-ju in the National Confucian Shrine began with the request of Third Inspector Chŏng Sun-bung that Chŏng Mong-ju and Kil Chae be honored for faithful adherence to their vows of loyalty by the appointment of their posterity to government posts and by other marks of public esteem. Chŏng Sun-bung asked further that Sŏng Sam-mun and Pak P'aeng-nyŏn (two of the famed Six Martyred Subjects) also be honored for their loyalty to Tanjong. He was supported in both requests by such stalwarts of the 1519 group as Cho Kwang-jo, Kim Chŏng, Ki Chun, and Yi Ch'ŏng in the OSC and Yi Cha in the Royal Secretariat. In the ensuing discussion, Chief State Councillor Chŏng Kwang-p'il led the high officials in noting that such honors for Chŏng and Kil had been carried out in previous reigns and in asserting that it was "too early" to think about so honoring Sŏng and Pak. Third Minister of Personnel Kim Al-lo, however, suggested that the posterity of Kim Koeng-p'il (Cho Kwang-jo's mentor) and Chŏng Yŏ-ch'ang be treated exceptionally as the descendants of sages and that other honors be conferred upon these two victims of 1498 (1517.8.5).

At this point there appeared a memorial from a group of National Academy students led by Kwŏn Chŏn, setting forth the attainments of Chŏng Mong-ju and Kim Koeng-p'il in respect to Neo-Confucian scholarship and asking that both be canonized. This request was promptly seconded by Cho Kwang-jo (1517.8.7). The *Sillok* historians have provided an engrossing, if tendentious, sidelight on the Kwŏn Chŏn memorial:

At this time many men of learning attached themselves to the Cho Kwang-jo group. They esteemed Chu Hsi-ism and did not hold in high regard the literary arts. Beginning students, too, fell under Cho's spell; they did not study texts but all day long sat rigidly as if in Zen-like meditation. Their teachers all deplored this, but yet did not have the courage to rectify this harmful practice.

Kwŏn Chŏn was on intimate terms with the Cho Kwang-jo group . . . When the Office of Special Counselors wanted to request the canonization of Kim Koeng-p'il, in response to their solicitation, Kwŏn Chŏn took the lead in presenting a memorial so requesting. . .

To begin with, Classics Licentiates An Ch'ŏ-gyŏm, An Chŏng, etc., took the lead from within the National Academy in advocating that Chŏng Mong-ju and Kim Koeng-p'il be canonized and on a certain day wished to bring the discussion to a close. But the other students felt that while in the case of Chŏng Mong-ju they could approve without hesitation, the case for Kim Koeng-p'il was by no means clear-cut and ought not be hastily

presented but, rather, slowly mulled over on a wait and see basis. Since the disapproval
of the other students was manifested in their faces, An Chŏng, etc., not daring to press
the matter, withdrew unceremoniously in high dudgeon. For they were bent on
canonizing Kim Koeng-p'il and using this as the fulcrum in the building of a faction.
Aware, however, that no one would go along with them if they proposed Kim
Koeng-p'il alone, they could not help but propose Chŏng Mong-ju as well. At the outset
it was not in behalf of Chŏng Mong-ju that they laid their plans.

Some days later, with the issue still undecided, the students of the National Academy
were telling each other: "To approve or disapprove of canonization is a function of the
government and is not something we can foretell. Even though we are not agreed in our
views, what harm is there in memorializing?" Whereupon they did memorialize. Now the
fact of the matter is that An Chŏng etc. did this in response to the exhortations of one
or two Counselors in the OSC. (1517.8.7 S)[72]

The views of the State Councillors, Six Boards Ministers, OSC and Censorate officials, all of
whom were summoned by the king to discuss the proposal, were predictably disparate. Chŏng
Kwang-p'il again led the higher echelons in arguing against canonization of either candidate. They
reasoned in this way:

Chŏng Mong-ju is the father of Korean Neo-Confucianism . . . His achievements in
[promoting] Confuciansim are great and moreover he died in defense of his code of
loyalty at the end of the Koryŏ period . . . Thus he could be installed in the National
Confucian Shrine without fear of reproach. Yet successive reigns have omitted doing so.
How can this be accounted for other than by the great stain [on his career] of having
zealously served the False Sin's [U and Ch'ang]?

Kim Koeng-p'il was deeply sincere in scholarship and conduct and was accorded great
esteem and deference by his contemporaries. But I have not been made aware that his
elucidations of the Classics or other contributions to Confucian studies can be viewed
as meriting such an honor . . ." (1517.8.9 S)

A majority of the Censorate, on the other hand, regarded the canonization of Chŏng as proper
but held it sufficient to honor Kim in lesser degree. Two Censorate officials, Chŏng Sun-bung and
Yun Ŭn-p'il, maintained that both should be canonized, and the OSC added the name of Chŏng
Yŏ-ch'ang as a third deserving figure. Chŏng Kwang-p'il and his colleagues then suggested that the
honors already accorded Kim Koeng-p'il and Chŏng Yŏ-ch'ang earlier in the reign were inadequate
and proposed certain additional measures. For his part, the king temporized with a non-committal
statement leaving the door open to further debate (1517.8.9 S).

The discussion now continued with Censorate and OSC rebuttals of the charge that Chŏng
Mong-ju's service under the False Sin's was reprehensible[73] and with assertions of the great contributions to Confucianism made by Kim Koeng-p'il and Chŏng Yŏ-ch'ang. The canonization of the three,
they argued, would do much to bring about the flourishing of Neo-Confucianism and the rectification
of literati mores. Again with Kwŏn Chŏn in the van, students of the National Academy memorialized
in a similar vein (1517.8.11 S, 8.12 S, 8.18 S). Presently, the king referred the question once more

to a broad assemblage of the officialdom, at the same time expressing his personal desire to see both Chŏng Mong-ju and Kim Koeng-p'il installed in the National Confucian Shrine (1517.8.18 S). However, after hearing opposition to canonizing Kim Koeng-p'il voiced with unanimity by the middle level officials, Chungjong contented himself with ordering the canonization of Chŏng Mong-ju and official recognition of the sites where Kim Koeng-p'il and Chŏng Yŏ-ch'ang had expounded the Confucian texts.[74] The latter order, however, was not carried out, for Chŏng Kwang-p'il and other State Councillors protested that the term "exposition site" was a misnomer, since Kim and Chŏng had merely assembled and taught the neighboring children. Accordingly, the king authorized instead that the government subsidize private rites for both and bestowed on each the posthumous office of Third State Councillor (1517.8.20).

The question of the canonization of Kim Koeng-p'il and Chŏng Yŏ-ch'ang was not raised again by the 1519 group, and nearly one hundred years were to pass before they, together with Cho Kwang-jo, were installed in the National Confucian Shrine (1610.9.4).

The Classics versus the Literary Arts

A closely related effort of the 1519 group, for it was based on the same premises, was aimed at modifying existing institutions and practices in favor of greater stress on textual knowledge, at the expense of traditional emphasis on literary accomplishments. Chungjong himself, from the early years of his reign, frequently had indicated that he personally was inclined in this direction. He had ordered Neo-Confucianism expounded in the Royal Lectures and the *Hsing-li ta-ch'üan* (the Ming dynasty's *Great compendium of Neo-Confucianism)* studied in the OSC and by other specially selected young civil officials (1509.6.10, 1511.11.24, 1513.9.21, 10.7). He had had texts of the Chu Hsi school published and distributed (1511.3.12). He had approved proposals for the selection of "teachers of Confucianism" who would be given long-term assignments to special duty in the National Academy and in the Four Colleges (1514.11.16, 12.21, 1516.5.30, 6.19). While the king had not neglected measures which would give stimulus to the literary arts (see 1508.2.19, 1511.3.14, 1518.7.12), he had left no doubt that, in his view, textual knowledge occupied a position of primacy. For example, in announcing his intention to administer a forthcoming civil examination on the basis of exposition of the Classics, Chungjong said: "Learning in the Confucian Classics is the root, and the art of literary composition is the branch. The literati of today all clamber toward the branch; they do not search out the root" (1511.3.8 S).

The men of 1519, however, were scarcely willing to accord the literary art even so subsidiary a status as this. They called it "spurious learning," a kind of "mechanical art," and asserted that its practitioners tended toward "superficiality and frivolity."[75] On many an occasion they asked the king to deemphasize literary skills and, by adopting a variety of specific proposals they were prepared to offer, esteem and encourage instead the study of Neo-Confucianism. Cho Kwang-jo, from his base in the OSC, was the undisputed leader of this movement and, indeed, in one storied instance took the matter of repudiation of the literary art into his own hands, when he refused to join in the Monthly Composition Trial (wŏlgwa; 1518.1.23).[76] *Sillok* historians aver that a similar long-established practice was omitted by Chungjong because of the views of the 1519 group:

The king bestowed wine on the Royal Secretariat and Office of Special Counselors. The historical officials said: "It is a tradition of the dynasty that on festival days the sovereign bestows wine and delicacies on the officials of the government who serve near to his person, and at some such times he announces a theme for the composition of poems. King Sŏngjong was exceedingly fond of this, and the present king, too, had done this repeatedly. But at this time Cho Kwang-jo and company, esteeming Neo-Confucianism and despising the literary arts, always argued at the Royal Lectures that the sovereign should not compose poetry and, moreover, should not command his officials to compose [poems] for presentation to him. Consequently, on [this] festival day, although the king awarded wine and delicacies in accordance with traditional practice, he did not order that poetry be composed." (1517.9.9 S)

This attitude of Cho and his group naturally did not go unchallenged by the High State Councillors and by others in the higher echelons of the government.[77] But it was Nam Kon, in these years alternating between Minister of Personnel and the secondary State Council posts, who was most articulate in defense of the importance and worth of the literary arts. In rebuttal to one attack of the Cho group he pointed out: "Our country not only has relations with China but also with other neighboring lands. The literary arts are vital, and we have no choice but to foster them" (1517.1.19 S). Some time later Nam Kon expanded on this theme:

It would behoove the nation to be concerned about the state of the literary art. I have often seen the compositions of various of my contemporaries, and in technical proficiency they rather fall short of their predecessors. Everyone follows personal whims and creates his own distinct style, paying no heed to prescribed format. . . . [In contrast,] men of yore exhaustively studied this art and only then could write without restraint. . . .

In the reign of Sejong the envoy Ni Ch'ien came from China. This was a time in which men of letters flourished in our country and, when they sang out or responded in poetical competition, their compositions were not inferior to those of China. Ni Ch'ien returned to his country and highly praised the brilliance of our literary artistry . . . . But if today an envoy such as Ni Ch'ien should come, how could we acquit ourselves as in the past? This should give us pause. (1518.6.8 S)

Furthermore, in refutation of the charge of superficiality and frivolity, Nam argued that:

Men today regard the literary skills [essential to the candidate] of the civil examination as repudiated learning and injurious to the proper learning. But [in all of history] since the Three Dynasties it has not been deemed advisable to repudiate the learning [essential to the candidate] of the civil examination. It may be all right to recruit officials by something like the Local Recommendation system [*hsiang-chü li-hsüan*] of the Three Dynasties [the Hsia, Shang and Chou dynasties of ancient Chinese history], on the basis of virtue of conduct and filial piety. But if it is not done in this way, then there is no alternative to recruiting officials by civil examination. Even though officials be so recruited, still sage men will appear among them . . . like the two Ch'eng's and Chu Hsi of the Sung, all of whom emerged via the examination route. Furthermore, how can those who practice the literary arts all be superficial and frivolous while those who pursue the study of the Classics all not be so? . . . The literary arts and study of the Classics must be regarded as two components of a single entity, neither one of which may be one-sidedly neglected. (1517.8.30 S)

Nam Kon's reference to the Local Recommendation system of ancient China had not been fortuitous, for it was very much in the minds of the 1519 group to repudiate the literary skills as the basis of the civil examination system. Earlier in the same year of 1517, OSC Second Counselor Yi Cha and Third Counselor Hong Ŏn-p'il had argued that an examination system based on poetical composition was extremely narrow and had urged that "idle literati" of preeminent learning and conduct be recommended and employed in accordance with this old Chinese prescription.[78] The reaction of such high officials as Chŏng Kwang-p'il and Nam Kon had been to stress the necessity of recruiting officials by means of an examination process rather than by recommendation. At this time Chungjong had ordered idle literati recommended throughout the country, but this was merely a familiar device for recruitment of quality personnel to staff the lower levels of the administrative structure (1517.2.21).[79]

With the passage of another year, the 1519 group was ready to make a startlingly radical proposal which would vitiate the objections previously raised to the recruitment of officials by recommendation. The authors of the proposal simply fused together the two divergent approaches: they would assemble a group of candidates by recommendation and subject them to a special type of examination; those who passed would then enjoy the full prerogatives of holders of the normal civil examination degree.

At a fateful session of the Royal Lectures in the spring of 1518, OSC First Counselor Cho Kwang-jo led off by repeating an earlier admonishment that Royal Lectures participants should be chosen on the basis of mature scholarship and proven virtue, not because of their attainments in the literary arts or their exalted lineage (1518.3.11). Third Royal Secretary Yi Cha then spoke as follows:

It is strange that the government should lament the insufficiency of qualified personnel. I could not venture an estimate of the able men of this day, but how can it be said definitely that there are none? The nation's method of recruiting personnel is extremely narrow. In consequence, many men are prevented from availing themselves of it and the task of the Boards of Personnel and War in making nominations is made difficult. Why not command the State Councillors and other participants in the Royal Lectures to determine in detail how best to find men whose ability and conduct make them worthy of employment? The concept of the special examination is not new to our dynasty and, if once we proceed along these lines, the benefits will be enormous. (1518.3.11 S)

As if by pre-arrangement, Cho Kwang-jo proceeded to elaborate:

> What Yi Cha has proposed is something I and my colleagues have long wanted to do.
> Men whose ability and conduct warrant their employment should be recommended by
> the Governors and Local Magistrates in the provinces and by the Office of Special
> Counselors, the Six Boards, and the Censorate in the capital, then assembled at the
> palace and examined by the king by the problem-essay method.[80] In this way, many
> men of parts can be found. This is a procedure which our dynasty has never followed;
> it is in the tradition of the Wisdom and Character Examination [*hsien-liang fang-cheng
> k'o*] of the Han. If men are widely recommended for virtue of conduct, there can be
> no question of dissimulation, and if we observe by means of the problem-essay how
> they apply their knowledge, then assurance is made doubly sure. (1518.3.11 S)

Among the high officials now summoned for discussion there were four who approved the
plan (Second State Councillor Sin Yong-gae, Fifth State Councillor An Tang, Inspector-General
Ch'oe Suk-saeng and Sixth State Councillor Yu Tam-nyŏn), but all the rest, with Chŏng Kwang-
p'il and Minister of Personnel Nam Kon in the lead, opposed. The gist of their argument was that
the scheme would undermine the traditional examination system, that unfairness in the recommendation of candidates would be inevitable, and that there would be "pernicious repercussions"
(1518.3.11). But the real concern of both sides is perhaps best revealed in the following exchange:

> [Minister of War] Chang Sun-son said: "To widely recommend the sage and
> talented, ascertain their views, and employ them is fine. [But] . . . it is not proper
> to term such a procedure a Government Service Examination." . . .
>
> [Fourth Censor] Yi Ch'ŏng said: "If it is not called by the term Government
> Service Examination, then [those selected under this plan] cannot be employed
> in the Office of Special Counselors. This would be profitless."
>
> [Chief State Councillor] Chŏng Kwang-p'il exclaimed: "Why must [such men]
> be employed in the Office of Special Counselors? Rather should they be used as
> ordinary clerks!" (1518.3.13 S)

Chungjong, however, would not give ear to the repeated protests and ordered the Board of
Rites to draw up detailed procedures. This proved to be a difficult task, for Chŏng Kwang-p'il was
uncompromising in his opposition and, indeed, soon succeeded in reopening formal discussion of
the issue. This time only An Tang and Ch'oe Suk-saeng (now Minister of Personnel and Seventh
State Councillor respectively) voiced approval. Nevertheless, the king determined to proceed with
the implementation of his previous decision (1518.3.11, 3.28, 4.22, 4.25).

Meanwhile, Nam Kon had continued to argue against the proposed plan by asserting that its
model, the Wisdom and Character Examination of the Han dynasty, had been marked by unfairness
(1518.3.22 S). He was concerned, too, that it was intended to replace lower echelon officials who
were being released on grounds of general unfitness (in accordance with frequent and accepted
practice) with "idle literati" already recommended or to be nominated as candidates of the new
examination course.[81] Before long, Nam had occasion to show how strongly he felt on the subject.

When his turn came to offer an explanation for the occurrence of an unusually severe earthquake, he frankly implied that it was Heaven's response to the idea of recruiting government personnel by recommendation (1518.5.15 S). But Nam Kon was already on his way off the scene, having been named the previous day to head an important embassy to China. He owed this honor, if such it was, to the Censorate and OSC officials, who made it clear that they wanted the appointment to go to Nam (1518.5.11 S, 5.14 S).[82]

Preparations to hold the Recommendation Examination (ch'ŏn'gŏ-kwa), as it was known,[83] now went smoothly forward. In mid-year the State Council and Board of Rites announced detailed procedures to govern the recommendation and processing of candidates (1518.6.5). Since the king already had ordered that "even though possessed of a single talent or a single accomplishment, all should be searched out and brought forward" (1518.4.19), a number of candidates had appeared on the scene and in some cases had been given posts even before the procedures were determined (1518.5.21, 5.27, 5.30, 6.1).[84] By year's end, a roster of one hundred twenty candidates had been prepared and, at the order of the king, had been scrutinized by the Board of Rites to eliminate the less worthy. Kim Chŏng, An Tang, and others, however, objected that the forty-odd candidates selected by the Rites Board were far too few and that such a screening was a violation of the concept of recommendation. Accordingly, the king ordered that the number of candidates authorized to proceed to the examination be increased (1518.12.1, 12.1 S, 12.17 S, 12.18 S).[85] This was done and, in the spring of 1519, the Yi dynasty's only Recommendation Examination was held and twenty-eight men awarded the crimson certificate of the civil examination final degree holder (1519.4.13).

Publication of the results of the Recommendation Examination could not have dispelled the suspicion that it would be administered unfairly. The most intriguing coincidence was that the three sons of Third State Councillor An Tang all were among the passers. On this point the *Sillok* historians offer us the following innuendo:

> An Tang's three sons passed at the same time and the king despatched a palace servant with a bountiful gift of wine and meat, as an expression of congratulations, and men all accounted this a signal honor. But discerning men were aware that this was not due simply to the good fortune of the An family. An Tang gave a congratulatory banquet and the whole government turned out to join in the festivities.
> [Recent Magistrate of Seoul] Han Hyŏng-yun said: "If they really passed, then how great a cause for rejoicing it would be!" Han Hyŏng-yun meant that he considered the Recommendation Examination to have been lacking in impartiality. (1519.4.20 S)

An Tang, of course, had been a staunch supporter of the Recommendation Examination plan, but this is not the only indication of his sympathies and ties with the Cho Kwang-jo group. When he was Minister of Personnel he singled out Cho and others among the men of 1519 for rapid advancement.[86] He spoke out strongly against punishing Kim Chŏng and Pak Sang for their ill-advised memorial. But above all, the way in which An Tang came to occupy the exalted position of Third State Councillor is convincing evidence that the 1519 group regarded An Tang as their man.[87]

With the removal of Second State Councillor Kim Ŭng-gi at the end of 1517 (i12.26), there occurred a vacancy among the High State Councillors for the first time in almost two years. Now it was the all but unvarying practice of the early Yi dynasty for incumbent and former High State Councillors alone to nominate candidates for appointment to such a vacancy. In accordance with this tradition, Chief State Councillor Chŏng Kwang-p'il and Third State Councillor Sin Yong-gae proposed to the king the names of Kim Chŏn and Yi Kye-maeng, respectively the Fourth and the Sixth State Councillor. Cho Kwang-jo and Kim Chŏng, however, took the lead in persuading the king to have nominations made by a broad assemblage of officials, thus, they argued, to ensure the appointment of a man of virtue and high repute (1518.1.4). But when the king convened such a broad assemblage, including the Censorate and OSC, the evident displeasure of Chŏng and Sin caused everyone else to decline to participate in the discussion. Thereupon, asked by Chungjong to submit nominations again, the two High State Councillors added the name of Nam Kon. When the king took the unusual step of referring for consideration the name of An Tang, they protested that he lacked the requisite official rank (1518.3.5).

Chungjong lost no time in making up An Tang's rank deficiency, appointing him Fifth State Councillor (1518.3.11 S).[88] Then he asked Chŏng and Sin once more to propose nominees and this time Chŏng gave his blessing as well to the candidacy of An Tang. Sin being indisposed at his home, a Royal Secretariat Recorder was despatched to ascertain his view, which was that, while An too was qualified, the appointment preferably should be made from among the original three nominees. When the Recorder returned to his office, Third Royal Secretary Kim Chŏng asked him whether Sin had recommended An Tang and was told that such was not the case. However, in writing up what Sin had said for presentation to the king, the Recorder, pressed for time, omitted to note Sin's expression of preference for one of the original three nominees, thus leaving the impression that he had equally endorsed An Tang's candidacy.[89] A few days later An Tang was appointed Third State Councillor (1518.5.15).

On the surface, it would appear that An Tang's candidacy was pushed on the sole initiative of the king. It is alleged, however, that from beginning to end Chungjong was playing out a role created by the enterprising Cho Kwang-jo group. The High State Councillor vacancy had occurred because of the removal of Kim Ŭng-gi, who had been removed because he had absented himself from his duties for a period of some six months. Serious illness, in fact, had made it impossible for Kim to attend his office, but he had abandoned his desk in the first place only after suffering character assassination at the hands of the Censorate (see 1517. i12.26 S, i12.27 S). The Censorate, without citing the specifics, earlier had impeached him thus: "Second State Councillor Kim Ŭng-gi is of inferior talent and limited capabilities, of paltry wisdom and weak moral purpose; he does not distinguish between right and wrong, nor differentiate good from evil. . . .Of affairs he does not decide the propriety and impropriety, of men he does not determine the upright and the wicked. . . .We beg that he be quickly removed" (1517.7.7 S). To this the *Sillok* historians have appended the following observations:

> At this time . . . the newly emerged officials were bent on attaining good government overnight. Those of the Cho Kwang-jo group regarded Minister of Taxation An Tang as being of State Council caliber because once, as Inspector-General [error for Minister of Personnel], he had succored Kim Chŏng and Pak Sang, and they wanted to recommend that he be speedily placed in High State Councillor position. But, among the incumbent High State Councillors, Chŏng Kwang-p'il was held in such widespread and high esteem and Sin Yong-gae was such a prepossessing figure that neither could be impugned. Only Kim Ŭng-gi remained, a man excessively complaisant and inclined toward indecisiveness of action. Accordingly, the Cho Kwang-jo group wanted to drive out Kim Ŭng-gi, thereby making an opening for An Tang. (1517.7.7 S)[90]

And an unofficial source further alleges that the king's extraordinary action of requesting that An Tang be considered as a candidate for High State Councillor position was done at the instance of OSC officials.[91]

As remarkable as the presence of the three sons of An Tang on the Recommendation Examination list was the inclusion of the names of Kim Sik and Pak Hun. Kim, who placed first in the examination, was well known to be one of Cho Kwang-jo's most intimate associates, and only a month was required for him to attain the high station of OSC First Counselor (1519.5.16). Pak Hun too was a leading member of the Cho group. Immediately following the examination, he was appointed a Fourth Inspector (1519.4.17), a post he had held at least once before (see 1518.8.21 S), and within a few months he rose to Second Censor (1519.9.24) and Sixth Royal Secretary (1519.10.6). Both Kim and Pak joined Cho and Kim Chŏng among the eight primary victims of the Purge of 1519.

No others among the passers of the Recommendation Examination quite so arrest the attention,[92] but it is not difficult to find further indications that, even if such was not its purpose, this examination was used to bulwark the political position of those who brought it into being. In the seven month period from the holding of the examination to the opening of the purge, perhaps half of the twenty-eight passers received appointments to the Censorate or OSC.[93] On the day the purge began they occupied five of the seventeen OSC duty posts and three of the eleven Censorate positions, and they also could boast of the Headmaster of the National Academy (Kim Sik) and a Royal Secretary (Pak Hun). These numbers plus the large group of acknowledged Cho Kwang-jo partisans then in other crucial posts resulted in a formidable force indeed.

The Heyday of the Cho Group

This thought undoubtedly troubled the minds of many men of that day. While some who felt such concern continued to wage a losing fight in the councils of the government, others were turning their attention to cruder but more effective methods of opposition. Thus the plot of a Chungjong Merit Subject, Kim U-jŭng, which came to light not long before the Recommendation Examination was held, was a harbinger of events to come.

A fellow Merit Subject reported the Kim U-jŭng plot in these words:

> This day Kim U-jŭng came to my house . . . [and said:] "Nowadays the king heeds the entirety of the Censorate's words and in consequence those who suffer crime charges are many. Moreover, recently one hears that Kim Chŏng, etc., want to open Pak Wŏn-jong's coffin and behead the corpse and then get rid of all the Chungjong Merit Subjects . . . Kim Chŏng, etc., recently wanted to precipitate [such] a crisis, but Cho Kwang-jo, wishing to wait for the return of Yi Cha, who has not yet come back from Peking, put a stop to it for the time being. The arrows recently shot into the Kŏnch'un Gate [in the eastern wall surrounding the Kyŏngbok Palace, the royal residence] and within the palace precincts all carried [messages about] this scheme of Kim Chŏng and his ilk.[94] Yet the king pays no heed and the High State Councillors, too, do not memorialize and urge the removal [of these men]. If the passers of the Wisdom and Character [i.e., the Recommendation] Examination are arrayed in the government, then unquestionably all the older officials will be ousted. Such men as myself wish to move first to get rid of [Kim Chŏng, etc.]. Adherents [to our cause] are already standing by . . ." [Then] . . . he clasped my hand and said: "This is a matter of the utmost importance. You must not let drop a word of it, even in the presence of your wife and sons." (1519.3.2 S)

Kim U-jŭng and three alleged collaborators (two of them also Merit Subjects) were immediately brought under arrest and interrogated but, when none confessed, the other three were released. Presently, when the rod was used on Kim U-jŭng, he admitted to all except that there were others prepared to act with him, and this he stubbornly denied having said. Accordingly, the sentence proposed to the king was beating and distant banishment, on the charge of "inflammatory words." Chungjong accepted this judgment and, with the support of his High State Councillors, resisted the strong representations of the censoring bodies (Cho Kwang-jo, Kim Chŏng, Kim Ku, and Pak Se-hŭi in the lead) for further investigation of the case and execution of Kim U-jŭng (1519.3.2, 3.3, 3.4).

The fear expressed by Kim U-jŭng that the "older officials" and Merit Subjects would all be ousted was well founded, in part upon events that had recently transpired, in part upon a sound reading of the probable future. I have already noted the persistent attacks of the censoring bodies on High State Councillors Sŏng Hŭi-an, Song Chil, and Yu Sun earlier in Chungjong's reign, as well as the more recent removal of Kim Ŭng-gi from his Second State Councillor position. It scarcely need be said that in the period when the influence of the Cho Kwang-jo group was at its height there was no lack of similar occurrences. Inquiry into a few such instances will help set the background for the Purge of 1519.[95]

The discharge of Merit Subject Second Class Cho Kye-sang from his post of Second Minister of Rites is exceptional in that it resulted from a direct and vehement attack on the 1519 group. On the day following the great earthquake of 1518 (which coincided with An Tang's appointment to Third State Councillor), when the king called the officialdom together to seek the reason for the calamity, Cho Kye-sang was moved to speculate as follows:

> Of late there have been exceedingly many startling calamities, and the earthquake disaster of yesterday is the most appalling of them all. The king has offered the view that it is a symbol of the waxing of the *yin* and the waning of the *yang;* what else can this mean than the presence of amoral men [of waxing influence in the government]? Yet, though there be amoral men present, it is in truth difficult to become aware of it. For on the surface they resemble men of principle and only within are they amoral men. Now the amoral men of this ilk are possessed of manifold talents; how can one expect them to provide visible evidence wherein their true form would be manifested? The way these men act, then, gives the appearance of being righteous, but should the king yearn after the olden days, then he will be able to regard their true stripe. For they show no concern for the restraints imposed by the realities of the times, but rather, pretending to guide the king by the ways of yore, in reality wish to carry out their personal desires. Accordingly, in the absence of a man-made calamity involving this crowd, there has inevitably occurred Heaven's admonition, that in the end they can surely not escape defeat and ruin. (1518.5.16 S)

At this, naturally, the censoring bodies loosed a roar of pained indignation, accusing Cho Kye-sang of "scheming to destroy the men of principle" and asking that he be banished afar. First Counselor Cho Kwang-jo, by chance then on leave outside the capital, quickly returned and stated the case against Cho Kye-sang in the strongest terms. At first, in accordance with the counsel of such high-placed figures as Chǒng Kwang-p'il, the king refused to heed the demands for punishment of Cho Kye-sang. Presently, however, Chungjong succumbed to the unceasing outcry and not only discharged Cho but also divested him of office warrants (1518.5.16, 5.17 S, 5.18 S, 5.20 S).

In the course of their denunciation of Cho Kye-sang, the Censorate and OSC, apparently gratuitously, leveled grave charges against Minister of War Chang Sun-son, saying:

> Chang Sun-son, though at bottom a sinister and base fellow, has attained high office and rank, far beyond his capabilities. Yet still he knows not humility. His greed for private gain is insatiable and he hates those who criticize him. Indeed he vilifies the literati and not only regards them as an enemy but cherishes malicious designs against them. He is secretly agitating in many quarters, and his stratagem is to strike down all in one fell swoop. This is exactly the method employed by Yu Cha-gwang in the past, and now Chang Sun-son is modelling himself after this pattern. Happily, availing themselves of the sovereign, the high officials have so far thwarted Chang's ambition. However, though his villainous scheming has not borne fruit, his malevolent intent

remains at unabated pitch. Should he but find the opportunity, the disaster he would wreak would be indescribable. (1518.5.16 S)

Chang Sun-son, too, did not lack defenders among the State Councillors. Chŏng Kwang-p'il observed that Chang had urged the high officials to stand with utmost firmness against the efforts of those who wished to change old laws and traditions of the dynasty. But Chŏng went on to point out that not only Chang but all the high officials had spoken out against such changes and that this could not be construed as intent "to strike down all in one fell swoop" (1518.5.17 S). Second State Councillor Sin Yong-gae recounted that Chang had spoken to him of the injustice of the condemnation of Yi Haeng but added that he had never heard from anyone the words that Chang wished to fell the literati. All agreed, however, that Chang had a reputation for avariciousness, and on this basis they were willing to see him shifted to another post (1518.5.17 S, 5.22 S). This was done (1518.5.17 S), but presently, due to the unrelenting assault of the censoring organs, Chang Sun-son met the same fate as Cho Kye-sang (1518.5.20 S).

Cho Kye-sang, of course, had invited attack, and despite a record substantially free of conflict with the censoring bodies his ouster at this time is not surprising. Chang Sun-son, too, appears never to have come under heavy fire before, although being on a higher level than Cho Kye-sang he had had occasion more frequently to express his opposition to the views of the 1519 group. It is difficult to understand, however, why he should have been singled out as a special target.[96] Perhaps the explanation of the incident, as well as its significance, lies in the operational techniques of the censoring organs. Chang Sun-son was neither so highly placed nor so vocal an opponent of the Cho group as some, but he was relatively more vulnerable, and this may have been the basis of his undoing. At any rate, both Chang and Cho now had been thrust off the scene and were either unwilling or unable to return in time to avenge themselves by joining in the fabrication of the Purge of 1519.

A very different case was that of another Merit Subject, Sim Chŏng, who had a considerable history of collision with the censoring bodies. The first major encounter occurred when Sim was named Second Minister of Personnel in 1514 (10.27) and the Censorate asserted, without effect, that his personal stature was incommensurate with his post (1514.11.2 S, 11.24 S). Again, when he was appointed Seventh State Councillor in 1518 (3.11), the Censorate averred that he was a man of little repute and quickly secured his removal (1518.3.12 S, 3.18 S). With his next assignment to a duty post, Sim suffered still harsher onslaught; the OCG termed him a man of "wickedly deceitful bent" and demanded that he be removed as Magistrate of Seoul and from his concurrent post of Special Participant in the Royal Lectures as well (1518.12.9, 12.13). For a time the king rejected this demand, but after the Censorate (with the OIG) had hammered away for more than a month, Chungjong finally transferred Sim from his position as Magistrate of Seoul but still refused to remove him from the Royal Lectures post (1518.12.26, 1519.1.23). Subsequently, Sim Chŏng again was prevented by Censorate attack from taking up a new assignment, that of concurrent

Second Magistrate of the State Tribunal. In the few months remaining before the purge Sim Chǒng was not again named to a duty post, but he made his presence felt in the very forefront of the purge coup.

There are a great many other instances which might be cited to further demonstrate the way in which the censoring organs operated in these years of ascendancy of the 1519 group or to lengthen the list of those who had personal reasons to participate in or applaud the purge. At the same time, there were other high-placed officials who were relatively immune from Censorate attack, despite repeated and forceful opposition to the program of the Cho Kwang-jo group. Particularly noteworthy in this regard were Nam Kon, Kim Chǒn, and Ko Hyǒng-san, all of whom had been attacked from time to time over the years by the censoring bodies. But, in spite of the unpopularity of their views, none of them experienced great difficulty in remaining in high office and, indeed, the efforts of the censoring bodies against them seem at first glance surprisingly sporadic and feeble. This was because each in his own way presented a very difficult target. Nam Kon was a man of great and versatile talent, of sound judgment and restrained temper, and his official and private life was well ordered. Kim Chǒn was that rarity, an official of high station renowned in his own lifetime for the highly prized virtue of "perfect probity," a man conspicuously modest in his way of life and staunchly incorruptible in the conduct of public business. Ko Hyǒng-san was the leading authority of his day on northern frontier affairs and, to his military knowledge, brought the learning necessary to the successful civil examination degree candidate. His public morals were impeccable. Since they both had been banished in the Purge of 1504, neither Nam nor Kim was in the least vulnerable to the charge of collaboration; nor was Ko, though he had not been touched at all by the purge. Nam and Kim both are accounted disciples of Kim Chong-jik, while additionally in Ko's favor was the fact of his undistinguished lineage, for this would diminish the possibility of condemnation by association. Nor was any of the three a Merit Subject or the close kin of a Merit Subject. The point is that the actions of these men, who were possessed of such integrity of character and of such unassailable background, would not be motivated by personal considerations; in the climactic events ahead, their concern would be with basic principles.

The men of 1519, some surface indications to the contrary, were also concerned with principles — specifically, they were attempting rapidly to effect a radical program of institutional and human engineering. By mid-1519 they had made considerable progress, both in realizing certain features of the program and in preparing the ground for presentation of what remained. For example, the term of office of provincial governors was doubled to two years, thus easing the burden on the people of frequent welcomings and leave-takings; and the so-called "village code" system was established, an attempt to place important responsibility for social order and well-being in the hands of the local populace. At the same time, however, the men of 1519 were responsible for a mounting crisis in the government, resulting from the hostility and resistance to their program of other segments of the power elite. In such a setting, they launched their most audacious campaign, the effort to obliterate for the most part the record of meritorious service in the enthronement of King Chungjong. This effort was to mark their undoing.

Revision of the Merit Roster

It was not until late in 1519 that the formidable problem of the Chungjong Enthronement Merit Subjects was essayed. Along with Censor-General Yi Sŏng-dong and his other colleagues in the Censorate,[98] Inspector-General Cho Kwang-jo argued that the Chungjong Enthronement merit enrollment in 1506 had been promiscuous and excessive. Many Merit Subjects, their memorial noted, had been favorites of Yŏnsangun and, while some of these nonetheless deserved enrollment, others were without a particle of merit. Yu Cha-gwang, it was added, wishing to exalt his sons and marriage relations, had manipulated the selection of the Merit Subjects in the direction of such excess. The result had been to foster mores of avarice and cupidity, which in turn were at the root of the numerous plots and alarums of plots against the king and government. This perilous urge toward material gain might be checked, it was concluded, by expunging the undeserving from the merit roster.[99] To this category the Censorate assigned eight Second Class, nine Third Class, and the entire Fourth Class of "more than fifty" Merit Subjects (1519.10.25 S).[100]

The king refused consent and remained steadfast in the face of unceasing Censorate demands, which were abundantly supported by the OSC and Royal Secretariat. Meanwhile, the Censorate officials had resigned and stubbornly resisted all efforts to lure or force them back to their duties (1519.10.26S, 10.27S, 10.28S, 10.29S, 10.30S, 11.4S). This deadlock lasted for about a week before the State Council, for the first time, entered into the debate. Their initial recommendation was that, although in principle deletion of merit was wrong, the uncompromising stand taken by the Censorate required that the most flagrant cases of undeserved enrollment, in Class Four only, be rectified. When summoned for a personal interview with the king, the State Council joined the other officials of high station in "severally expressing the conviction that [the merit roster] must be revised" (1519.11.1.S, 11.2 S).

The king was now beset by all levels of the officialdom with the demand that he bow to the public consensus. The State Council, the Board Ministers, the Board Section Chiefs, the Diarists of the Office of Royal Decrees, and the Seoul Magistracy all added their weight to the incessant advocacy of the Censorate and OSC. Moreover, a few individual Merit Subjects now came forward to urge approval of the deletion proposal or to offer to resign their own merit status (1519.11.4 S, 11.7 S).[101] Such unrelenting pressures at last proved too much for Chungjong and, indicating willingness to delete the most flagrant cases, he handed back down a list on which he indicated approval of the deletion of fifty-eight names and marked nineteen others for further discussion (1519.11.8 S, 11.9 S, 11.10 S).

There now ensued a final, bitter two days of controversy in which the king was firm in his insistence that deletion be limited to flagrant cases. But he stood utterly alone. The Censorate presented a detailed case against the totality of the Class Four enrollees. When time and time again the king sought to except a specific figure, often on the basis of personal knowledge of what had transpired in 1506, his leading officials (most frequently in the persons of Chŏng Kwang-p'il and Cho Kwang-jo) rose in determined opposition. At length the king fell silent. Seeing then that decision was coming no nearer to hand, Cho Kwang-jo suggested that he and his colleagues retire to continue their deliberations (1519.11.9 S).

Presently the officials returned with their new deletion proposals. But the only change from the original request was the addition of three names from the Third Class of merit enrollment; just as before, it was asked that the entire Fourth Class roster be expunged. At this, the king expressed indignation that his wishes of the morning had been so blithely disregarded and proceeded to dictate certain exceptions, insisting the while that he would approve deletion only of the flagrant cases. Chŏng Kwang-p'il, however, in mild tone, and the Censorate quite sharply, asserted that the king had gone back on his word, while Chungjong in turn, at times with evident anger, accused the State Councillors and Censorate of inconsistency and once more refused to take the action desired of him (1519.11.9 S). Finally, after another day of listening to alternating entreaties and recriminations, the king gave up the unequal struggle and agreed to the deletion of seventy-six names. This was nearly three-quarters of the total roster of men rewarded for merit in raising him to the throne (1519.11.10 S, 11.11 S).[102]

The Purge Unfolds

The purge started only four days later when, in the middle of the night,

At the second watch, there was commotion in the palace courtyard. The duty officers, Royal Secretaries Yun Cha-im and Kong Sŏ-rin, Recorder An Chŏng and Third Diarist Yi Ku, rushed out and found the Yŏngch'u Gate [in the west wall surrounding the Kyŏngbok Palace] open and Minister of War Yi Chang-gon, Second Minister-without-Portfolio [error for Minister of Works] Kim Chŏn, Minister of Taxation Ko Hyŏng-san, the Lord of Hwach'ŏn Sim Chŏng, and Fourth Minister of War Sŏng Un sitting outside the Royal Lecture Hall, while blue uniformed troops were standing on guard at the left and right of the Kŭnjŏng Audience Hall. Yun Cha-im asked Yi Chang-gon and the others how they came to enter the palace precincts. They replied: "Because we have a special gate pass from within."

Suddenly, from the royal quarters, Sŏng Un was appointed a Royal Secretary and [through him] it was ordered that the Royal Secretariat duty officers and the OSC duty officers, Fourth Counselor Ki Chun and Junior Sixth Counselor Sim Tal-wŏn, be handed over to the State Tribunal, that Seventh State Councillor Yi Cha, Minister of Punishments Kim Chŏng, Inspector-General Cho Kwang-jo, First Counselor Kim Ku, Headmaster of the National Academy Kim Sik, and Royal Secretaries Yu In-suk, Pak Se-hŭi, Hong Ŏn-p'il, and Pak Hun be arrested and imprisoned, and that the entire personnel of the Royal Secretariat, the Office of Special Counselors, the Office of the Inspector-General, the Office of the Censor-General, and the Office of Royal Decrees be removed. Then, by verbal instruction, the king had Minister of Rites Nam Kon exchange posts with Minister of Personnel Sin Sang and made Third Minister of War Kim Kŭn-sa a Royal Secretary.

At the fifth watch, [Office of Royal Decrees] First Diarist Ch'ae Se-yŏng and Second Diarists Kwŏn Ye and Yi Kong-in were ordered restored to their posts, for no one remained to record events. Chŏng Kwang-p'il, Hong Kyŏng-ju, Kim Chŏn, Yi Chang-gon, Ko Hyŏng-san Sim Chŏng, Son Chu, Pang Yu-nyŏng, Kim Kŭn-sa, Sŏng Un, and Yun Hŭi-in entered and memorialized a bill requesting charges of crime against Cho Kwang-jo, Kim Chŏng, etc. The king then called near Chŏng Kwang-p'il, etc., and An Tang and Hong Suk to discuss this. Except for Cho Kwang-jo, Kim Chŏng, Kim Sik, Kim Ku, Yun Cha-im, Pak Se-hŭi, Pak Hun and Ki Chun, all were released and Nam Kon was ordered to draft a royal minute on judicial proceedings against the eight remaining prisoners for transmission to the State Tribunal.

This royal minute said:

"Cho Kwang-jo, Kim Chŏng, Kim Sik, and Kim Ku have bound themselves together in a clique, advancing those who adhere to them and repudiating those who differ with them. Each throwing his weight behind the other, they have entrenched themselves in positions of authority and have lured over to their side the newly emerged young officials. Making a habit of vituperative bombast, with each passing day they inflict more injury on the government. But the present officialdom, fearing the enormous power of these men, do not dare speak out. As for Yun Cha-im, Pak Se-hŭi, Pak Hun, and Ki Chun, they have willingly lent themselves to this practice of government by vituperation. Let judicial proceedings be conducted along these lines."

Dawn had already broken. (1519.11.15)

At first, the Purge of 1519 was surprisingly limited in scope. After judicial proceedings lasting less than two days, sentence was adjudged on the eight remaining prisoners. The harsh punishments initially proposed quickly were mitigated: the first four (Cho Kwang-jo, Kim Chŏng, Kim Sik, Kim Ku) were ordered beaten one hundred strokes and banished afar under confinement, while the other four (Yun Cha-im, Pak Se-hŭi, Pak Hun, Ki Chun) were fined in lieu of beating and banished in mild degree. All eight were completely divested of office warrants (1519.11.16 S).

This initial display of moderation was due to strenuous efforts on all sides in behalf of the accused. The voice of Chief State Councillor Chŏng Kwang-p'il was the most prominent and the most tireless in this advocacy. Often seconded by Third State Councillor An Tang and Minister of Rites Sin Sang, Chŏng repeatedly insisted that the charges being brought against Cho and the others were far too severe. For, Chŏng argued in essence, their only crime was their "extremism" and this was the result of the excessive tolerance of the king, who "extraordinarily raised them all to vital positions" and "failed to heed not a single word they uttered" (1519.11.16 S). In Chŏng's view, the king would be amply justified in censuring the accused for their extremism, but to charge them with grave crime would endanger the principle of freedom of remonstrance and would cause men's minds to be seriously unsettled (1519.11.16 S). As he had observed at the very outset: "The actions of this group always and in every case were in the name of right. It will be difficult to find words to specify their crime" (1519.11.15 S).

Chŏng Kwang-p'il by no means stood alone; succor was literally everywhere at hand.[103] Several Second and Third Ministers of the Six Boards and the Second and Third Seoul Magistrates expressed their astonishment at the king's desire to lodge serious charges against the accused, who had merely endeavored to revitalize the nation's mores and purify the government (1519.11.16 S). The newly appointed Censor-General, Yun Hŭi-in, who on the previous day had joined in memorializing the bill requesting that crime be charged against Cho, now echoed the plea that the Cho group was guilty of no more than extremism (1519.11.16 S). The former Royal Secretaries, who had been jailed and then quickly freed, asked that they be recommitted to prison, while the former Censorate personnel joined the temporarily removed OSC officials in requesting that they be imprisoned and punished alike with Cho and the others (1519.11.16 S). A large group of National Academy students forced their way through the gates of the palace compound and carried to the very door of the king's residence their laments and protestations that the accused were innocent of crime (1519.11.16 S).[104]

The king countered these pleas with the dogged assertion that the government had requested that charges of crime be preferred and that he would proceed to prosecute on this basis.[105] The Investigation Officers then interpreted the law to require that the four headed by Cho Kwang-jo be beheaded, their wives and children enslaved, and their property confiscated, and that the lesser four be beaten and banished afar.[106] This touched off a further wave of protest. After the State Council, Six Boards, and Seoul Magistracy had argued that the victims had not confessed to cliquism and that no evidence existed to substantiate this charge, the king was moved to mitigate the sentence to decreed suicide for Cho and Kim Chŏng, the rod and banishment to desert isles for Kim Sik and Kim Ku, and fines in lieu of beating, banishment in light degree, and loss of office warrants for the other four (1519.11.16 S). But this was not palliative enough; appeals for leniency continued unabated, especially from Chŏng Kwang-p'il and An Tang, and these eventually brought a promise from Chungjong to weigh his decision once again (1519.11.16 S).

The result of the king's further reflection was the far more lenient punishment decree already noted, but not even so drastic an amelioration as this could quiet the pro-Cho clamor. Chŏng Kwang-p'il now took the lead in arguing that application of the rod to Cho and the three others might result in their deaths and in urging that this portion of the sentence be suspended (1519.11.16 S). The Censor-General, citing the pernicious effect on the literati spirit of laying charges of crime against men who had only endeavored to serve their country, asked that the king exhibit still greater magnanimity (1519.11.16 S). Inspector-General Yu Un echoed and elaborated this plea (1519.11.17 S), while his colleagues in the new Censorate resigned their posts, averring that they could not prosecute their duties unless Cho and his fellow victims were restored to grace (1519.11.17 S, 11.18 S). The newly appointed Royal Secretaries lamented the resort to numerous irregular procedures on the night the purge began, a theme which was further developed by Chŏng Kwang-p'il and An Tang and by the official historians. The OSC officials submitted a written brief in defense of the Cho group and sought also to resign their posts (1519.11.17 S).[107]

The king, however, was adamant in his refusal to make further concessions. In fact, he had already ordered the sentences quickly carried into effect (1519.11.16 S).

This great current of protest had delayed but could not prevent the logical development of the purge pattern. For a while an uneasy peace prevailed, marked by clear indications that a climate of opinion uncompromisingly hostile to the Cho Kwang-jo group was in the making. The Censorate officials who had openly declared themselves to be on Cho Kwang-jo's side were replaced and, in a few cases, the replacements were removed when indications of a pro-Cho attitude became apparent. Similar changes occurred also in the composition of the OSC,[108] and there were drastic changes on the State Council level as well (1519.11.20, 11.25, 11.26, 12.1, 12.4, 12.6).

At first the effect of these changes was limited to the negation of some of the institutional changes wrought by the 1519 group,[109] but presently the revamped Censorate launched a drive to increase the severity and scope of the purge. In conjunction with requests that the Recommendation Examination be invalidated, the Censorate pressed for the discharge of An Tang, now Second State Councillor, on the ground of lack of stature, and Chungjong soon yielded to the extent of transferring An to a non-portfolio post (1519.12.2, 12.6). Then the Censorate succeeded in having judicial proceedings instituted against three incumbent officials and one former OIG Third Inspector, adducing a variety of charges only tenuously, if at all, related to the crucial consideration that all four were acknowledged Cho Kwang-jo partisans (1519.12.9, 12.10).[110] At the same time, the State Councillors were called to task for their irresolution in the critical period following Cho's downfall, and Chŏng Kwang-p'il in particular was denounced for opposing the Censorate and OSC case against the Recommendation Examination (1519.12.9, 12.11).

Emboldened, no doubt, by the king's sympathetic response to these probes, the Censorate now abandoned the indirect approach. Drawing up a roster of thirty-five "Cho Kwang-jo clique members," headed by An Tang, the Censorate asked punishment on the same basis as in the case of the minor four of the original eight purge victims, i.e., banishment on charges of willingly following Cho's lead (1519.12.14 S, 12.15 S).[111] Upon hearing this request, Chungjong averred that "the reason why right and wrong have not been determined and men's minds are not yet settled is because of the failure of the High State Councillors to perform their proper function." He then recalled the lenience that had been shown Cho Kwang-jo and, asserting that in his view the Censorate had not struck at the root of the problem, Chungjong now announced his intention to "kill this root" (1519.12.15 S, 12.16 S). Nam Kon in particular, who would be named Second State Councillor on the next day (1519.12.17 S), strenuously opposed the king's desire to apply the full extent of the law to the original purge victims and the Censorate's demands for punishment of its list of Cho partisans (1519.12.16 S). These efforts, however, met with only limited success. In the end, the king commanded Cho Kwang-jo to kill himself, banished in harsher degree the other seven primary accused, and, selecting eighteen from the Censorate list, sentenced them to punishments ranging from banishment to loss of office warrants (1519.12.16 S).[112] Moreover, the king also complied with the repeated demand that the Recommendation Examination be abrogated (1519.12.16 S).

Before the new and harsher judgment against him could be carried into effect, Kim Sik fled his place of banishment (1519.12.29), and the next concentration of purge victims, albeit minor figures all, is found in the denouement of this event. After more than four months had passed he was betrayed and he hung himself, leaving behind a document denouncing Sim Chŏng for his leading role in fashioning the purge (1520.4.16, 5.22). His suicide saved him only from the rigors of the judicial process; formal sentence soon was passed on the basis of sedition and called for beheading and confiscation of property (1520.6.6).

Several isolated cases further swelled the purge toll. For the most part at the instance of the Censorate, generally mild punishments were meted out to three others who had been named on the list of thirty-five Cho Kwang-jo bedfellows (1519.12.25), to one of the Diarists whose duty it had been to make a record of events as the purge unfolded (1519.12.18), to an unsuccessful Recommendation Examination candidate who had gone on to pass the special examination held later that fall (1519.12.25), to the Magistrate of Samch'ŏk on the ground that, during earlier service as a Royal Secretary, he had exceeded the prerogatives of his office (1520.1.11 S), to the former Royal Secretariat Recorder whose incomplete report had given An Tang an indirect boost to appointment as a High State Councillor (1520.3.21), and to the Governor of Kyŏngsang on a charge convenient to hand but which contained no mention of the man's identification with the Cho Kwang-jo group (1520.2.9, 3.9).

After a brief period of quiet Kim Se-p'il, who was courageous—and foolish—enough to speak up publicly in defense of Cho Kwang-jo, was purged. Entering into attendance at the Royal Lectures as a Special Participant, Kim Se-p'il argued that Cho had been without evil intent and that, in consequence, the death sentence had been excessive. The High State Councillors and the Censorate impeached him for this, and, after judicial inquiry by the State Tribunal, Kim was sentenced to three years banishment at post station servitude (1520.9.13). Although pardoned before expiration of term, he was not requalified for public office and so did not serve again.[113]

In mid-1521, just when it seemed that the Purge of 1519 had fully spent itself, the Censorate moved to stir up the dying embers and feed them with fresh fuel. Reviling An Tang and seven others in scurrilous terms and charging them with servile acquiescence in the schemes of the 1519 clique, the OIG asked that An Tang be divested of office warrants and the others demoted. The OCG immediately echoed the charges, but found the king unreceptive. However, after listening to numerous and insistent Censorate denunciations over a period of nearly three months, Chungjong at length ordered all of the accused divested of their office warrants. Without exception they were experienced officials of Junior Second or Senior Third Rank, with from ten to nearly thirty years service behind them (1521.7.8, 9.27).

It was not entirely coincidental that this further punishment of An Tang was followed in only a matter of days by a final and great convulsion of the Purge of 1519, which was caused by an accusation of criminal conspiracy laid against his sons. An Tang's first son, An Ch'ŏ-gyŏm, was charged with plotting with the second son, An Ch'ŏ-gŭn, kinsman An Hyŏng, royal clansman Yi Chŏng-suk, and Kwŏn Chŏn to kill a number of the highest officials. The motivation of the plotters was said to be deep dissatisfaction with the prevailing political climate. The State Tribunal was immediately activated under Chŏng Kwang-p'il[114] and began interrogation of the alleged leaders of the plot, who at first did not confess. The case was soon broken wide open, however, by the confession of the royal clansman Yi Chŏng-suk who, after very liberal application of the rod, admitted to having plotted with An Ch'ŏ-gyŏm and others to launch an attempt to compel the king by force of arms to get rid of the incumbent high officials. If the king failed to heed their demands, he was to have been deposed (1521.10.11, 10.12, 10.13, 10.14, 10.15).

In view of the greater gravity imparted to the case by Yi Chŏng-suk's revelation, Chungjong ordered that more severe methods of interrogation be employed on the leading suspects and that An Tang as well be jailed. The further confessions thus wrung from the other principals corroborated Yi Chŏng-suk's testimony and, indeed, went further in naming the king's half-brother, Yi Ch'im, as the man the plotters had decided to raise to the throne. Accordingly, these ringleaders were summarily executed and, in accordance with the law, their fathers and grown sons strangled. An Tang, of course, was among those executed (1521.10.15, 10.17).

A number of ramifications of the An brothers plot further swelled the toll of victims. An intimate of the leading 1519 figures was beheaded, accused of independent designs against the current high officials (1521.10.16). Another royal clansman was executed after confessing to an expanded version of Yi Chŏng-suk's admissions (1521.10.17). A Recommendation Examination candidate, belatedly brought under arrest, confessed to plotting with the principals and was executed by dismemberment (1521.10.28, 10.29). A prominent 1519 victim, Han Ch'ung, was brought to Seoul from his place of banishment and shortly died in prison (1521.10.28, 10.29, 11.3). It was also at this time that death sentences were passed on primary 1519 purge victims Kim Chŏng and Ki Chun (1521.10.17).[115]

A final by-product of the 1521 affair was the victimizing of Yi Chang-gon, Minister of War when the purge began in 1519 and subsequently elevated to Fifth State Councillor. The Censorate at this time charged that he was the top leader of the "evil gang" and asked that he be banished afar. The king refused but presently, with apparent great reluctance, agreed to divest Yi of his office warrants (1521.10.17, 10.29, 10.30). Beginning as early as the end of this same year, Chungjong several times sought to make redress but was repeatedly thwarted by Censorate protest (1521.12.25, 1523.i4.22, 1528.9.28, 1533.12.15, 1538.4.12). Accordingly, Yi Chang-gon was unable to serve again in the government. Yi Chang-gon certainly was not a leader of the men of 1519 and, in fact, appears to have been unsympathetic to most of their aims. However, he had exercised a restraining influence at the outset of the purge and presumably this was his undoing.[116]

One can only speculate as to how much substance there was to the charges and confessions made in the An brothers conspiracy case. On the face of it the conclusion is inescapable that, at the least, seditious thoughts were harbored and spoken. Yet there are obvious difficulties in the way of full acceptance of the view that seditious action was contemplated as charged, much less as admitted to under torture. Whatever the facts of the case really were, the important thing is that it inevitably contributed to the bitterness of the memories which mention of the Purge of 1519 came to evoke, and that it enhanced as well the aura of martyrdom which came to surround the names of the "men of 1519."[117]

The Aftermath: Reform Rescinded

The purge of the men of 1519 was accompanied by the undoing of many of the changes they had wrought. This, even more than the purge of men, was a sporadic effort but it was accomplished with equal thoroughness. One of the first such acts, logically enough, was to rescind the order for the deletion of the Chungjong Merit Subjects. This was done at the instance of the king, with the reluctant approval of the highest officials (1519.11.20 S, 11.21 S).

The restoration of the former regulations governing term of office and jurisdiction of provincial governors was a second major instance of return to pre-purge patterns. At the urging of such figures among the 1519 group as Kim Chŏng, Cho Kwang-jo, Ki Chun, Yi Cha, and Yu In-suk, a "long-term tenure and concurrent magistracy" system for provincial governorships had been adopted in 1519. This meant that the prescribed tour of duty would be two years instead of one (which in practice, apparently, was often less than one), and that the Governor would concurrently serve as Magistrate of the leading, or capital, city of his province. This was a system that long had been in effect for the two northern provinces. At the same time, it had also been decided to split Kyŏngsang into two provinces, a left and a right.

The main consideration advanced in support of long-term tenure was that a Governor could not acquaint himself with provincial conditions, formulate a program, and carry his policies into effect in the short span of one year. Particular emphasis was placed upon the beneficent effect on mores and education that a long-term tenure system would have (1518.1.14 S, 4.17 S, 1519.4.29 S, 5.17 S, 5.20 S). The opponents of long-term tenure, such as Chŏng Kwang-p'il, Sin Yong-gae, Nam Kon, and Pang Yu-nyŏng, principally relied upon the sanctions of tradition: one year tenure had been the uniform practice of the dynasty; moreover, Sejong had introduced a long-term tenure and concurrent magistracy system at the end of his reign and "it must have been because of harmful consequences that [the experiment] was abandoned" after only three years (1519.4.29 S, 5.6 S,

5.11 S, 5.18 S). As for concurrent magistracy, the opponents pointed out that, as concurrent Magistrate, a Governor would be required to remain at his administrative seat and thus could not undertake the usual circuits of his province. This would be injurious to the interests of people living far from the capital city, who then could not easily bring their problems to the attention of the Governor (1519.5.11 S). Furthermore, concurrent magistracy would necessitate new construction and additional staff personnel (1519.5.19 S, 5.20 S).

The discussion of these proposed changes, although protracted, did not assume the proportions of a major controversy. While the date and nature of the final disposition of the problem appears not to have been explicitly recorded, *Sillok* entries indicate that the ultimate decision was to divide only Kyŏngsang, to appoint Governors to two-year terms and make them concurrent Magistrates (the Kyŏnggi Governor, logically, was excepted), and to appoint new Deputy Magistrates for the capital cities of all the provinces affected except Kangwŏn (1519.11.5 S, 11.29 S, 11.30 S).

In asking for a return to traditional practice, Kim Chŏn and Chŏng Kwang-p'il asserted merely that, as was found to be the case in Sejong's time, the long-tenure system would produce harmful effects, and that it should be abandoned before this stage was reached. However, both the context in which Kim and Chŏng spoke and the wording of the rescission decree suggest that a more important factor may have been the general post-purge reaction against the "promiscuous changes" in the established order wrought by the Cho group (1519.11.29 S, 11.30 S).

The Recommendation Examination, a storm center of controversy when it was established, was the subject of further dispute when, a fortnight after the purge began, the Censorate sought to have it invalidated. Now largely rid of potential pro-Cho voices, the Censorate attacked the Recommendation Examination as unfair, pointing to the suspicious coincidence of An Tang's stand in favor of it and the successful candidacy of his three sons. After discussing the question with his high officials, the king adopted the view of Kim Chŏn and Nam Kon that the passers should not be employed in "vital posts," thus rejecting the demand of the Censorate (supported by Yi Chang-gon and Yi Yu-ch'ŏng) that this examination list be canceled (1519.12.2).[118]

Interestingly enough, the Recommendation Examination now found its only determined champion in its earlier most adamant opponent, Chief State Councillor Chŏng Kwang-p'il. Chŏng's approach, however, was not really out of character, being based as ever on conservative instincts, which demanded that he oppose all unsettling efforts to change accomplished fact. Chŏng denied that there was credible evidence of unfairness in the administration of the Recommendation Examination and insisted that its products were men of talent well fitted for government employment (1519.12.2, 12.3 S). When the king chided him for opposing the consensus in discussion both of the establishment and abolition of the examination, Chŏng is said to have replied: "At the outset I stoutly maintained that the Recommendation Examination was improper. But now that it has been established, certificates awarded, and appointments made, is it not unthinkable to abolish it? To now enact and now rescind—the country's statutes ought not evidence such irresolution."[119]

But Chŏng Kwang-p'il's was a futile struggle. Two Fourth Inspectors who did not concur with the majority view against the Recommendation Examination were replaced by more amenable men, and the Censorate went on to press its attack. Presently the Censorate coupled its list of thirty-five men of the Cho Kwang-jo clique to a repeated demand that the examination be invalidated. At this point the king replaced his High State Councillors and then consented to abrogation of the Recommendation Examination (1519. 12.11, 12.14 S, 12.16).[120]

Another pre-purge innovation of some magnitude had been the effort to put into practice on the local administration level the so-called *hyangyak,* or village code.[121] Authorization to do this had been given provincial governors in 1517 in consequence of the memorial of a Kyŏngsang province literatus. Predisposed himself in this direction, the king acted at the urging of the State Council, which warmly endorsed the view of the proponent that the village code could serve as an instrument for "the transformation of popular mores" (1517.6.30 S, 7.6 S, 7.26 S).

After the village code system had been in operation for a year or so, critiques of its efficacy began to be heard. Members of the Cho group praised it with little reservation, claiming for example that in the areas where it was being assiduously practiced it had put a stop to such evils as the impressment of free men into unfree status and the extortions of petty officials (1518.9.5 S). One enthusiast, who was not a member of the Cho group, went so far as to suggest that penal law might eventually be dispensed with (1518.9.5 S), while another offered eye-witness testimony to the great change wrought by the village code in one locality, where now an object of value dropped on the road would be left unmolested (see 1519.12.9).

High State Councillors Chŏng Kwang-p'il and Sin Yong-gae, however, while conceding the educational value of the doctrine when properly applied, publicly lamented that its operation had weakened the authority of the Local Magistrates, had dulled the distinction between high born and commoner, and, because it stipulated precedence in seating arrangements in accordance with age, regardless of social status, had produced considerable turbulence on the local scene (1518.9.5 S, 9.14 S). But the king was by no means inclined to abandon the experiment. In the middle months of 1519 he admonished his provincial governors to exhibit greater zeal in putting the village code into effect (1519.4.5 S), he spoke of similarly enjoining the Local Magistrates (1519.5.19 S), and he refused to forbid establishment of the village code system in Seoul itself (1519.6.8 S).[122] Here the village code experiment stood on the eve of the purge.

Before the purge was a week old, Chungjong had banned the assembling of "village code men" for the purpose of discussing and carrying out penal administration. Chŏng Kwang-p'il expressed approval of this decision, adding that he had observed also that artisans in Seoul had neglected their work in consequence of participation in such village code meetings (1519.11.20 S). Then, at the beginning of the next year, Chungjong readily acquiesced in Censorate requests to call a complete halt to the village code program (1520.1.4 S, 1.11 S).[123]

A number of other instances of restoration of the *status quo ante* may be noted briefly. At Nam Kon's request, Yi Haeng was summoned back to the government as Director of the Office of Special Counselors, the post which above all others paid tribute to the appointee's mastery of the literary arts, and, with Nam, was set to the task of revising the rules of literary style (1519.12.18, 12.28, 1520.1.17). Also by the agency of Nam Kon, all of the minor posts abolished at the urging of Cho Kwang-jo were reestablished and those who had been discharged were reappointed (1520.1.24). The practice of employing female musical entertainers at various official functions held in the capital and provinces was reinstituted (1520.8.7).[124] The testing of civil examination candidates by "recitation of the Classics" was ordered stopped (1521.12.12).[125] On the level of personalities, a judicial case which Cho Kwang-jo, as Inspector-General, had "wrongly judged" was reopened (1519.12.8), and a project initiated at the instance of Kim An-guk, then the Governor, to reclaim and settle certain Chŏlla wastelands was discontinued (1519.6.6, 1520.2.20).

On the other side of the balance sheet, the king attempted without success, at least for the time being, to restore the *Sogyŏksŏ* and to lift a ban "imposed by the Cho Kwang-jo group" on the wearing of silk finery by high officials. In both these instances the opposition of the High State Councillors was decisive (1519.12.10, 1520.1.21).

Why did it happen? What did it mean?

A typical account, dating from the late eighteenth century, which contains much of the lore and bias in which traditional historiography had come to clothe the Purge of 1519, describes it in this way:

> In 1510 Cho Kwang-jo took a first in the Literary Licentiate examination and in 1515, recommended for filial piety and probity, he was posted as Overseer of the Paper Manufactory. Cho was not pleased at this and said: "To gain office by virtue of groundless repute is not the same as qualifying via the examinations." Now it so happened that Chungjong was about to conduct an examination on the occasion of a royal visit to the National Confucian Shrine, and Cho passed this examination. He was appointed Librarian of the National Academy, but presently was transferred to the post of Fourth Censor. Then he was selected and assigned to the Office of Special Counselors, where he served progressively as Sixth, Fifth, and Fourth Counselor. After a stint as a Royal Secretary, he was transferred back to the OSC, becoming First Counselor.[126]

> Chungjong, who always held the Confucian arts in high esteem and was keenly interested in enlightened civil administration, placed the greatest reliance on Cho Kwang-jo. Cho, in turn, deeply conscious of the sovereign's grace, made it his mission to exalt the royal virtue and promote the flourishing of Confucianism. Whenever he spoke forth in the presence of the king, he was unfailingly as respectful and devoted as if he were standing before Heaven itself; never did he refrain from speaking what was in his mind and never did his words lack utter candor. When the government was about to despatch Yi Chi-bang to ambush and capture [a barbarian troublemaker] . . . Cho Kwang-jo asked leave to speak and said in admonishment:

"This is akin to the crafty schemes of the sneak-thief; it is not the way of a sovereign in defending against barbarian peoples. In my heart I feel shame at this." Whereupon Chungjong ordered that the question be reopened to discussion. At this, those in attendance clamored to protest: "In the military art there is both the doctrinal and the expedient approach; in defending against the barbarian there is both the normal and the extraordinary procedure. The plan has already been decided upon. It ought not be rashly changed at the word of one man alone." And the Minister of War, Yu Tam-nyŏn, said: "In tilling one ought to ask the bondsman, and in spinning the bondswoman. I have passed in and out of the North Gate [so often that] I can recite the conditions of the border entirely by heart. The present plan truly should be carried out." Yet Chungjong rejected the overwhelming consensus and desisted from sending the expedition. This was a measure of the king's regard for Cho Kwang-jo.

By extraordinary royal decree Cho Kwang-jo was promoted to Inspector-General and concurrently occupied the position of Third Mentor to the Crown Prince. By this time, the worthies of the period all were being accorded exceptional preferment and those thus honored by the king's favor strove in concert to write a record of achievement. They rooted out long-standing evils and revised and clarified the nation's statutes, thus gradually carrying into effect the precepts of the kings of yore.

The government wanted to establish a Recommendation Examination course whereby to pick out men of talent. Cho Kwang-jo memorialized, saying: "Your Majesty has long aspired to good government but as yet has not met with complete success. This is because it has not been possible to obtain men of talent. If this law is put into effect, obtaining men of talent will cease to be a matter for concern." Then . . . one hundred twenty men were recommended and, in the fourth month of 1519, . . . twenty-eight were taken. At this juncture, the iniquitous skulked away and superior men of wisdom were arrayed in the government.

However, the newly emerged young men often were impatient and their proposals involved many radical innovations. Always at the Royal Lectures they had so many matters to talk about that the sun set before they were finished. Chungjong was mentally and physically tired, at times yawned and stretched himself and reclined upon the throne with such willful abandon that it groaned and creaked. The Nam Kon-Sim Chŏng crowd, who had been forced to back off into non-portfolio positions, harbored malice on this account and, ever watchful, soon surmised that the king had become disenchanted. Cho Kwang-jo, too, early perceived this danger and, realizing that the ideal kingly rule could not be easily achieved, constantly desired to forsake government position. When he was named Inspector-General, in all humility at his very rapid rise in station he forcefully sought to decline the appointment but instead was favored still more with the royal grace, and the more stoutly he declined the more firmly the king refused consent. Though sore distressed at heart, there was nothing Cho Kwang-jo could do. It was now that the impulsive and imprudent literati saw that, indeed, Cho had become irresolute and tractable, and there were even some who thought to seek his expulsion [from his key position].

In the tenth month of this year of 1519, Cho Kwang-jo jointly memorialized with Censor-General Yi Sŏng-dong and others attacking the great excesses in merit enrollment at the time of Chungjong's enthronement and asking that the undeserving be deleted from the roster.

First Counselor Kim Ku, too, presented a memorial on the subject and the State Councillors and Board Ministers as well offered their views [in support of deletion], but still Chungjong would not agree. At length, then, the Censorate officials resigned their posts and, with no help for it, Chungjong summoned the State Council and Censorate and determined upon the selection and deletion of the unjustified enrollments. Because of this the men of petty stripe, apprehensive at the imminent loss of their merit listings, came to regard Cho with still greater loathing.

Even before this, Hong Kyŏng-ju, who long had harbored resentment at having been impeached [by the Censorate] and removed as [Fourth] State Councillor, had joined forces with such men as Nam Kon and Sim Chŏng. Now, then, Hong Kyŏng-ju had his daughter, a royal concubine, reiterate day and night that the hearts of the people of the entire country had turned to Cho Kwang-jo. Sim Chŏng, too, secretly made contact with a slave attendant of the royal concubine Madame Pak and persuaded her to spread the story in the palace that the affairs of the government were entirely controlled by Cho Kwang-jo and his cohorts, that the people all rejoiced in this, and that they wished to elevate him to the throne. Employing another stratagem, [Sim Chŏng] caused a bug to eat out a leaf of a tree in the palace garden so as to form the four characters "the running image will become king."[127] Then he had the leaf discovered and brought to the king's attention by someone within the palace. In these and myriad other ways it was sought to perturb the king's mind; nor was Chungjong insusceptible to such agitation.

Sim Chŏng then had Hong Kyŏng-ju take a secret letter around to the houses of a number of high ranking officials of frustrated ambitions to enlist them in a plot to kill Cho Kwang-jo and his followers. This done, together with First Minister-without-Portfolio Kim Chŏn and others,[128] Hong Kyŏng-ju secretly memorialized as follows: "Although we wish to report an imminent crisis to the throne, those in close attendance upon Your Majesty all are Cho Kwang-jo cronies. The situation being of the utmost urgency, we ask that the Sinmu Gate [in the northern wall around the Kyŏngbok palace compound] be opened so that under cover of night we may enter and memorialize."

At dusk of the 15th, then, Hong Kyŏng-ju and those with him entered through the Sinmu Gate, proceeded to the outside of the palace, and presented this written memorial: "We, your subjects, . . . beg to offer our view that Cho Kwang-jo has bound himself to others in a clique, advancing those who adhere to him and repudiating those who differ with him . . . The present officialdom . . . , fearing the enormous power of these men, do not dare speak out. Truly it may be said that the situation has reached a dread and shocking extreme. We ask that . the matter be turned over to the judicial authorities for clear determination of the crimes of these men." . . . Hong Kyŏng-ju and Nam Kon entered into the royal presence and said: "The matter is urgent; there ought to be no preliminary interrogation. We ask that the duty officers of the Royal Secretariat and Office of Special Counselors be imprisoned forthwith." . . . [After this had been done] Kim Chŏn and the others also entered into the royal presence and requested that . . . Inspector-General Cho Kwang-jo, Headmaster of the National Academy Kim Sik, First Counselor Kim Ku, First Royal Secretary Yu In-suk and Royal Secretaries Pak Se-hŭi, Hong Ŏn-p'il and Pak Hun be apprehended, brought under arrest to the area outside the palace, and there executed.

It was only now that [Minister of War] Yi Chang-gon realized that Hong Kyǒng-ju, Nam Kon, and the others had plotted to have their victims beaten to death on this very night, and he forcefully remonstrated, saying: "It is wrong thus to perform the act of a brigand, and it is wrong to shun the presence of the Chief State Councillor. I ask that the Chief State Councillor be summoned to discuss the matter." Hong Kyǒng-ju wanted to advance and urge that judgment be passed on the spot, but Yi Chang-gon blocked him with an outstretched arm . . . and Hong was unable to leave his seat.

Chungjong's anger had now somewhat abated, and so he ordered that Chief State Councillor Chǒng Kwang-p'il be summoned. Chǒng Kwang-p'il entered and tearfully remonstrated in these words:

"The young literati are not conscious of what is appropriate to the times and what is not; they seek only to evoke the past and apply it straightway to the present. But surely they are guilty of no other intent. Let us display a little tolerance. I ask that the matter be discussed with all the high officials."

He spoke in a choked voice, and his flowing tears completely drenched his lapels and sleeves. Chungjong swiftly arose and was about to retire, but Chǒng Kwang-p'il pulled at the King's trailing skirt, kowtowing the while. Then, at last, the King ordered . . . [the accused] remanded to prison and summoned An Tang, the Third State Councillor . . . Kim Chǒn, Nam Kon, and Sim Chǒng were busily engaged in drafting a crime specification decree, while time and time again Chǒng Kwang-p'il and An Tang spoke out in exculpation . . .

It had now become dawn.[129]

The explanation of the purge offered at the time by Chungjong is in significant contrast to this traditional account. Although sentence had just been passed on the eight primary purge victims, the Censorate was continuing with undiminished vigor its efforts to succor the victims. After an unsuccessful attempt to persuade Inspector-General Yu Un and his Censorate colleagues to attend their posts, the king remarked:

The political authority of the state ought to reside in the officialdom, and among the officialdom political authority is to be wielded by the high officials . . . Of yore it was said: "When political authority resides in the Censorate there will then be disorder." During recent years political authority lay not with the high officials but with the Censorate . . . Extremism became the established practice, resulting in the experienced high officials all being impeached and ousted. This was a situation affecting the very foundations of the state. This malignant condition had to be rectified; only then could the government know tranquility. That is why I acted. In the discussion yesterday I heard all say: "This was done by the villainous crew." This action was planned and taken in concert with the high officials, for the sake of the larger interests of the state; it was not the action of a single man of evil. (1519.11.18 S)

To this the Censorate instantly retorted:

If Cho Kwang-jo and the others committed acts for which crime might justifiably be charged, the matter should have been handled openly and with due process. . . . To charge them with crime in this way, on the basis of a secret memorial presented after nightfall by one or two men, constitutes perfidy in the extreme. . . . We heard yesterday about the secret memorial of the evil crew, and now we have heard further that Your Majesty sent a clandestine communication to Hong Kyŏng-ju, saying:

> "The clique of the Cho Kwang-jo group already is formed. In the beginning, when [Cho and his partisans] wished to establish the Recommendation Examination, I viewed it with favor. But, as I consider it now, [I realize that] they were creating a supporting force. I want to get rid of them all, but your son-in-law, Kim Myŏng-yun, is among them,[130] and for this reason I have not acted."

... To outwardly show trust while harboring purge designs within—such an attitude in the sovereign is a portent of national disaster. We, your subjects, cannot restrain our bitter lamentations, our flowing tears. (1519.11.18 S)

Stung, perhaps, by such a sharp reproach, the king for the first time elaborated his earlier simple insistence that the purge victims had been charged with crime at the request of "the government," saying:

> This the Censorate has wrongly heard. I now wish to speak, so that the officialdom may clearly understand. At the outset, Hong Kyŏng-ju, at the houses of Nam Kon, Song Chil, Kim Chŏn, etc., heard that some thirty or so military men wished to strike down the civil officials ... Despite their good intentions, the Cho Kwang-jo group had made a habit of calumny, thus giving rise to such as this [military plot]. The proper way to deal with the situation was for the government to rectify existing literati mores. On this basis I reached agreement with the Ministers of the Six Boards, who then memorialized. The fact that I did not inform the Royal Secretariat does give the appearance of clandestine action, and I myself realize that this was wrong. But the story of a secret communication is false, and the rumor concerning Kim Myŏng-yun is also false. (1519.11.18 S)

It is just at this point in the record, as if by prearrangement, that Chief State Councillor Chŏng Kwang-p'il, Third State Councillor An Tang, Fourth State Councillor Yi Chang-gon, and Sixth State Councillor Yi Yu-ch'ŏng memorialized, saying: "We have an urgent matter to report; we request a personal audience." Granted their wish, they told of learning of a scheme hatched by some thirty or forty military men to kill members of the Cho group because, in the view of the plotters, those who had been punished had been punished too lightly, while others of the Cho clique had escaped their just desserts (1519.11.18 S).[131]

Chungjong quickly siezed upon this opportunity to further justify his acquiescence in the purge, making this revelation:

> Now that the subject has been broached, I too may speak of it. Recently Hong Kyŏng-ju ... came and said he had an urgent matter to report. When I asked him what it was he replied: "Certain military officials are deeply resentful at these men [of the Cho group] and are plotting to kill them all. If the government does not take action first, then I fear there will be grave disorder. Should the government fail to charge crime against these newly risen men, then it will not be possible to avoid a purge." I felt that, if these newly risen officals were curbed ... then the anger of the military men would subside of itself, and there would be no purge of the officialdom. Thus it was that I could not but charge crime against Cho

Kwang-jo. Yet now, because the punishment has been light, the military men remain unmollified, and so have dared [to plot in] this way. That the government recognized the crisis and preferred charges of crime first, before the military men could act—this was the great good fortune of the Cho Kwang-jo group. (1519.11.18 S)

Not quite fifty years had passed since the Purge of 1519 when the boy king Sŏnjo inquired of the aged philosopher-statesman Yi Hwang about the scholarship and character of Cho Kwang-jo. The great T'oegye replied:

Cho Kwang-jo was a man of superlative natural endowment. He early set himself to the study of orthodox Neo-Confucianism, and in his family relationships he was filial and brotherly. Chungjong, who yearned after enlightened government as a thirsty man craves water, was of a mind to reintroduce the precepts of the Three Dynasties of yore. Cho Kwang-jo saw this as an unexampled opportunity and, in cooperation with such like-minded men as Kim Chŏng, Kim Sik, Ki Chun, and Han Ch'ung, wrought a vast reformation. They effected statutes, they made the *Hsiao-hsüeh* the foundation of moral education, and they sought to put the village code into operation—nothing was left unaffected. Had but their efforts remained uninterrupted, the way of enlightened government would not have been difficult of attainment.

The young men of that time, however, were impatient to reach their goal, so that the evil of precipitousness was not absent. The older, established officials who had been shunted aside were dismayed at the loss of their posts and, with great guile, furtively sought an opening, the meanwhile fabricating the vilest of slanders. Then the literati of the time suffered either banishment or death, while the repercussions of the purge spread out widely. Even today, should there be among the literati one whose mind is fastened upon scholarship and upright conduct, his detractors will quickly designate him as one of the 1519 ilk. What man in his heart does not fear purge? That literati mores have become corrupted and that no Confucianist figure of repute appears in public office is attributable to this . . .

The Purge of 1519 stemmed directly from the villainy of Nam Kon and Sim Chŏng, villainy which in the end enmeshed Chungjong as well. The enormity of their crimes may be said to reach to Heaven.[132] (1568.9.21 S)

These several accounts of the purge all stress the repudiation of the older, established officials by the youthful, overzealous members of the Cho Kwang-jo group. The two non-contemporary interpretations strongly imply, if they do not state, that it was these casualties of the righteous remonstrance of the Cho group who, out of personal rancor, turned the tables on their young tormenters. Meanwhile the king, already out of patience with Cho Kwang-jo and his followers, was duped into subserving the ends of the blackguardly plotters. Chungjong's explanation, on the other hand, credits the purge plotters with patriotic motives in moving incisively to rescue the government from imminent peril of bloody civil strife.

Enough has been said in the foregoing pages to justify attaching the labels of "disingenuous," "tendentious," or "contrived" to each of these interpretations of the purge. Yet, at bottom, are they not merely variant elaborations of a single hypothesis? A simple statement of this hypothesis would be that the men of 1519 suffered purge because, whether by accidental configuration or by design, they constituted an exclusivistic clique. This was their crime and, indeed, this was the charge originally laid against them.

What is the implication of a conflict such as this between established older officials and a young newly emerged element? It is, for one thing, the clash of the cautious conservatism normal to men of experience and responsibility with the idealism and radicalism of impetuous youth. Circumstances peculiar to that time contributed intensifying factors to this not uncommon phenomenon. Among the experiences of the older officials were those gained in serving or suffering under Yŏnsangun and in being rewarded or redeemed on the occasion of the enthronement of Chungjong. Where these experiences did not provide grounds for condemnation, they did constitute obstacles to understanding and tolerance by those who did not share in them.

But the most important aspect of this clash of age and youth is that, while such conflict was unexceptional, its denouement was uncommon in the extreme. Youth's repudiation of its elders is not to be wondered at, but the manner and the totality of the rejection are indeed remarkable. While the phenomenon of the political purge is scarcely noteworthy, an institutional framework which encouraged, perhaps required, conflict and resultant purge of this severity merits close scrutiny.

Clique forming, in that society and age, was perhaps second in heinousness only to overt treason in the roster of crimes against the state. In fact, clique forming was regarded, quite soundly, as the seedbed of full-blown treason, as the unfailing preliminary to the overt act. By definition, the underlying motivations of a clique were selfish, its ultimate aims seditious. No matter how public spirited the actions of a concert of government officials, no matter how effective their policies or program in promoting the common weal, they posed a real threat to the throne.

This was because, in Chosŏn, public spiritedness consisted above all else in working to buttress the established order, and the common weal was inseparably bound to the continuation of the ruling house. The "public" was the government, an aggregation of individuals privileged to serve the king at his pleasure, ever conscious of the privilege and ever constrained to preserve the individual character of their allegiance. In the background were the common, and less than common, people, the conglomeration of the variously unprivileged. The loyalty of these, too, was required to be unitary: if it were attracted elsewhere it would be lost to the sovereign. Hence, in a certain sense, the more popular, the more effective, the policies espoused by a group of government officials, the greater the menace to the occupant of the throne that group must be regarded as constituting.

In the context of the times it was perhaps inevitable that the Cho Kwang-jo group should be designated a clique. The existence of an acknowledged leader who commanded a high degree of respect and loyalty, the intolerance exhibited toward those who did not bow to the group's views or subserve its ends, the manifest dissatisfaction with numerous aspects of the established order and of traditional practice—all these were familiar and authentic earmarks. It follows, then, that those who set themselves in opposition to the Cho Kwang-jo clique and ultimately brought about its downfall may have been impelled by motives as pure as those history has decided moved the cliquists.

Desires for revenge and personal aggrandizement no doubt contributed importantly to the motivations of some opponents of the Cho group, and perhaps decisively to those of others. The conclusion is inescapable, however, that history has dealt unjustly with leading purgers such as Nam Kon and Kim Chŏn. Neither called into question the fundamental devotion to the throne of the Cho Kwang-jo group, which was a unique feature of this third purge, and neither proved to be vindictive in triumph. They believed, rather, that the Cho group was misguided, that much of its program was inimical to the health of the body politic, and that the turbulence brought to the public scene by its actions held a grave and growing danger to the foundations of the state.

For the officials who plotted the purge, then, the crucial considerations were the radical nature of the program of the Cho group and the extreme nature of its anti-personnel actions. To these opponents of Cho Kwang-jo the final anathema must have been the Recommendation Examination, a key item in the Cho program which contained frightening implications for the established practices of personnel recruitment. The Merit Subject issue, on the other hand, was important to these officials mainly for the additional leverage it gave them in securing support or sympathy for the purge undertaking in the palace and in other quarters. Few Merit Subjects now remained who served, or could aspire to serve, in central capacities in the government, and the merit enrollment of the most important of this handful was not in jeopardy.

But to Chungjong, the ultimate key to the purge equation, the attack against the Merit Subjects quite likely was decisive. He had less reason to be disturbed by the implications of the Recommendation Examination, which posed no direct threat to his position. On the other hand, the serious consequences of disaffection among his Merit Subjects had been forcefully impressed upon him time and time again, for the men who set Chungjong upon the throne had proven themselves to be a highly volatile group. Granted such a foundation on which to build, and granting, too, some validity to the classical thesis that the king was growing weary of the pressure tactics of the Cho Kwang-jo group, it is not surprising, especially in that credulous age, that Chungjong's mind could be so quickly and so firmly turned against those in whom he had recently reposed such boundless trust.

Chapter V

THE SUMMING UP

In speculating on the meaning of the Literati Purges, it is useful to distinguish between the specific factors that gave rise to the purges themselves and the general factors that underlay the appearance of factionalism in the Yi dynasty. In other words, we must make clear whether we are talking about the particular manifestation of factionalism in Yi Korea known as the Literati Purges, or about why the phenomenon of factionalism came into existence at all in the Yi dynasty.

While there were subsidiary factors peculiar to each purge, there is one great theme that is common to all of them. In each case, a purge was the climax to sustained conflict between the censoring organs and the more highly constituted authority of the government and the palace. In each case, a purge represented a severe but temporary reversal of a trend toward allowing the censoring organs a greater voice in the councils of government.

Beneath this broad similarity shared by the purges, elements of difference can be detected which reflect stages in the enhancement of the role of the censoring organs and the heightened acceptance of this role as proper. The purge of 1498 took as its target an abstraction of the objectionable features of the new concept of remonstrance; the identity of the victims of the purge has little other significance, I feel, than the symbolic. But because the attack was indirect, it was largely ignored, if not misunderstood. This factor, in conjunction with the abnormalities of Yŏnsangun's character, led quickly to the Purge of 1504. This time there was no attempt to disguise the object of the purge: it was aimed at the very root of the political turbulence of that day, the concept of remonstrance itself; it was aimed at individuals only insofar as they proved to have been exponents of the concept.

The Purge of 1504 had the very opposite effect from that intended. Suppressed by force and terror, the principle of remonstrance reemerged upon the fall of Yŏnsangun with new vigor and with still wider acceptance as an indispensable ingredient of the art of government. Enveloped in the aura of martyrdom generated by the suffering of those who had been victimized in 1504, the concept of remonstrance could no longer be seriously challenged in principle. In a complete reversal of the situation of 1504, it no longer could be suppressed but could be controlled only by manipulation.

Cho Kwang-jo and the other "men of 1519" were purged because the way they wielded their paramount influence menaced other concentrations of power in the government. Their means to power had been the new weapon of remonstrance, and the bastion of their power had been the censoring organs. They had constituted themselves into a clique, cemented together by a common idelaism, a common program of reform, and a common intolerance for viewpoints different from their own. They had left no room to satisfy the claims of others to a share in the ordering of the state, and the king—alike the sovereign of other aggregates of the politically privileged—at length felt compelled to sanction their destruction.

Probably the most significant aspect of the downfall of the men of 1519 was the role of the censoring organs in encompassing it. The original authors of the purge apparently would have remained content with a far less harsh and widespread purging than actually occurred and it was, then, the Censorate that cried and cried again for increased severity and scope of punishment. It is precisely at this point in Yi Korean history that the censoring bodies came of age as the supreme instrument of political change. But, at the same time that the organs of remonstrance were being brought to this institutional apogee, they were being subverted. So long as they stood solely on the principle of freedom of remonstrance, the censoring bodies might aspire to fill the role of chief arbiter of the political arena. From the moment they came to subserve the parochial interests of a single grouping of the power elite, the censoring organs in effect abdicated their role as arbiter and became a mere instrument of power.

Thus it was that only a decade after the end of the Purge of 1519, Kim Al-lo became the first figure of the Yi dynasty (excepting Sejo, of course) individually to wield unchallenged authority in the government. His path to power had been opened by the acquiescence of a docile Censorate, and his six-year sway was marked by manipulation of the Censorate in a series of criminal proceedings aimed at destroying his present and potential enemies. Even more revealing of the altered role of the censoring organs is the manner of Kim Al-lo's demise. When, at length, King Chungjong once again was faced with an ultimate choice and determined that Kim Al-lo must go, he moved against Kim not by royal fiat but by manipulation of the Censorate. An elaborate set of signals was arranged whereby the worried Inspector-General, newly appointed for the occasion, could be reassured of the king's intention to support a denunciation of Kim Al-lo. The Inspector-General rose on cue to deliver his indictment, whereupon Chungjong accepted the formal charges requested against Kim Al-lo and executed him. Again, a few years later, the first thought of the men who prosecuted the Purge of 1545 was to turn the weapon of the Censorate against their intended victims.

The era of the Literati Purges, then, was not primarily an early chapter in the history of political schism in Yi Korea but was most importantly a period of major institutional developments. The evidence of the present study strongly suggests that it is not particularly fruitful for an analysis of this phenomenon to focus on the issue of factionalism. All political systems, to survive, must work out effective mechanisms for allocating power positions and resolving political differences. Further study may well show that the traditional Korean approach to these problems, however it may reflect unique Korean social and cultural configurations, was neither markedly different nor colored more by factionalism than was the case in other pre-modern societies. In fact, the traditional Korean approach, despite the periodic trauma of the purges, may be said to have served well the ultimate purpose of insuring the longevity of the dynasty. And a highly developed remonstrance institution played a vital part in achieving this end.

APPENDIX A
LIST OF GOVERNMENT OFFICES AND POSTS
with indication of rank

(*denotes the concurrent holding of
more then one official appointment)

Border Inspector		Sunch'alsa	巡察使
Censorate		Taegan	臺諫
Censor-General,		Saganwŏn	司諫院
Office of the (OCG)			
Censor-General	Sr. 3	Taesagan	大司諫
Second Censor	Jr. 3	Sagan	司諫
Third Censor	Sr. 5	Hŏnnap	獻納
Fourth Censor (2)	Sr. 6	Chŏngŏn	正言
Commander-in-chief of		Sŏjŏng Towŏnsu	西征都元師
the Western Expedition			
Crown Prince Tutorial		Seja Sigangwŏn	世子侍講院
Office			
Director*	Sr. 1	Sa	師
Deputy Director*	Sr. 1	Pu	傅
Second Deputy	Jr. 1	Isa	貳師
Director*			
First Mentor*	Sr. 2	Chwabingaek	左賓客
Second Mentor*	Sr. 2	Ubingaek	右賓客
Third Mentor*	Jr. 2	Chwabubingaek	左副賓客
Fourth Mentor*	Jr. 2	Ububingaek	右副賓客
First Tutor*	Jr. 3	Podŏk	輔德
Second Tutor	Sr. 4	P'ilsŏn	弼善
Third Tutor	Sr. 5	Munhak	文學
Fourth Tutor	Sr. 6	Sasŏ	司書
Fifth Tutor	Sr. 7	Sŏlsŏ	說書
Diplomatic Correspondence,		Sŭngmunwŏn	承文院
Office of*			
Editor	Sr. 3	P'angyo	判校
Assistant Editor	Jr. 3	Ch'amgyo	參校

First Drafter	Jr. 4	Kyogam	校勘
Second Drafter (2)	Jr. 5	Kyori	校理
Third Drafter (2)	Sr. 6	Kyogŏm	校檢
Reference Consultant (2)	Sr. 7	Paksa	博士
First Copyist (2)	Sr. 8	Chŏjak	著作
Second Copyist (2)	Sr. 9	Chŏngja	正字
Third Copyist (2)	Jr. 9	Pujŏngja	副正字

Director of the Veritable
Records Office — Saguk (Sillokch'ŏng) Tangsang 史局 (實錄廳) 堂上

Editorial Review, Office of — Kyosŏgwan 校書館

Examinations, Office of* — Sagwanso 四館所

Five Military Commands — Owi 五衛

Commanding General (12)	Jr. 2	Chang	將
First Deputy Commander (9)	Sr. 3	Sanghogun	上護軍
Second Deputy Commander (14)	Jr. 3	Taehogun	大護軍
Third Deputy Commander (12)	Sr. 4	Hogun	護軍
Fourth Deputy Commander (54)	Jr. 4	Puhogun	副護軍
Fifth Rank Military Officer (14)	Sr. 5	Sajik	司直
Junior Fifth Rank M.O. (123)	Jr. 5	Pusajik	副司直
Sixth Rank M.O. (15)	Sr. 6	Sagwa	司果
Junior Sixth Rank M.O. (176)	Jr. 6	Pusagwa	副司果
Battalion Commander (25)	Jr. 6	Pujang	部將
Seventh Rank M.O. (5)	Sr. 7	Sajŏng	司正
Junior Seventh Rank M.O. (309)	Jr. 7	Pusajŏng	副司正
Eighth Rank M.O. (16)	Sr. 8	Samaeng	司猛
Junior Eighth Rank M.O. (483)	Jr. 8	Pusamaeng	副司猛
Ninth Rank M.O. (42)	Sr. 9	Sayong	司勇
Junior Ninth Rank M.O. (1939)	Jr. 9	Pusayong	副司勇

Five Military Commands Headquarters — Owi Toch'ongbu 五衛都摠府

Commander	Sr. 2	Toch'onggwan	都摠官
Deputy Commander	Jr. 2	Puch'onggwan	副摠官
Adjutant (4)	Jr. 4	Kyŏngnyŏk	經歷
Auditor (4)	Jr. 5	Tosa	都事

Fortifications, Office of		Ch'uksŏngsa	築城司
Four Colleges		Sahak	四學
Great Lord		Puwŏngun	府院君
Great Prince		Taegun	大君
Hall of Reading		Toksŏdang	讀書堂
Hall of Worthies		Chiphyŏnjŏn	集賢殿
High State Councillors		Samgong	三公
Historian		Sagwan	史官
Horse Assayer		Chŏmma	點馬
Inspector-General, Office of the (OIG)		Sahŏnbu	司憲府
Inspector-General	Jr. 2	Taesahŏn	大司憲
Second Inspector	Jr. 3	Chibŭi	執義
Third Inspector (2)	Sr. 4	Changnyŏng	掌令
Fourth Inspector (2)	Sr. 5	Chip'yŏng	持平
Bailiff (24)	Sr. 6	Kamch'al	監察
Investigation Officer (State Tribunal)		Ch'ugwan	推官
Kaesŏng Magistracy		Kaesŏngbu	開城府
Local Magistrate		Suryŏng	守令
Lord		Kun	君
Magistrate (of a county, etc.)		(see Provincial Administration, Civil)	
Marketing Control Office		P'yŏngsisŏ	平市署
Director*		Chejo	提調
Merit Awards Administration		Ch'unghunbu	忠勳府
Military Training Administration		Hullyŏnwŏn	訓鍊院
Ministers-without-Portfolio, Office of		Chungch'ubu	中樞府
First Minister	Sr. 1	Yŏngsa	領事
Second Minister(2)	Jr. 1	P'ansa	判事
Third Minister (6)	Sr. 2	Chisa	知事
Fourth Minister (7)	Jr. 2	Tongjisa	同知事
Fifth Minister (8)	Sr. 3	Ch'ŏmjisa	僉知事

Secretary	Jr. 4	Kyŏngnyŏk	經歷
Auditor	Jr. 5	Tosa	都事

National Academy		Sŏnggyungwan	成均館
Director*	Sr. 2	Chisa	知事
Assistant Director*	Jr. 2	Tongjisa	同知事
Headmaster	Sr. 3	Taesasŏng	大司成
Assistant Master (2)	Jr. 3	Sasŏng	司成
Second Assistant Master (3)	Sr. 4	Saye	司藝
Lecturer (4)	Sr. 5	Chikkang	直講
Librarian (13)	Sr. 6	Chŏnjŏk	典籍
Reference Consultant (3)	Sr. 7	Paksa	博士
First Proctor (3)	Sr. 8	Hakchŏng	學正
Second Proctor (3)	Sr. 9	Hangnok	學錄
Third Proctor (3)	Jr. 9	Hagyu	學諭
National Confucian Shrine		Munmyo	文廟

Palace Guards Headquarters		Naegŭmwi	內禁衛
Commandant (3)*	Jr. 2	Chang	將
Palace Guardsmen		Naegŭmwi in	內禁衛人
Palace Supply Office		Naesusa	內需司
Paper Manufactory		Chojisŏ	造紙署
Overseer	Jr. 6	Saji	司紙
Personnel, Board of		Ijo	吏曹
Minister	Sr. 2	P'ansŏ	判書
Second Minister	Jr. 2	Ch'amp'an	參判
Third Minister	Sr. 3	Ch'amŭi	參議
Section Chief (3)	Sr. 5	Chŏngnang	正郎
Assistant Section Chief (3)	Sr. 6	Chwarang	佐郎
(Provincial Administration, Civil)			
Governor	Jr.2	Kwanch'alsa	觀察使
Magistrate, Special Capital	Jr. 2	Puyun	府尹
Deputy Magistrate, Special Capital	Jr. 4	Sŏyun	庶尹
Magistrate, Special City	Sr. 3	Taedohobusa	大都護府使
Magistrate, City/Island	Sr. 3	Moksa	牧使
Magistrate, Town	Jr. 3	(Toho)busa	(都護)府使

Magistrate, Great County	Jr. 4	Kunsu 郡守
Magistrate, County	Jr. 5	Hyŏllyŏng 縣令
Magistrate, Small County	Jr. 6	Hyŏngam 縣監
Inspector, Province	Jr. 5	Tosa 都事
Governor's Aide/Magistrate's Aide	Jr. 5	P'angwan 判官
Superintendent of Post Stations	Jr. 6	Ch'albang 察訪
Education Officer	Jr. 6	Kyosu 教授
(and others)		

(Provincial Administration, Military)

Army Commander	Jr. 2	Pyŏngma Chŏltosa 兵馬節度使
Army Deputy Commander	Sr. 3	Pyŏngma Chŏlchesa 兵馬節制使
Army Second Deputy Commander	Jr. 3	Pyŏngma Ch'ŏmjŏlchesa 兵馬僉節制使
Army Third Deputy Commander	Jr. 4	Pyŏngma Tongch'ŏmjŏlchesa 兵馬同僉節制使
Army Inspector	Jr. 3	Pyŏngma Uhu 兵馬虞候
Army Aide	Sr. 6	Pyŏngma P'yŏngsa 兵馬評事
Navy Commander	Sr. 3	Sugun Chŏltosa 水軍節度使
Navy Deputy Commander	Jr. 3	Sugun Ch'ŏmjŏlchesa 水軍僉節制使
Navy Inspector	Sr. 4	Sugun Uhu 水軍虞候
Navy Sub-area Commander	Jr. 4	Sugun Manho 水軍萬戶
(and others)		

Punishments, Board of		Hyŏngjo 刑曹
Minister	Sr. 2	P'ansŏ 判書
Second Minister	Jr. 2	Ch'amp'an 參判
Third Minister	Sr. 3	Ch'amŭi 參議
Section Chief (4)	Sr. 5	Chŏngnang 正郎
Assistant Section Chief (4)	Sr. 6	Chwarang 佐郎
(and others)		

Recorder		Sagwan 史官
Rites, Board of		Yejo 禮曹
Minister	Sr. 2	P'ansŏ 判書
Second Minister	Jr. 2	Ch'amp'an 參判
Third Minister	Sr. 3	Ch'amŭi 參議

Section Chief (3)	Sr. 5	Chŏngnang	正郎
Assistant Section Chief (3)	Sr. 6	Chwarang	佐郎
Royal Decrees, Office of		Yemungwan	藝文館
Superintendent*	Sr. 1	Yŏngsa	領事
Director*	Sr. 2	Taejehak	大提學
Deputy Director*	Jr. 2	Chehak	提學
Second Deputy Director*	Sr. 3	Chikchehak	直提學
Drafter*	Sr. 4	Ŭnggyo	應敎
First Diarist (2)	Sr. 7	Ponggyo	奉敎
Second Diarist (2)	Sr. 8	Taegyo	待敎
Third Diarist (4)	Sr. 9	Kŏmyŏl	檢閱
Royal House Administration		Tollyŏngbu	敦寧府
Director	Sr. 1	Yŏngsa	領事
Deputy Director	Jr. 1	P'ansa	判事
Second Deputy Director	Sr. 2	Chisa	知事
Third Deputy Director	Jr. 2	Tongjisa	同知事
First Secretary	Sr. 3	Tojŏng	都正
Second Secretary	Sr. 3	Chŏng	正
Third Secretary	Jr. 3	Pujŏng	副正
Fourth Secretary (2)	Jr. 4	Ch'ŏmjŏng	僉正
Auditor (2)	Jr. 5	P'angwan	判官
(and others)			
Royal Lectures, Office of the*		Kyŏngyŏn	經筵
Director (3)	Sr. 1	Yŏngsa	領事
Deputy Director (3)	Sr. 2	Chisa	知事
Second Deputy Director (3)	Jr. 2	Tongchisa	同知事
Participant (7)	Sr. 3	Ch'amch'angwan	參贊官
Expositor	Sr. 4	Siganggwan	侍講官
Reader	Sr. 5	Sidokkwan	侍讀官
Commentator	Sr. 6	Kŏmt'ogwan	檢討官
First Secretary	Sr. 7	Sagyŏng	司經
Second Secretary	Sr. 8	Sŏlgyŏng	說經
Third Secretary	Sr. 9	Chŏngyŏng	典經
Royal Secretariat		Sŭngjŏngwŏn	承政院
First Royal Secretary	Sr. 3	Tosŭngji	都承旨
Second Royal Secretary	Sr. 3	Chwasŭngji	左承旨
Third Royal Secretary	Sr. 3	Usŭngji	右承旨

Fourth Royal Secretary	Sr. 3	Chwabusŭngji	左副承旨
Fifth Royal Secretary	Sr. 3	Ubusŭngji	右副承旨
Sixth Royal Secretary	Sr. 3	Tongbusŭngji	同副承旨
Recorder (2)	Sr. 7	Chusŏ	注書
Royal Secretary		Sŭngji	承旨
Royal Stables Administration		Saboksi	司僕寺
Superintendent		Chejo	提調
Seoul Magistracy		Hansŏngbu	漢城府
Chief Magistrate	Sr. 2	P'anyun	判尹
Second Magistrate	Jr. 2	Chwayun	左尹
Third Magistrate	Jr. 2	Uyun	右尹
Assistant Magistrate	Jr. 4	Sŏyun	庶尹
Chief Clerk (2)	Jr. 5	P'angwan	判官
Bailiff (3)	Sr. 7	Ch'amgun	參軍
Six Boards		Yukcho	六曹
Slave Administration, Bureau of		Changnyewŏn	掌隸院
Chief	Sr. 3	P'angyŏlsa	判決事
First Secretary (3)	Sr. 5	Saŭi	司議
Second Secretary (4)	Sr. 6	Sap'yŏng	司評
Sogyŏkchŏn			
Sogyŏksŏ			
Special Counselors, Office of the		Hongmungwan	弘文館
(OSC)			
Superintendent*	Sr. 1	Yŏngsa	領事
Director*	Sr. 2	Taejehak	大提學
Deputy Director*	Jr. 2	Chehak	提學
First Counselor	Sr. 3	Pujehak	副提學
Second Counselor	Sr. 3	Chikchehak	直提學
Third Counselor	Jr. 3	Chŏnhan	典翰
Fourth Counselor	Sr. 4	Ŭnggyo	應敎
Junior Fourth Counselor	Jr. 4	Puŭnggyo	副應敎
Fifth Counselor (2)	Sr. 5	Kyori	校理
Junior Fifth Counselor (2)	Jr. 5	Pugyori	副敎理
Sixth Counselor (2)	Sr. 6	Such'an	修撰
Junior Sixth Counselor (2)	Jr. 6	Pusuch'an	副修撰
Seventh Counselor	Sr. 7	Paksa	博士

Eighth Counselor	Sr. 8	Chŏjak	著作
Ninth Counselor (2)	Sr. 9	Chŏngja	正字
Special Mentor of the Crown Prince		Wŏnja Poyanggwan	元子輔養官
Special Participant (Office of the Royal Lectures)		T'ŭkchingwan	特進官
State Council		Ŭijŏngbu	議政府
Chief State Councillor	Sr. 1	Yŏngŭijŏng	領議政
Second State Councillor	Sr. 1	Chwaŭijŏng	左議政
Third State Councillor	Sr. 1	Uŭijŏng	右議政
Fourth State Councillor	Jr. 1	Chwach'ansŏng	左贊成
Fifth State Councillor	Jr. 1	Uch'ansŏng	右贊成
Sixth State Councillor	Sr. 2	Chwach'amch'an	左參贊
Seventh State Councillor	Sr. 2	Uch'amch'an	右參贊
First Secretary (2)	Sr. 4	Sain	舍人
Legal Secretary	Sr. 5	Kŏmsang	檢詳
Copyist (2)	Sr. 8	Sarok	司錄
State Records, Bureau of*		Ch'unch'ugwan	春秋館
Director	Sr. 1	Yŏngsa	領事
Deputy Director (2)	Sr. 1	Kamsa	監事
Second Deputy Director (2)	Sr. 2	Chisa	知事
Third Deputy Director (2)	Jr. 2	Tongjisa	同知事
Editor	Sr. 3	Such'angwan	修撰官
Compiler (4)	Sr. 3-Jr. 4	P'yŏnsugwan	編修官
Drafter (2)	Sr. 5-Jr. 5	Kijugwan	記注官
Copyist (6)	Sr. 6-Sr. 9	Kisagwan	記事官
State Tribunal		Ŭigŭmbu	義禁府
Chief Magistrate* ⎫	Jr. 1	P'ansa	判事
Second Magistrate* ⎬(4)	Sr. 2	Chisa	知事
Third Magistrate* ⎭	Jr. 2	Tongjisa	同知事
Captain ⎫(10)	Jr. 4	Kyŏngnyŏk	經歷
Lieutenant ⎭	Jr. 5	Tosa	都事
Supernumerary Third Copyist (Office of Diplomatic Correspondence)		Kwŏnji Pujŏngja	權知副正字

Taxation, Board of		Hojo 戸曹	
Minister	Sr. 2	P'ansŏ	判書
Second Minister	Jr. 2	Ch'amp'an	參判
Third Minister	Sr. 3	Ch'amŭi	參議
Section Chief (3)	Sr. 5	Chŏngnang	正郞
Assistant Section Chief (3) (and others)	Sr. 6	Chwarang	佐郞

Vertiable Records Office		Sillokch'ŏng 實錄廳

War, Board of		Pyŏngjo 兵曹	
Minister	Sr. 2	P'ansŏ	判書
Second Minister	Jr. 2	Ch'amp'an	參判
Third Minister	Sr. 3	Ch'amŭi	參議
Fourth Minister	Sr. 3	Ch'amji	參知
Section Chief (4)	Sr. 5	Chŏngnang	正郞
Assistant Section Chief (4)	Sr. 6	Chwarang	佐郞

Works, Board of		Kongjo 工曹	
Minister	Sr. 2	P'ansŏ	判書
Second Minister	Jr. 2	Ch'amp'an	參判
Third Minister	Sr. 3	Ch'amŭi	參議
Section Chief (3)	Sr. 5	Chŏngnang	正郞
Assistant Section Chief (3)	Sr. 6	Chwarang	佐郞

APPENDIX B
SILLOK LOCATIONS OF DATE CITATIONS

This list contains all date citations used in the text and footnotes, including both those referring to *Chōsen shi (CSS)* and those citing the *Sillok* directly. The *CSS* cites many sources other than the *Sillok* but essentially attempts an abridgement of *Sillok* data; since its dates provide both cyclical character notation for a particular day and the appropriate number date for that day, reference back to *CSS* for any date I have cited will be an easy matter. The *Sillok,* on the other hand, even in its modern editions offers only the cyclical character notation for the day, usually putting it wherever it may haphazardly come in amongst the data-filled columns. The location of any particular day's record thus often is a tedious process. This list, then, is aimed at making reference to the *Sillok,* too, an easy matter. It must be noted, however, that the *Sillok* page citations refer to the location of the beginning of that day's record, not necessarily to the location of that portion of the record I have used.

A few corrections of *Sillok* and *CSS* datings are noted in footnotes hereto.

SILLOK LOCATIONS

King	Year of Reign	Date citation		Cyclical date for day	volume	page
T'aejo	1	1392	8.20	己巳	1	52b
			9.16	甲午	2	2a
			9.27	乙巳	2	7a
			10.9	丁巳	2	8a
			11.1	戊寅	2	11a
			11.19	丙申	2	14b
	2	1393	7.22	乙丑	4	2a
			7.27	庚午	4	4a
			7.29	壬申	4	4b
			8.10	癸未	4	5b
			8.15	戊子	4	6a
			8.17	庚寅	4	6b
	3	1394	6.16	甲申	6	2b
	5	1396	1.10	己巳	9	1a
			1.20	己卯	9	1b
	7	1398	9.17	己丑	15	5a
			10.1	癸卯	15	6b
			12.15	丁巳	15	11a
T'aejong	1	1401	1.14	甲戌	1	2b
			1.15	乙亥	1	8b
	2	1402	1.27	庚戌	3	6a
	3	1403	11.15	己丑	6	25a
	4	1404	3.27	戊辰	7	11a
	17	1417	11.17	戊辰	34	31b
Sejong	8	1426	9.4	甲午	33	15b
Tanjong	1	1453	10.11	甲午	8	10b
			10.15	戊戌	8	17a
			10.17	庚子	8	19a
			10.18	辛丑	8	22a
			11.4	丙辰	9	2b
	2	1454	1.28	庚辰	10	25a

Sejo	1	1455	9.9	辛巳	2	19b
			12.27	戊辰	2	53b
	2	1456	3.28	丁酉	3	24b
			6.2	庚子	4	10a
			6.3	辛丑	4	12a
			6.6	甲辰	4	14a
			6.18	丙辰	4	18a
	3	1457	6.21	癸丑	8	8b
			6.26	戊午	8	10a
			10.24	甲寅	9	28a
	10	1464	8.6	丁亥	34	9a
	12	1466	1.15	戊午	38	4b
	13	1467	9.20	壬午	43	61a
			11.2	甲子	44	23a
Yejong		1468	10.28	甲寅	1	43a
			10.30	丙辰	1	44b
	1	1469	5.20	癸卯	5	28a
			7.3	甲申	6	31b
Sŏngjong	2	1471	3.27	庚子	9	35a
			8.25	乙丑	11	15b
	7	1476	1.13	戊午	63	8a
	8	1477	i2.24	壬戌	77	17b
			3.29	丙申	78	11b
			7.8	癸酉	82	3a
			7.9	甲戌	82	4a
			7.12	丁丑	82	5b
			7.14	己卯	82	7a
			7.16	辛巳	82	8b
			7.17	壬午	82	9a
			7.23	戊子	82	28b

Sŏngjong	8	1477	7.24	己丑	82	29b
			8.15	己酉	83	8a
			8.16	庚戌	83	8b
			8.17	辛亥	83	9a
			8.18	壬子	83	11a
			8.19	癸丑	83	11b
			8.20	甲寅	83	12b
			8.23	丁巳	83	15a
			8.26	庚申	83	20a
			8.27	辛酉	83	22a
			8.29	癸亥	83	24b
			8.30	甲子	83	26a
			9.5	己巳	84	3a
			9.8	壬申	84	13b
			9.28	壬辰	84	27a
			9.29	癸巳	84	30a
			10.1	乙未	85	1a
			10.2	丙申	85	2a
	9	1478	1.22	乙酉	88	12b
			1.25	戊子	88	17b
			1.27	庚寅	88	18a
			2.20	癸丑	89	16b
			3.9	辛未	90	3b
			4.3	甲午	91	1b
			4.8	己亥	91	8b
			4.9	庚子	91	13a
			4.15	丙午	91	16a
			4.21	壬子	91	24a
			4.24	乙卯	91	29a
			4.27	戊午	91	31a
			4.28	己未	91	34b

138

Sŏngjong	9	1478	4.29	庚申	91	41a
			4.30	辛酉	91	48b
			5.1	壬戌	92	1a
			5.6	丁卯	92	6b
			5.7	戊辰	92	11a
			5.8	己巳	92	14b
			5.15	丙子	92	18a
			6.2	壬辰	93	1b
			9.5	癸亥	96	1b
			9.17	乙亥	96	8b
			9.19	丁丑	96	9a
			10.7	乙未	97	2b
			10.29	丁巳	97	10a
			12.10	丁酉	99	5b
	10	1479	6.2	丁亥	105	1a
			6.5	庚寅	105	6b
	11	1480	11.12	戊子	123	4b
			11.14	庚寅	123	6a
			11.15	辛卯	123	6b
			11.21	丁酉	123	7a
			11.22	戊戌	123	7b
			12.16	辛酉	124	4b
			12.18	癸亥	124	6b
	13	1482	7.22	己丑	143	28a
			8.16	壬子	144	21a
	16	1485	1.27	庚戌	174	35b
			2.2	甲寅	175	2b

Sŏngjong	16	1485	7.3	辛亥	181	2a
			7.6	甲寅	181	10a
	17	1486	3.6	辛亥	189	5a
	18	1487	9.28	甲子	207	11b
	19	1488	9.4	甲子	220	2a
			9.23	癸未	220	7b
			9.28	戊子	220	11b
			10.2	壬辰	221	2b
			11.15	甲戌	222	14a
			11.29	戊子	222	27a
			11.30	己丑	222	28a
			12.1	庚寅	223	1a
			12.15	甲辰	223	19a
	20	1489	7.13	己巳	230	9b
			7.14	庚午	230	10b
			11.14	戊辰	234	15a
	21	1490	4.27	己酉	239	16b
			5.10	辛酉	240	2b
			5.11	壬戌	240	3a
			6.7	戊子	241	4a
			6.12	癸巳	241	9b
			6.17	戊戌	241	11b
			6.19	庚子	241	13a
			6.20	辛丑	241	13b
			9.5	甲寅	244	5a
	22	1491	1.19	丙申	249	13a
			3.21	丁酉	251	8b
			4.11	丙辰	252	5b

Sŏngjong	22	1491	4.17	壬戌	252	9b
			4.19	甲子	252	12a
			4.21	丙寅	252	14a
			5.7	壬午	253	8a
			5.8	癸未	253	13a
			5.9	甲申	253	17a
			6.5	庚戌	254	5b
			6.16	辛酉	254	14a
			6.17	壬戌	254	14b
			6.19	甲子	254	17a
			6.20	乙丑	254	21a
			6.21	丙寅	254	23a
			6.22	丁卯	254	23b
			6.23	戊辰	254	25b
			6.24	己巳	254	27b
			10.17	庚申	258	9a
			12.2	甲辰	260	1a
			12.7	己酉	260	3a
			12.8	庚戌	260	3b
	23	1492	1.6	丁丑	261	3b
			1.16	丁亥	261	10b
			1.19	庚寅	261	13b
			2.3	甲辰	262	1b
			2.7	戊申	262	3b
			2.17	戊午	262	12a
			2.27	戊辰	262	18a
			5.19	戊子	265	17a
			8.7	乙巳	268	8b
			8.8	丙午	268	9a
			8.19	丁巳	268	18b
			8.30	戊辰	268	25b

Sŏngjong	23	1492	9.4	壬申	269	2a
			9.8	丙子	269	5a
			9.10	戊寅	269	5b
			10.23	庚申	270	9a
			11.21	戊子	271	13b
			11.23	庚寅	271	16a
			11.24	辛卯	271	17a
			11.25	壬辰	271	19a
			11.26	癸巳	271	20a
			11.28	乙未	271	24b
			11.29	丙申	271	27a
			12.2	戊戌	272	2b
			12.3	己亥	272	6a
			12.4	庚子	272	8b
			12.5	辛丑	272	11b
			12.6	壬寅	272	13b
			12.7	癸卯	272	15a
			12.8	甲辰	272	16b
			12.10	丙午	272	18a
			12.14	庚戌	272	23a
	24	1493	6.27	己丑	279	18a
			7.6	戊戌	280	6a
			7.12	甲辰	280	19b
			7.13	乙巳	280	21b
			7.14	丙午	280	24a
			7.15	丁未	280	25b
			7.16	戊申	280	28a
			7.18	庚戌	280	28b
			7.19	辛亥	280	31b
			7.29	辛酉	280	39b
			7.30	壬戌	280	41a
			8.1	癸亥	281	1a

Sŏngjong	24	1493	8.4	丙寅	281	8b
			8.6	戊辰	281	12a
			8.7	己巳	281	13b
			8.10	壬申	281	18b
			8.11	癸酉	281	22a
			8.16	戊寅	281	29a
			8.21	癸未	281	35a
			9.1	壬辰	282	1a
			9.2	癸巳	282	3a
			9.5	丙申	282	7a
			10.6	丁卯	283	4b
			10.23	甲申	283	29b
			10.29	庚寅	283	44a
			10.30	辛卯	283	47b
			11.3	甲午	284	2b
			11.18	己酉	284	18b
	25	1494	2.15	甲戌	287	12b
			3.23	壬子	288	21b
			6.11	戊辰	291	7a
			12.8	癸亥	297	4a
			12.9	甲子	297	4a
			12.10	乙丑	297	5a
			12.11	丙寅	297	5b
			12.12	丁卯	297	6b
			12.13	戊辰	297	8a
			12.14	己巳	297	8b
			12.15	庚午	297	9b
			12.16	辛未	297	10a
			12.17	壬申	297	11a
			12.18	癸酉	297	12a
			12.19	甲戌	297	12b
			12.20	乙亥	297	13a
			12.24	己卯	297	15b

Yŏnsangun		1494	12.25	庚辰	1	1a
			12.27	壬午	1	3b
			12.28	癸未	1	5b
			12.29	甲申	1	7a
	1	1495	1.1	乙酉	2	1a
			1.2	丙戌	2	3a
			1.7	辛卯	2	7a
			1.22	丙午	2	20b
			1.24	戊申	2	22a
			1.27	辛亥	2	27a
			1.30	甲寅	2	29b
			2.28	壬午	3	30a
			3.20	癸卯	4	7a
			5.11	癸巳	5	9b
			5.22	甲辰	5	18a
			5.24	丙午	5	19a
			5.25	丁未	5	19b
			5.28	庚戌	5	22a
			6.3	甲寅	6	2a
			6.6	丁巳	6	4b
			6.7	戊午	6	5b
			6.12	癸亥	6	7a
			6.15	丙寅	6	8a
			6.26	丁丑	6	9b
			6.28	己卯	6	10b
			6.29	庚辰	6	11b
			6.30	辛巳	6	14b
			7.1	壬午	7	1a
			7.3	甲申	7	2b
			7.7	戊子	7	9a
			7.11	壬辰	7	15b
			7.12	癸巳	7	17a
			7.13	甲午	7	18b

Yŏnsangun	1	1495	7.15	丙申	7	22b
			7.18	己亥	7	27a
			7.19	庚子	7	30a
			7.21	壬寅	7	33b
			7.23	甲辰	7	40a
			7.25	丙午	7	42a
			7.26	丁未	7	43b
			8.2	壬子	8	1a
			8.8	戊午	8	3b
			8.9	己未	8	4b
			8.11	辛酉	8	6b
			8.22	壬申	8	9a
			8.25	乙亥	8	11a
			9.3	癸未	9	1a
			9.5	乙酉	9	5a
			9.8	戊子	9	7a
			9.15	乙未	9	9b
			9.16	丙申	9	10a
			11.6	乙酉	10	4b
			11.15	甲午	10	8a*
			12.30	己卯	11	9a
	2	1496	1.1	庚辰	12	1a
			i3.30	丁丑	14	15a
			4.11	戊子	14	23a
			5.15	辛酉	15	4b
			6.3	戊寅	15	9b
			6.5	庚辰	15	11a
			6.7	壬午	15	11b

*CSS erroneously has 14th.

Yŏnsangun	2	1496	6.13	戊子	15	17b
			6.29	甲辰	15	26b
			7.2	丁未	16	1b
	3	1497	2.14	丙戌	21	32a
			3.16	戊午	22	9b
			6.1	辛未	24	1a
			6.2	壬申	24	1b
			6.6	丙子	24	6b
			6.13	癸未	24	11a
			6.14	甲申	24	11b
			6.15	乙酉	24	11b
			6.16	丙戌	24	12b
			6.28	戊戌	24	25a
			7.3	壬寅	25	3a
			7.8	丁未	25	12b
			7.14	癸丑	25	24b
			7.15	甲寅	25	25b
			7.17	丙辰	25	30a
			7.18	丁巳	25	32a
			7.20	己未	25	35a
			7.21	庚申	25	35a
			7.22	辛酉	25	36a
			7.23	壬戌	25	36b
			7.24	癸亥	25	37b
			7.28	丁卯	25	41b
			7.29	戊辰	25	42a
			7.30	己巳	25	42b
			8.2	辛未	26	3b
			8.4	癸酉	26	7a
			8.6	乙亥	26	9a
			8.11	庚辰	26	11a

Yŏnsangun	3	1497	9.13	辛亥	27	6b
			10.2	庚午	28	1a
			10.9	丁丑	28	7a
			11.20	丁巳	28	27a
			12.25	壬辰	28	35b
			12.26	癸巳	28	36b
	4	1498	2.1	丁卯	29	4b
			2.13	己卯	29	6a
			2.24	庚寅	29	8a
			4.11	丙子	29	11b
			4.18	癸未	29	12a
			4.30	乙未	29	15a
			6.1	丙寅	29	20a*
			6.6	辛未	29	21a
			6.13	戊寅	29	21a
			7.1	乙未	30	1a
			7.6	庚子	30	1b
			7.7	辛丑	30	2a
			7.8	壬寅	30	2a
			7.11	乙巳	30	3b
			7.12	丙午	30	4a
			7.13	丁未	30	6a
			7.14	戊申	30	7a
			7.15	己酉	30	8a
			7.17	辛亥	30	9b
			7.18	壬子	30	12b
			7.19	癸丑	30	13b
			7.21	乙卯	30	19b
			7.26	庚申	30	22a

Sillok erroneously has 戊寅.

Yŏnsangun	4	1498	7.27	辛酉	30	23b
			7.28	壬戌	30	24b
			7.29	癸亥	30	25a
			8.1	甲子	31	1a
			8.10	癸酉	31	2a
			8.14	丁丑	31	2b
			8.16	己卯	31	3a
			8.20	癸未	31	4a
			9.6	己亥	31	5b
			9.8	辛丑	31	5b
			9.11	甲辰	31	7a
			9.18	辛亥	31	8b
			11.9	辛丑	31	11b
			11.29	辛酉	31	13b*
			i11.6	丁卯	31	14b
			i11.8	己巳	31	15a
			i11.9	庚午	31	15a
			i11.11	壬申	31	15a
			i11.12	癸酉	31	15a
			i11.14	乙亥	31	15b
			i11.17	戊寅	31	16a
			i11.19	庚辰	31	17a
			12.19	庚戌	31	20a
			12.28	己未	31	23a
	5	1499	1.10	庚午	32	1b
			1.17	丁丑	32	4a
			1.18	戊寅	32	5b
			1.22	壬午	32	6b
			1.24	甲申	32	9b
			1.25	乙酉	32	10a

Sillok erroneously has 壬戌 , the first day of 1498.i11; *CSS* has assumed this to be an error for 辛酉 , but since there are no *Sillok* entries for 1498.11 after the 26th day, except this one, there is no way to establish the date intended.

Yŏnsangun	5	1499	2.1	辛卯	32	11a
			2.18	戊申	32	16a
			2.23	癸丑	32	18a
			3.2	辛酉	32	20a
			3.27	丙戌	32	23b
			4.3	壬辰	33	1a
			4.29	戊午	33	5a
			5.3	壬戌	33	5a
			5.9	戊辰	33	5b
			5.12	辛未	33	7a
			5.21	庚辰	33	11b
			5.28	丁亥	33	12b
			5.29	戊子	33	15a
			6.7	乙未	33	16a
			6.17	乙巳	33	17b
			6.27	乙卯	33	18a
			6.28	丙辰	33	19a
			7.2	庚申	34	1a
			7.11	己巳	34	5b
			7.12	庚午	34	6b
			7.20	戊寅	34	8b*
			7.23	辛巳	34	11a
			7.24	壬午	34	11b
			7.28	丙戌	34	13b
			8.7	甲午	34	16a
			9.10	丁卯	35	1b
			9.12	己巳	35	2b
			9.22	己卯	35	7a

Sillok erroneously has 戊辰.

Yŏnsangun	5	1499	10.7	癸巳	35	9a
			10.8	甲午	35	9a
			10.12	戊戌	35	9b
			10.23	己酉	35	12b
			12.24	己酉	35	32a
	6	1500	1.9	甲子	36	2a
			1.12	丁卯	36	4a
			1.20	乙亥	36	8a
			1.21	丙子	36	8b
			1.22	丁丑	36	10a
			2.9	癸巳	36	15b
			6.25	丁未	38	6a
			7.14	丙寅	38	11b
			7.18	庚午	38	12b
			7.28	庚辰	38	14a
			8.4	丙戌	38	15b
			8.13	乙未	38	16b
			9.18	己巳	39	2a
			9.27	戊寅	39	5b
			10.27	戊申	39	12b
	7	1501	1.30	己卯	40	4b
			2.3	壬午	40	8b
			4.5	壬午	40	10b
			4.21	戊戌	40	11b
			4.23	庚子	40	12a
			4.26	癸卯	40	12a
			4.28	乙巳	40	12b
			5.6	癸丑	40	13a

Yŏnsangun	7	1501	5.25	壬申	40	14a
			6.18	甲午	40	15a
			6.30	丙午	40	15b
			7.5	辛亥	40	16b
			8.7	壬子	41	2a
			8.9	甲寅	41	4a
			8.11	丙辰	41	4b
			8.14	己未	41	5a
			8.20	丁卯	41	5b
			8.29	甲戌	41	6a
			9.16	壬辰	41	7b
			9.27	癸卯	41	9b
			9.29	乙巳	41	10b
			10.7	壬子	41	11a
			10.11	丙辰	41	11b
			10.12	丁巳	41	11b
			10.22	丁卯	41	13a
			10.26	辛未	41	14a
			10.29	甲戌	41	14b
			11.6	庚辰	41	14b
			11.10	甲申	41	15a
			11.11	乙酉	41	15a
			11.12	丙戌	41	15b
			11.16	庚寅	41	16a
			11.17	辛卯	41	17a
			11.23	丁酉	41	19a
			12.25	戊辰	41	21a
	8	1502	1.9	壬午	42	4a
			1.13	丙戌	42	7a

Yŏnsangun	8	1502	1.22	乙未	42	12a
			1.28	辛丑	42	18b
			1.30	癸卯	42	21b
			2.5	戊申	42	25a
			2.16	己未	42	28b
			3.10	壬午	43	3b
			3.25	丁酉	43	14a
			4.20	辛酉	43	24a
			5.2	癸酉	44	3a
			5.10	辛巳	44	4a
			5.12	癸未	44	4b
			6.3	癸卯	44	13a
			6.16	丙辰	44	19a
			6.28	戊辰	44	24b
			7.29	己亥	45	9a
			8.12	辛亥	45	13b
			8.30	己巳	45	19b
			9.16	乙酉	46	3b
			9.23	壬辰	46	8a
			9.28	丁酉	46	10b
			10.4	癸卯	46	13b
			10.12	辛亥	46	16a
			10.28	丁卯	46	23a
			11.27	丙申	47	13a
			11.29	戊戌	47	13b
	9	1503	1.2	庚午	48	1a
			2.19	丙辰	48	17a
			2.30	丁卯	48	25b

Yŏnsangun	9	1503	3.1	戊辰	49	1a
			4.3	己亥	49	13b
			4.28	甲子	49	22b
			5.5	庚午	49	24b
			5.22	丁亥	49	29a
			6.9	甲辰	50	2a
			6.12	丁未	50	2b
			6.13	戊申	50	2b
			6.29	甲子	50	8a
			9.8	辛未	50	19b
			9.15	戊寅	50	21a
			9.20	癸未	50	23b
			9.21	甲申	50	23b
			11.1	甲子	51	6b
			11.6	己巳	51	10a
			11.9	壬申	51	11a
			11.10	癸酉	51	11b
			11.16	己卯	51	14b
			11.20	癸未	51	15b
			11.22	乙酉	51	16b
			11.23	丙戌	51	18a
			12.22	乙卯	51	23a
			12.25	戊午	51	23a
			12.26	己未	51	23b
	10	1504	1.6	戊辰	52	1b
			1.11	癸酉	52	2b
			3.3	甲子	52	10b
			3.11	壬申	52	12a
			3.12	癸酉	52	14a
			3.13	甲戌	52	15a
			3.14	乙亥	52	16a

Yŏnsangun	10	1504	3.16	丁丑	52	17b
			3.17	戊寅	52	18a
			3.18	己卯	52	19a
			3.19	庚辰	52	20a
			3.20	辛巳	52	20b
			3.23	甲申	52	22a
			3.24	乙酉	52	23a
			3.26	丁亥	52	24b
			3.27	戊子	52	25a
			3.28	己丑	52	25b
			3.30	辛卯	52	26b
			4.1	壬辰	52	27b
			4.3	甲午	52	28b
			4.10	辛丑	52	31a
			4.14	乙巳	52	32b
			4.18	己酉	52	34a
			4.19	庚戌	52	34b
			4.21	壬子	52	35a
			4.22	癸丑	52	35b
			4.23	甲寅	52	36a
			4.24	乙卯	52	36b
			4.25	丙辰	52	37a
			4.27	戊午	52	38a
			i4.5	乙丑	53	2a
			i4.6	丙寅	53	3a
			i4.8	戊辰	53	3b
			i4.10	庚午	53	4b
			i4.11	辛未	53	5a
			i4.12	壬申	53	6a
			i4.13	癸酉	53	7a
			i4.15	乙亥	53	8a*
			i4.16	丙子	53	8b
			i4.17	丁丑	53	9a
			i4.19	己卯	53	12a

Sillok erroneously has 己亥 .

Yŏnsangun	10	1504	i4.20	庚辰	53	12b
			i4.23	癸未	53	14b
			i4.25	乙酉	53	16a
			i4.26	丙戌	53	16b
			i4.27	丁亥	53	17b
			i4.28	戊子	53	19a
			i4.29	己丑	53	20b
			5.1	庚寅	53	22b
			5.2	辛卯	53	23a
			5.3	壬辰	53	23b
			5.4	癸巳	53	24b
			5.6	乙未	53	27a
			5.7	丙申	53	28a
			5.8	丁酉	53	29b
			5.9	戊戌	53	30a
			5.10	己亥	53	31a
			5.11	庚子	53	32b
			5.12	辛丑	53	33b
			5.14	癸卯	53	34b
			5.15	甲辰	53	34b
			5.18	丁未	53	38b
			5.19	戊申	53	39b
			5.21	庚戌	53	40b
			5.22	辛亥	53	41b
			5.23	壬子	53	42b
			5.25	甲寅	53	44a
			5.26	乙卯	53	45a
			5.27	丙辰	53	45b
			5.30	己未	53	47a
			6.1	庚申	54	1a
			6.2	辛酉	54	1b
			6.4	癸亥	54	2b
			6.6	乙丑	54	5a
			6.7	丙寅	54	6a
			6.8	丁卯	54	7a

Yŏnsangun	10	1504	6.9	戊辰	54	7b
			6.10	己巳	54	8b
			6.12	辛未	54	9a
			6.13	壬申	54	9b
			6.15	甲戌	54	11a
			6.16	乙亥	54	12b
			6.20	己卯	54	16a
			6.27	丙戌	54	19a
			7.6	甲午	54	21b
			7.10	戊戌	54	24a
			7.13	辛丑	54	26b
			7.16	甲辰	54	28a
			7.17	乙巳	54	28b
			7.19	丁未	54	29b
			7.20	戊申	54	31a
			7.22	庚戌	54	32a
			7.23	辛亥	54	32b
			7.25	癸丑	54	33b
			8.2	己未	55	2a
			8.5	壬戌	55	3a
			8.7	甲子	55	4a
			8.8	乙丑	55	4b
			8.10	丁卯	55	7a
			8.14	辛未	55	10a
			8.15	壬申	55	11a
			8.16	癸酉	55	12a
			8.17	甲戌	55	12b
			8.18	乙亥	55	13b
			8.20	丁丑	55	14a
			8.26	癸未	55	16b
			8.27	甲申	55	17a
			9.1	戊子	55	19a
			9.6	癸巳	55	20b
			9.8	乙未	55	21b

Yŏnsangun	10	1504	9.10	丁酉	55	22a
			9.18	乙巳	55	23a
			9.19	丙午	55	23b
			9.24	辛亥	55	24b
			9.25	壬子	55	25a
			9.26	癸丑	55	25a
			9.27	甲寅	55	26b
			9.28	乙卯	55	26b
			9.30	丁巳	55	26b
			10.1	戊午	56	1a
			10.4	辛酉	56	2b
			10.7	甲子	56	3b
			10.8	乙丑	56	4a
			10.11	戊辰	56	5b
			10.14	辛未	56	6b
			10.15	壬申	56	7a
			10.18	乙亥	56	8a
			10.21	戊寅	56	9a
			10.22	己卯	56	9b
			10.23	庚辰	56	10a
			10.24	辛巳	56	10b
			10.25	壬午	56	11b
			10.27	甲申	56	12b
			10.28	乙酉	56	12b
			10.29	丙戌	56	13a
			11.5	辛卯	56	14b
			11.6	壬辰	56	15a
			11.9	乙未	56	15b
			11.13	己亥	56	18a
			11.24	庚戌	56	21b
			11.27	癸丑	56	22b
			11.30	丙辰	56	23b
			12.2	戊午	56	24b
			12.5	辛酉	56	25a

Yŏnsangun	10	1504	12.14	庚午	56	27b
			12.15	辛未	56	27b
			12.16	壬申	56	28a
			12.17	癸酉	56	28b
			12.19	乙亥	56	29a
			12.20	丙子	56	29b
			12.22	戊寅	56	29b
			12.23	己卯	56	30a
			12.24	庚辰	56	30b
			12.26	壬午	56	31a
			12.27	癸未	56	32a
	11	1505	1.4	庚寅	57	2a
			1.6	壬辰	57	4a
			1.8	甲午	57	5a
			1.13	己亥	57	7b
			1.15	辛丑	57	8b
			1.16	壬寅	57	9a
			1.29	乙卯	57	12b
			2.8	甲子	57	13b
			2.9	乙丑	57	15a
			2.12	戊辰	57	15b
			2.19	乙亥	57	17a
			3.2	丁亥	57	18b
			3.24	己酉	57	22a
			4.6	辛酉	57	24a
			4.8	癸亥	57	24b
			4.15	庚午	57	26a
			5.22	丙午	58	5b
			5.25	己酉	58	6a
			6.5	戊午	58	8b
			6.15	戊辰	58	13a
			6.16	己巳	58	13b

Yŏnsangun	11	1505	6.30	癸未	58	16b
			7.2	乙酉	58	17b
			7.7	庚寅	58	18b
			7.9	壬辰	58	19a
			8.4	丙辰	59	1a
			8.10	壬戌	59	2a
			8.24	丙子	59	5b
			9.14	乙未	59	14b
			9.18	己亥	59	16a
			10.1	壬子	60	1a
	12	1506	1.14	甲午	61	5b*
			1.17	丁酉	61	6b
			2.14	甲子	61	15b
			2.17	丁卯	61	16a
			2.26	丙子	61	18a
			3.1	辛巳	61	19b
			3.23	癸卯	61	24b
			4.1	庚戌	62	1a
			4.6	乙卯	62	1b
			4.20	己巳	62	5b
			4.25	甲戌	62	7a
			5.1	庚辰	62	8b
			5.28	丁未	62	14b
			6.15	癸亥	62	18a

*From 1505. 12.23 癸酉 , erroneously recorded as 癸未 , the *Sillok's* cyclical dates for the days of the month are uniformly ten days off, through the end of 1506. 3. For all date citations within this period I have supplied the correct cyclical characters.

Yŏnsangun	12	1506	7.1	戊寅	63	1a
			7.24	辛丑	63	7b
			7.29	丙午	63	9a
			8.14	辛酉	63	14b
			8.17	甲子	63	16a
			9.2	戊寅	63	20a
Chungjong	1	1506	9.2	戊寅	1	1a
			9.3	己卯	1	5a
			9.5	辛巳	1	7a
			9.8	甲申	1	10a
			9.9	乙酉	1	11a
			9.10	丙戌	1	12a
			9.13	己丑	1	13b
			9.16	壬辰	1	14b
			9.17	癸巳	1	15b
			9.19	乙未	1	17a
			9.20	丙申	1	18b
			9.23	己亥	1	20a
			9.26	壬寅	1	21b
			9.27	癸卯	1	23a
			10.2	丁未	1	25b
			10.3	戊申	1	26b
			10.5	庚戌	1	29b
			10.7	壬子	1	30b
			10.14	己未	1	35a
			10.19	甲子	1	36a
			10.20	乙丑	1	37b
			10.25	庚午	1	40a
			10.27	壬申	1	42a
			11.5	庚辰	1	47a
			11.6	辛巳	1	48a
			11.12	丁亥	1	50b
			11.16	辛卯	1	52a
			12.3	丁未	1	59a

Chungjong	2	1507	1.7	辛巳	2	2a
			i1.2	丙午	2	14b
			i1.25	己巳	2	17b
			i1.26	庚午	2	21a
			i1.27	辛未	2	23b
			2.2	丙子	2	28b
			2.3	丁丑	2	30a
			3.18	辛酉	2	42b
			4.12	乙酉	2	49b
			4.23	丙申	2	66b
			6.10	壬午	3	16b
			6.11	癸未	3	22a
			6.17	己丑	3	23b
			6.28	庚子	3	26a
			7.4	乙巳	3	29a
			7.10	辛亥	3	31b
			7.12	癸丑	3	32b
			7.15	丙辰	3	34b
			7.18	己未	3	36b
			7.21	壬戌	3	39b
			7.22	癸亥	3	39b
			8.8	己卯	3	45a
			8.20	辛卯	3	52a
			8.23	甲午	3	53a
			8.26	丁酉	3	55b
			8.27	戊戌	3	62a
			8.28	己亥	3	64a
			8.29	庚子	3	70a
			9.1	辛丑	4	1a
			9.2	壬寅	4	3b

Chungjong	2	1507	9.6	丙午	4	7b
			9.7	丁未	4	8a
			9.19	己未	4	17b
			9.20	庚申	4	17b
			10.2	壬申	4	27a
			10.6	丙子	4	28a
			11.1	庚子	4	37a
			11.22	辛酉	4	47a
			11.24	癸亥	4	49b
			11.30	己巳	4	53a
			12.18	丁亥	4	63a
			12.26	乙未	4	69b
	3	1508	1.5	癸卯	5	2a
			1.26	甲子	5	14b
			1.30	戊辰	5	18a
			2.3	辛未	5	21a
			2.17	乙酉	5	28a
			2.19	丁亥	5	29b
			2.21	己丑	5	30b
			2.24	壬辰	5	32a
			3.1	戊戌	5	36b
			4.1	戊辰	5	50a
			4.7	甲戌	5	51b
			4.23	庚寅	5	58b
			4.26	癸巳	5	62b
			5.23	庚申	6	10b
			6.6	壬申	6	18a
			6.11	丁丑	6	20a
			6.23	己丑	6	24a
			6.25	辛卯	6	25b

Chungjong	3	1508	7.14	庚戌	6	32b
			7.17	癸丑	6	35a
			7.22	戊午	6	40b
			7.26	壬戌	6	42b
			7.28	甲子	6	43b
			8.7	壬申	6	47b
			8.21	丙戌	6	51b
			9.6	辛丑	6	55a
			10.8	壬申	7	2b
	4	1509	1.23	丙辰	7	56a
			3.21	癸丑	8	10b
			6.1	辛酉	8	46b
			6.10	庚午	8	50b
			6.11	辛未	8	51a
			6.13	癸酉	8	51b
			7.1	辛卯	8	55a
			7.9	己亥	8	61a
			8.5	乙丑	9	3a
			i9.16	乙亥	9	37a
			i9.17	丙子	9	40a
			i9.18	丁丑	9	41a
			i9.27	丙戌	9	46a
			10.20	戊申	9	58b
			11.4	壬戌	10	2a
			11.11	己巳	10	8a
	5	1510	3.6	辛酉	10	55b
			10.18	辛丑	12	35a
			10.19	壬寅	12	35a
			10.21	甲辰	12	35b
			12.21	癸卯	12	63b

Chungjong	6	1511	3.8	戊午	13	27b
			3.12	壬戌	13	28a
			3.14	甲子	13	33a
			4.11	庚寅	13	42a
			4.24	癸卯	13	47a
			5.4	癸丑	13	52a
			5.10	己未	13	56b
			5.15	甲子	13	60b
			6.2	庚辰	14	1a
			6.4	壬午	14	2a
			6.5	癸未	14	3b
			6.12	庚寅	14	5b
			7.4	壬子	14	14b
			7.5	癸丑	14	15a
			7.18	丙寅	14	17a
			8.19	丙申	14	21a
			8.26	癸卯	14	23a
			10.11	戊子	14	32a
			10.21	戊戌	14	40a
			11.1	丁未	14	45a
			11.24	庚午	14	48a
	7	1512	6.15	丁巳	16	22b
			10.7	丁未	17	3b
			11.22	壬辰	17	17a
			11.26	丙申	17	22a
	8	1513	3.2	辛未	18	1b

Chungjong	8	1513	4.2	庚子	18	14a
			7.27	癸巳	18	45b
			8.20	乙卯	18	54a
			9.21	丙戌	18	62b
			10.7	辛丑	19	3a
			10.22	丙辰	19	11a
			10.24	戊午	19	24b
			11.12	丙子	19	38a
	9	1514	1.16	庚辰	19	56a
			2.14	戊申	20	6b
			2.22	丙辰	20	10a
			4.17	庚戌	20	23b
			4.19	壬子	20	24a
			5.28	庚寅	20	31a
			6.4	乙未	20	32a
			6.8	己亥	20	32b
			6.18	己酉	20	34b
			6.19	庚戌	20	35b
			6.23	甲寅	20	37a
			7.15	丙子	20	41b
			7.16	丁丑	20	41b
			9.28	丁亥	20	60b
			10.27	丙辰	21	17a
			11.2	庚申	21	17b
			11.12	庚午	21	19a
			11.16	甲戌	21	22a
			11.24	壬午	21	24a
			12.11	己亥	21	32a
			12.21	己酉	21	35b

Chungjong	10	1515	2.25	癸丑	21	61a
			3.2	己未	21	63a
			6.8	癸亥	22	28a
			6.28	癸未	22	41a
			8.8	壬戌	22	53b
			8.11	乙丑	22	58a
			8.12	丙寅	22	59a
			8.22	丙子	22	65a
			8.23	丁丑	22	65b
			8.26	庚辰	22	66b
			8.29	癸未	22	68b
			9.4	丁亥	23	2b
			9.5	戊子	23	4a
			11.20	壬寅	23	34b
			11.22	甲辰	23	35a
			11.27	己酉	23	36b
			11.28	庚戌	23	38a
			12.3	乙卯	23	42b
			12.6	戊午	23	46b
	11	1516	1.5	丁亥	23	52b
			1.14	丙申	23	59a
			1.23	乙巳	23	64a
			3.6	丁亥	24	19b
			3.8	己丑	24	20b
			3.28	己酉	24	29b
			5.8	戊子	25	3b
			5.19	己亥	25	19a
			5.30	庚戌	25	33b

Chungjong	11	1516	6.3	癸丑	25	44a
			6.19	己巳	25	54a
			6.28	戊寅	25	56b
			7.15	甲午	25	67a
			10.12	庚申	26	36b
			10.16	甲子	26	37b
			11.13	庚寅	26	63b
			11.29	丙午	26	72b
			12.8	甲寅	27	4a
			12.10	丙辰	27	4b
			12.12	戊午	27	6a
	12	1517	1.19	乙未	27	23a
			1.21	丁酉	27	30b
			1.22	戊戌	27	30b
			2.1	丁未	27	33a
			2.3	己酉	27	34a
			2.21	丁卯	27	37b
			2.26	壬申	27	39b
			3.14	己丑	27	47b
			3.24	己亥	27	51a
			5.15	己丑	28	5a
			5.28	壬寅	28	8a
			6.30	甲戌	28	23a
			7.6	庚辰	28	27a
			7.7	辛巳	28	28a
			7.22	丙申	28	38b
			7.26	庚子	28	46a
			7.28	壬寅	28	52b

Chungjong	12	1517	8.3	丙午	29	4b
			8.4	丁未	29	6a
			8.5	戊申	29	6b
			8.7	庚戌	29	13a
			8.8	辛亥	29	15a
			8.9	壬子	29	18a
			8.11	甲寅	29	19b
			8.12	乙卯	29	20a
			8.16	己未	29	25a
			8.18	辛酉	29	28a
			8.20	癸亥	29	33a
			8.21	甲子	29	37a
			8.22	乙丑	29	41a
			8.24	丁卯	29	44a
			8.27	庚午	29	47a
			8.28	辛未	29	49a
			8.30	癸酉	29	52a
			9.9	壬午	29	55b
			9.12	乙酉	29	55b
			9.17	庚寅	29	57b
			9.24	丁酉	29	61b
			9.29	壬寅	29	63a
			10.8	辛亥	30	5a
			10.10	壬子	30	5b*
			10.19	辛酉	30	9b
			10.20	壬戌	30	14a
			10.22	甲子	30	18b
			10.23	乙丑	30	18b
			10.26	戊辰	30	24a
			10.27	己巳	30	24b
			10.30	壬申	30	28a
			11.4	丙子	30	32b
			11.18	庚寅	30	50a

*CSS erroneously gives this date as the 9th and continues to thus wrongly convert all subsequent tenth month dates.

Chungjong	12	1517	11.21	癸巳	30	54a
			11.22	甲午	30	54b
			12.30	辛未	31	19b
			i12.13	甲申	31	29b
			i12.26	丁酉	31	40a
			i12.27	戊戌	31	41a
	13	1518	1.4	甲辰	31	42a
			1.5	乙巳	31	44a
			1.10	庚戌	31	46a
			1.12	壬子	31	47b
			1.14	甲寅	31	49a
			1.15	乙卯	31	51b
			1.23	癸亥	31	58b
			2.8	丁丑	32	4b
			2.26	乙未	32	14b
			3.5	甲辰	32	21a
			3.8	丁未	32	24a
			3.11	庚戌	32	27a
			3.12	辛亥	32	29a
			3.13	壬子	32	31b
			3.18	丁巳	32	34a
			3.22	辛酉	32	35b
			3.26	乙丑	32	38a
			3.28	丁卯	32	42a
			4.6	甲戌	32	49a
			4.8	丙子	32	49b
			4.17	乙酉	32	53a
			4.19	丁亥	32	56b
			4.22	庚寅	32	59b
			4.25	癸巳	32	62b
			4.26	甲午	32	64b

Chungjong	13	1518	5.2	庚子	33	1a
			5.5	癸卯	33	4a
			5.7	乙巳	33	4b
			5.11	己酉	33	7b
			5.14	壬子	33	9a
			5.15	癸丑	33	10b
			5.16	甲寅	33	13a
			5.17	乙卯	33	18a
			5.18	丙辰	33	22a
			5.20	戊午	33	26b
			5.21	己未	33	27b*
			5.22	庚申	33	30a
			5.27	乙丑	33	34a
			5.30	戊辰	33	36b
			6.1	己巳	33	39a
			6.5	癸酉	33	46a
			6.8	丙子	33	48b
			6.21	己丑	33	56b
			7.11	戊申	34	5a
			7.12	己酉	34	8b
			7.15	壬子	34	11b
			7.18	乙卯	34	13b
			7.19	丙辰	34	14a
			7.21	戊午	34	15a
			7.27	甲子	34	19a
			8.3	庚午	34	24a
			8.16	癸未	34	32a
			8.21	戊子	34	35b
			8.22	己丑	34	36b
			8.30	丁酉	34	39a
			9.1	戊戌	34	40a
			9.2	己亥	34	42a

Sillok erroneously has 乙未 .

Chungjong	13	1518	9.5	壬寅	34	43b
			9.14	辛亥	34	45a
			10.23	己丑	34	58a
			11.21	丁巳	34	72b
			12.1	丙寅	35	1a
			12.7	壬申	35	2a
			12.9	甲戌	35	2b
			12.13	戊寅	35	4b
			12.17	壬午	35	6a
			12.18	癸未	35	7a
			12.26	辛卯	35	9b
	14	1519	1.23	戊午	35	20a
			2.6	庚午	35	24a
			2.7	辛未	35	24a
			2.8	壬申	35	24a
			2.11	乙亥	35	26b
			2.18	壬午	35	30b
			2.29	癸巳	35	32b
			3.2	乙未	35	36a
			3.3	丙申	35	38b
			3.4	丁酉	35	40a
			3.15	戊申	35	47b
			4.5	戊辰	35	57a
			4.7	庚午	35	58b
			4.9	壬申	35	62b
			4.13	丙子	35	65a
			4.17	庚辰	35	65b
			4.20	癸未	35	69a
			4.29	壬辰	35	75b
			5.6	戊戌	36	3b
			5.11	癸卯	36	5a

Chungjong	14	1519	5.16	戊申	36	7b
			5.17	己酉	36	7b
			5.18	庚戌	36	8a
			5.19	辛亥	36	8a
			5.20	壬子	36	9b
			6.6	戊辰	36	16b
			6.8	庚午	36	18a
			7.18	己酉	36	46b
			7.30	辛酉	36	54a
			8.10	辛未	36	57a
			9.24	乙卯	36	73b
			10.6	丙寅	37	2a
			10.10	庚午	37	3a
			10.17	丁丑	37	4b
			10.25	乙酉	37	6a
			11.1	辛卯	37	8a*
			11.3	癸巳	37	9a
			11.5	乙未	37	10a
			11.13	癸卯	37	14b
			11.15	乙巳	37	15a
			11.16	丙午	37	16b
			11.17	丁未	37	22b
			11.18	戊申	37	26a
			11.19	己酉	37	30b
			11.20	庚戌	37	31a
			11.21	辛亥	37	31b
			11.25	乙卯	37	33b
			11.26	丙辰	37	33b
			11.29	己未	37	34a
			11.30	庚申	37	37b
			12.2	壬戌	37	38b
			12.3	癸亥	37	40b

Sillok erroneously has 辛酉.

Chungjong	14	1519	12.8	戊辰	37	47a
			12.10	庚午	37	48a
			12.11	辛未	37	51a
			12.14	甲戌	37	54a
			12.16	丙子	37	59a
			12.18	戊寅	37	66a
			12.27	丁亥	37	72a
			12.28	戊子	37	72a
	15	1520	1.4	癸巳	38	2a
			1.6	乙未	38	4a
			1.11	庚子	38	6a
			1.13	壬寅	38	10b
			1.14	癸卯	38	11b
			1.17	丙午	38	14b
			1.21	庚戌	38	18a
			1.24	癸丑	38	20b
			2.4	癸亥	38	25a
			2.20	己卯	38	33a
			2.28	丁亥	38	39b
			3.21	己酉	38	57b
			3.22	庚戌	38	60b
			3.27	乙卯	38	64a
			4.16	癸酉	39	13b
			4.26	癸未	39	26a
			5.12	己亥	39	39a
			5.21	戊申	39	42a
			5.25	壬子	39	43a
			5.28	乙卯	39	44b
			6.3	己未	39	46b
			6.17	癸酉	39	57a

Chungjong	15	1520	8.7	壬戌	40	10a
			8.13	戊辰	40	12a
			8.20	乙亥	40	14b
	16	1521	5.22	癸酉	42	13b
			10.11	己丑	43	3b
			10.17	乙未	43	17a
			10.20	戊戌	43	22a
			10.29	丁未	43	32a
			10.30	戊申	43	34b
			11.5	癸丑	43	37a
			12.12	庚寅	43	45a
	17	1522	12.14	丙戌	46	38a
	18	1523	1.25	丁卯	46	55a
			3.10	辛亥	47	24a
			12.11	丁未	49	50b
	22	1527	6.3	戊申	59	13b
	25	1530	4.23	壬午	68	14a
	26	1531	2.25	庚辰	70	23b
	28	1533	9.8	丁未	76	2b
			9.12	辛亥	76	3a
			9.15	甲寅	76	6a
	29	1534	7.8	癸酉	77	44a
Injong	1	1545	4.17	己酉	2	32b
			6.29	庚申	2	75b

Myŏngjong		1545	8.1	辛卯	1	34a
			8.2	壬辰	1	36a
			9.1	辛酉	2	1a
			10.10	己亥	2	61b
			11.24	癸未	2	98a
	5	1550	1.17	壬午	10	2a
	10	1555	5.16	己酉	18	33b
			6.16	己卯	18	63b
Sŏnjo		1567	12.23	癸卯	1	20a
	1	1568	9.21	丁卯	2	22a
			10.9	甲申	2	24a
	19	1586	9.7	戊戌	*	
	22	1589	10.2	丙子	23	15a
			12.16	己丑	23	28b
Kwanghaegun	2	1610	9.4	丙午	33	2a#
Sukchong	24	1698	11.6	丁丑	32B	23b

---

*CSS cites only a non-Sillok source for the events of this date.

#This is the Sillok location of 1610.9.5, the date under which the account of the previous day's enshrinement is carried.

NOTES

Abbreviations Used in the Notes

CJJ	*Chōsen jinmei jisho*
OCG	Office of the Censor-General
OIG	Office of the Inspector-General
OSC	Office of Special Counselors
Sillok	*Chosŏn wangjo sillok*
YK	Yi Kŭng-ik, *Yŏllyŏsil kisul*

I. *The Setting*

1. The factual data presented in the following sketch of the history and institutions of the early Yi dynasty, unless otherwise attributed, are drawn from three modern survey histories of Korea: *Kuksa taegwan*, by Yi Pyŏng-do; *Kuksa kaeron*, by Han U-gŭn and Kim Ch'ŏl-chun; and *Kuksa kaesŏl*, by the Seoul National University Society for the Study of Korean History. Verification and clarification of these data have been sought, largely, in the *Kyŏngguk taejŏn* and *Chōsen shi* (Keijō, 1932-1940).

2. The *kyŏl* is a complicated unit of measurement, and I cannot define it satisfactorily. In effect, it was a unit of area calculated in terms of the tax assessment on a predicted crop yield. Thus the size of a "one *kyŏl*" field would vary with such factors as the quality of the land, and, needless to say, the definition of the unit also varied somewhat in different periods of the Yi dynasty. In his dictionary, Gale defines *kyŏl* as "a numerative of tax payments—100 coolie loads." Tentatively, I would estimate that a typical *kyŏl* unit meant, at this time, something on the order of half an acre of land.

    The magnitude of the land grants given to Merit Subjects may be better appreciated by comparison with the scale of payments to office holders. The position of Chief State Councillor (Senior First Rank) carried with it an income of 110 *kyŏl*, while the holder of a Ninth Rank post received 10 *kyŏl* (see *Kyŏngguk taejŏn* 182-185). To be sure, this so-called "post land" was not the only perquisite of office.

    In a doctoral dissertation on Yi land tenure completed at Harvard in 1973 ("Land Tenure and the Agrarian Economy in Yi Dynasty Korea: 1600-1800") Susan S. Shin accepts a figure of approximately 2 1/4 acres to one *kyŏl* of the most fertile category of land in the early Yi dynasty.

3. See the photographic reproduction of the warrant of merit enrollment issued to one such Minor Merit Subject, at *Chōsen shi*, series 4, 1.118 opp.

4. I have found no evidence that a Minor Merit Subject roster was drawn up on this occasion.

5. The T'aejong Merit Subjects (*chwamyŏng kongsin*) were rewarded on a slightly reduced scale. Those in Class One received 150 *kyŏl* of land and 13 slaves, those in Class Two 100 *kyŏl* and 10 slaves, those in Class Three 80 *kyŏl* and 8 slaves, and those in Class Four 60 *kyŏl* and 6 slaves (1401.1.15 S). Again there seem to have been no Minor Merit Subjects.

6. Mid-Koryŏ military strongmen had protected themselves and their interests by maintaining large retinues of armed supporters. This practice had continued and in the first years of the Yi such small private armies were used by T'aejo's sons in their fratricidal struggles for the throne. King T'aejong had made use of this device in achieving power himself and he was wise and strong enough to ensure that the throne would be secure in future from such a threat.

7. The great reverence accorded these six men throughout the remainder of the dynasty's history can only be explained in terms of Chosŏn's increasing commitment to abstract Confucian morality. Inevitably, a body of folk-lore grew up around the history of the period and fact soon came to be colored by fancy. Less than a century after Sejo seized the throne, the *Kosa ch'waryo* was first compiled. This is a selective encyclopedia that attempts to provide basic data on important events in the relations of the Yi with China and Japan and on major aspects of domestic practice. Under one of its headings it lists the Merit Subject groups created from the beginning of the dynasty to the time of writing, giving the date, the number of men enrolled for merit, and the reason for each roster. But in the case of the Sejo-Enthronement Merit Subjects, after correctly assigning the roster to 1455, the *Kosa ch'waryo* records that the reason for the roster was to reward merit in crushing the plot of the Six Martyred Subjects. The plot, of course, occurred a year later and, in fact, one of the Six Martyred Subjects, Sŏng Sam-mun, had been enrolled both as a Sejo-Usurpation and as a Sejo-Enthronement Merit Subject. Whether or not the *Kosa ch'waryo* is the source of the error, it is repeated in reputable modern sources (for example, *K'ŭn sajŏn* 2779, *Chōsengo jiten* 756).

8. Actually, the temple name "Tanjong" was bestowed only after some 240 years had passed, in 1698 (11.6).

9. The rewards of land and slaves given to these Merit Subjects were somewhat less than the previous norm (see 1467.9.20, 11.2 S). There do not appear to have been any Minor Merit Subjects enrolled on this occasion.

10. The data in this paragraph were gathered in a preliminary investigation based on the listings of High State Councillors for each reign given in the *YK*. Obituary entries in the *Chōsen shi* were used to supplement the information of *YK*.

11. The information in these paragraphs is drawn from Suematsu Yasukazu, "Chōsen Giseifu kō," *Chōsen gakuhō* 9:12-26(1956), a detailed study, based on the *Sillok* materials, of the development of the State Council institution in the early Yi dynasty. Suematsu concludes that Chungjong's restoration of the *sŏsa* power to the State Council proved meaningless (p. 35); my own study of the period tends to confirm this view.

12. See *Kyŏngguk taejŏn* 52.

13. Ibid., pp. 112-132.

14. The statistics given in these paragraphs have been derived from an analysis of those who passed the final civil examination under the Yi, as listed in an appendix to the *CJJ*. This listing is based on comprehensive examination rosters (*pangmok*), which cover the entirety of the Yi dynasty. Since the *CJJ* rearranged the purely chronological order of the original to a listing by surname groups (chronological within each surname group), it was necessary for statistical purposes to reconstruct the original arrangement. The fidelity of this reconstruction was checked against information to be found in the *Chōsen shi* on the number who passed each examination.

II. *The Purge of 1498*

1. My discussion of events in the years 1477-1497 owes a heavy debt to the monograph, "Chōsen Seisō jidai no shin-kyū tairitsu," by Sin Sŏk-ho in *Kindai Chōsen shi kenkyū* (Keijō, 1944). The course that I have followed through the political turbulence of these years is very largely the one charted by Sin. In Sin's study, however, I found enough instances of incomplete documentation and of factual or textual inaccuracy to warrant a thorough effort to verify the descriptive statements he makes. Accordingly, I have examined the originals of sources that Sin cites specifically (very largely the *Sillok*) and have endeavored as well to locate the materials upon which Sin drew in making statements unsupported by explicit designation of authority. In the pages which follow, therefore, I nowhere cite Sin but instead provide reference to pertinent original sources. The reader is advised, however, to refer to the Sin monograph for more detailed treatment of many of the events described below.

2. Hyŏn Sŏk-kyu's five subordinates were Second Royal Secretary Yi Kŭk-ki, Third Royal Secretary Im Sa-hong, Fourth Royal Secretary Son Sun-hyo, Fifth Royal Secretary Han Han (brother-in-law of one of the plaintiffs), and Sixth Royal Secretary Hong Kwi-dal. Led by Hong, these officials pointed out that the plaintiffs could not have known marriage formalities had been performed, and they urged accordingly that charges against the plaintiffs be dropped (1477.7.8 S, 7.9 S).

3. Hyŏn Sŏk-kyu was related by marriage to the royal house (his wife was a granddaughter of a brother of Sejong), was renowned for literary talent and for integrity, and had rendered noteworthy service in penal administration. He enjoyed, therefore, Sŏngjong's esteem and trust.

4. The other Royal Secretary in office at the outset of this dispute, Yi Kŭk-ki, had been appointed a provincial governor two days before (1477.8.15).

5. The orthodox view of both Wang An-shih, the great Northern Sung reformer, and of Lu Ch'i, a confidante of the T'ang emperor Te Tsung, is that they gained the trust of the monarchs they served through guile and wielded power arbitrarily in ways harmful to the state.

6. The recommendation of the State Tribunal was that Kim Ŏn-sin be punished by one hundred strokes and three years banishment, which the king at first declared to be too mild. General outcry against such an infringement of the freedom of remonstrance, however, soon persuaded Sŏngjong to restore Kim to his post. No action was initiated against Yu Cha-gwang, presumably because of his status as a Merit Subject.

7. Im Sa-hong had just been named Second Royal Secretary (1477.8.15) when Sŏngjong effected his wholesale transfer of Royal Secretariat personnel, at which time Im became Censor-General (1477.8.17). In the following year, Im was appointed First Royal Secretary from Personnel Third Minister (1478.4.8).

8. The daughter of Han Myŏng-hoe was Sŏngjong's first queen. From her death in 1474 to the investiture of a successor queen (daughter of Yun Ho) in 1480, the so-called Deposed Lady Yun (mother of Yŏnsangun) was queen in all but formal title.

9. *Kuŏn:* a decree normally issued following a natural calamity or unusual natural phenomenon, inviting written advice from anyone in the official class on what steps to take to appease the forces of Heaven; in traditional concept, responses to such an appeal, no matter how distasteful or extreme their contents, were not to entail the risk of penal action against the writer.

10. At one point the Second Inspector had protested that aged military officers ought not be permitted to participate in the banquet, but Sŏngjong had rejected this view (1478.3.9).

11. Im Sa-hong was an uncle of Yi Sim-wŏn: Yi's father and Im's wife were brother and sister, great-grandchildren of T'aejong.

12. In his interview with the king, Yi Sim-wŏn alleged merely that Im Sa-hong had prevailed upon a confidante in the Censorate to dupe his colleagues into attacking Hyŏn Sŏk-kyu. This, said Yi Sim-wŏn, he had heard from P'yo Yŏn-mal. In the course of the inquiry that followed, it developed, in sum, that Im's tool in the Censorate had been the then Second Censor Pak Hyo-wŏn, that Im also had incited Kim Ŏn-sin and (through Kim) Yu Cha-gwang to attack Hyŏn, and that P'yo Yŏn-mal's source of information was the Fourth Censor of the time, Kim Maeng-sŏng (1478.4.29 S, 4.30 S).

13. The State Tribunal recommendation called for beheading of Im Sa-hong, Yu Cha-gwang, Pak Hyo-wŏn, and Kim Ŏn-sin, as well as enslavement of their wives and sons and confiscation of their properties. The king, however, overriding the objections of the Censorate (voiced, too, by such elder statesmen as Han Myŏng-hoe), declared his intent to mitigate the death penalties of Im and the others to distant banishment and debarment from public office for life. Presently, moved by the tearful appeals of Yejong's daughter and members of the distaff side of his own household, Sŏngjong acted further to commute to a fine the beating due Im. Yu Cha-gwang escaped the rod by reason of his Merit Subject status which, however, he now lost (1478.5.6, 5.7, 5.8).

14. A week or so after this punishment was meted out to Yi Sim-wŏn, Sŏngjong recalled Im Sa-hong from banishment, citing in answer to Censorate protest the grave illness of Im's daughter-in-law, Princess Hyŏnsuk (1478.9.17 S). Continuing Censorate concern persuaded the king to promise to send Im back to banishment after the recovery of the princess, and this eventually was done (1478.9.19 S, 10.7 S, 12.10). Meanwhile, Censorate officials had made the invidious comparison between the favored treatment accorded Im Sa-hong and the punishment of Yi Sim-wŏn, and so the king, with the expressed approval of No Sa-sin, ordered Yi released (1478.10.29 S). But two years later, when Yi Sim-wŏn's father charged his son with disobedience and unfilial conduct, Sŏngjong somewhat reluctantly heeded the counsel of his highest officials and banished Yi again (1480.12.16 S). The OSC argued that Yi Sim-wŏn's father had bowed to the demands of *his* father (Im Sa-hong's father-in-law), who still harbored rancor over Yi Sim-wŏn's role in the 1478 Case, but to no avail (1480.12.18 S).

15. Yu Cha-gwang, Kim Ŏn-sin, and Pak Hyo-wŏn were released at the same time as Im Sa-hong (1480.11.14 S); perhaps not entirely by coincidence this occurred but two days after the death of Hyŏn Sŏk-kyu (1480.11.12), who had risen by then to Seventh State Councillor. Office warrants were returned to Yu Cha-gwang in 1482 (7.22), but were withheld from Kim Ŏn-sin and Pak Hyo-wŏn until the date four years later when Im Sa-hong got his back (1486.3.6 S). I have been unable to determine when Yi Sim-wŏn was released from banishment, but in 1485 (1.27) he and Yu Cha-gwang were ordered requalified for office. Due to Censorate and other protest, however, Sŏngjong quickly rescinded this order as it affected Yi (1485.2.2). And even after Im Sa-hong had been appointed once more to government position, Sŏngjong refused to act on a plea from a son of Yi Sim-wŏn to requalify his father for office (1488.12.15 S).

16. It is recorded that the king ordered judicial proceedings instituted against Im Sa-hong at this time, in consequence of the OIG charge that he had composed the text of his son's protest (1488.10.2). But obviously, in view of the appointment to office Im was shortly to receive, nothing could have come of this. Sŏngjong, however, had long since ordered that the entire schedule of preliminary civil examinations be repeated in the following spring (1488.9.4).

17. Im Wŏn-jun's reward for his meritorious service as a physician was promotion for himself and the "enrollment for employment of his eldest legitimate son" (1488.11.15 S).

18. Such instances may be found at 1489.11.14; 1490.9.5; 1492.2.27; 1497.3.16, 6.15, 6.16, 6.28, 7.30.

19. The term tax conversion (*pangnap*) refers to the practice of exacting payment of local tribute levies in cash (at an inflated price) instead of in the stipulated locally produced commodities. This practice was prohibited in the National Code (*Kyŏngguk taejŏn* 481-482).

20. After more than a week of daily Censorate outcries on the subject of Yun Ŭl-lo's appointment, the king was moved to remark: "By and large when a kinsman of the queen obtains an appointment in the government, the Censorate invariably construes this as truckling to the inner [palace (to the queen and queen-mother)] and impeach the appointee. How is it that [only] among the Censorate officials there is none with a record of past misdemeanors? If a past error is to be subject to [unlimited] later indictment, there will be no personnel at all [left in the government]" (1493.7.6).

21. The essential facts of the case are set forth at 1494.6.11 S.

22. The Censorate officials were more than usually adamant in opposition to naming Pak to the Royal Secretariat and repeatedly sought to resign in the face of the king's rejection of their pleas. The State Council from the outset had joined in disapproving the appointment, and in the end it was in deference to a request by Chief State Councillor Yun P'il-sang and Second State Councillor No Sa-sin that Pak was transferred to Third Minister of Works (1492.8.8, 8.30, 9.4, 9.8, 9.10). Pak Wŏn-jong was but twenty-five years old at this time.

23. Sŏngjong brusquely dismissed this attempt by the Censorate to fasten responsibility for a slave's act upon the master, remarking that "these words of yours are laughable" (1493.9.2 S).

24. Two brief footnotes may be appended to the narrative of the Sin Su-gŭn episodes. The first is that the appointment of Sin to Fourth Royal Secretary late in Sŏngjong's reign evoked, apparently, no protest, although the simultaneous appointment of Pak Wŏn-jong to Sixth Royal Secretary was roundly attacked as noted (1492.8.7). The other is that on the very day of Sin's appointment to First Royal Secretary, Yŏnsangun instructed that "young men fond of creating disturbances are not to be appointed to the Censorate or OSC" (1497.6.14). (Yŏnsangun had just relieved a Censorate roster which had long and vigorously opposed promotions awarded Im Sa-hong and others, and the OSC had protested the king's action; 1497.6.1, 6.2, 6.6, 6.13). But the new Censorate rushed immediately to the defense of its predecessor and went on to attack Sin Su-gŭn's appointment (1497.6.15).

25. After considerable further ado, the king agreed to drop charges against Ch'oe Kwan and then permitted P'yo Yŏn-mal to resume his post (1491.6.22 S to 6.24 S)

26. *Kyŏngguk taejŏn* 296.

27. The protest of the two queen mothers laid stress on abuses in the enforcement of the anti-monk measures and made a point of asking for no more than strict observance of the provisions of the National Code. Their arguments necessarily turned on the harsh blows dealt the monkish profession: they found it possible to claim that no monks remained to staff the Vow Halls consecrated to preceding monarchs and also that the mountain fastnesses, now emptied of monks, had become the lairs of brigands.

28. Sŏngjong had first ordered Yi Mok barred from the examinations, but the censoring organs protested afresh on the basis that such a step would inhibit the freedom of remonstrance (1492.12.10). Among the other students who figured prominently in this incident were Sim Sun-mun, Cho Wŏn-gi, Yi Yun-t'ak, Nam Kon, and Kwŏn Min-su (1492.12.4, 12.8).

29. The term used in the *Sillok* is *sŏlchae,* "to establish a hall"; *chae* here is an abbreviation for *suryuk-chae* (*shui-liu-chai*).

30. At the same time, Sixth Counselor Son Chu adamantly refused to obey a royal command to compose texts to accompany the Buddhist rites, on the ground of his personal opposition and that of his office to the proposed practices. And again the king followed No Sa-sin's advice to have the Royal Secretariat undertake the urgent matter of these texts and to pass judgment on Son Chu later (1494.12.27 S, 12.28 S).

31. This was the third memorial in as many days presented by the National Academy students over the name of Cho Yu-hyŏng (1494.12.29, 1495.1.1, 1.2).

32. The banished students were Yi Mok, Chŏng Hŭi-ryang, and Yi Cha-hwa. It was not long before their punishment was mitigated to examination debarment, while the twenty-one who had been debarred were pardoned; Yŏnsangun took this action following requests by OSC and Censorate officials (1495.5.22). Presently, in accordance with the request of Fourth State Councillor Ŏ Se-gyŏm, these three also were pardoned (1495.8.25). Yi Mok and Chŏng Hŭi-ryang both passed the civil examination later in this same year (Yi Mok taking a first; 1495.11.6) and went on to become prominent victims of the Purge of 1498. Yi Cha-hwa passed in the next year and became a minor casualty of 1504.

      The twenty-one other students punished at this time offer an interesting study in diversity of future career. Kim Ch'ŏn-nyŏng died in the Purge of 1504 as did Im Sa-hong's son Im Hŭi-jae (who had been banished in 1498). Pak Kwang-yŏng suffered banishment in 1504, while Yun Wŏn, Yu Hŭi-jŏ, and Cho Yu-hyŏng all were minor victims of the same purge. Kim Su-gyŏng and Sŏng Mong-jŏng became Chungjong Merit Subjects. Sim Chŏng became an arch-villain of the Purge of 1519, and subsequent thereto was a High State Councillor. Sŏng Un also played the role of purger in 1519, while Yi Sŏng-dong was purged. Han Hyo-wŏn was a Chief State Councillor of the middle years of Chungjong's reign. Only five of the twenty-one later failed to pass the civil examination.

33. The Censorate memorial said: "When the Rites Board asked [about] establishing journey smoothing halls, then [No Sa-sin] actually regarded [establishing] them as proper and strongly endorsed it. When the National Academy students were ensnared in crime charges for justly rejecting Buddhism, then [No Sa-sin] said not one word to succor them." This was being unfair, for No, of the opinion that the students were innocent of malicious intent and simply were ignorant of proprieties, had urged that the charges against them be dropped (1495.1.24 S).

34. Ming envoys were then in Seoul, having brought the investiture rescripts for Yŏnsangun and his queen (1495.6.3). One of them (a eunuch of Korean birth) had incurred the abusive denunciation of the Censorate over a ritual question (1495.8.8). That Yŏnsangun was more concerned to curb the excesses of the Censorate than to redress the insult to the Ming envoy is indicated in the royal pronouncements of the time (e.g., 1495.8.8 S, 8.11 S).

35. No Sa-sin's title of enfeoffment heretofore had been simply Lord, his enrollments as a Merit Subject both having been in Class Three.

36. See 1497.8.2; 1497.8.6.

37. See 1497.8.2; 1498.2.13, 2.24, 4.18; 1498.4.30, 6.6.

38. See 1497.9.13, 10.2, 10.9; 1498.2.1.

39. See 1497.8.11; 1497.12.25, 12.26, 1498.2.1.

40. See 1497.11.20.

41. See 1498.6.13.

42. For example, when the Censorate criticized as excessive the promotions in rank conferred by the king on medical officers, and on the officialdom as a whole, in celebration of the birth of an heir, Yŏnsangun brusquely retorted: "You who speak like this are not subjects of mine. Though unpardonable, for the moment I will overlook your crime. Let there be nothing more said on the subject." (1497.12.25) Again, when the Censorate officials were stubbornly reluctant to acquiesce in a light sentence for a grasping Seoul merchant whom the king originally had wanted to absolve entirely, Yŏnsangun silenced them with these words:

> You hold to your opinions with glue-like tenacity. Though the matter be one that should be terminated, still it is not possible to render final judgment. Day after day in the palace swirls the din from the courtyard [where Censorate memorials were presented], in the government rises [the cacophony of] rejected remonstrance. This is not a seemly thing. From the time I ascended the throne there has not been a single day free from charge and confutation. My food is not sweet of taste, my sleep knows no tranquility. Already thus sore at heart, what shall prevent illness from developing? In your present memorializing your multitude of voices speak as one [making kingly] authority difficult to maintain The habit of subjects wringing victory [from their sovereign] has already hardened; the norm of concord between sovereign and subject has gradually died out. Thus it was that I deferred to your [earlier] memorials [but I will not do so now]. (1498.6.1 S)

43. Kim Il-son's most recent post of importance had been Third Censor, during which incumbency (late 1495) he had shown himself to be a highly vocal practitioner of the art of remonstrance. Transferred to the Board of Taxation as a Section Chief, he then suffered the death of his mother. He had now completed formal mourning and was nursing a cold at his home in Ch'ŏngdo, North Kyŏngsang. His tour as a Historian apparently occurred in the latter years of Sŏngjong's reign.

44. During this interlude, a Third Inspector urged that about a dozen recent appointments, mostly to minor posts, be rescinded and that the Board of Personnel be prosecuted for its bias in making them; the king refused (1498.7.6). The Censorate attacked four appointments to the post of Horse Assayer, citing the various grounds of nepotism, corruption and inexperience; the king removed only the one alleged to be inexperienced (1498.7.7). Still harking back to his endorsement of the jailing of the Censorate and his attitude in the Yun T'ang-no case, the Censorate levelled yet another attack against No Sa-sin; it was futile (1498.7.8 S). The Office of Special Counselors took advantage of recurrent earth tremors in Kyŏngsang province to urge the king to cease absenting himself from the Royal Lectures; again Yŏnsangun's response was in the negative (1498.7.8).

45. When the OSC and Office of Royal Decrees protested the king's personal perusal of *Sillok* raw material, Yŏnsangun handed them over to the State Tribunal on charges of trying to cover up the evidence of cliquism. But on the following day, stressing the magnanimity of his action, he released them (1498.7.13 S, 7.14 S).

46. She was the mother of the ill-fated King Tanjong (Nosan'gun). When Sejo banished his young nephew, he also reduced the status of Tanjong's mother to that of commoner and had her reburied away from the site of Munjong's tomb (1457.6.21, 6.26).

47. Hŏ Pan currently was Supernumerary Third Copyist in the Office of Diplomatic Correspondence. He was a nephew of Madame Kwŏn, a concubine of Tŏkchong (father of Sŏngjong and a son of Sejo; he did not reign).

48. Internal evidence indicates that both letters dated from two or more years earlier. Yi Mok had been a National Academy Librarian at the time and concurrently was participating in the *Sŏngjong Sillok* compilation work. Kwŏn O-bok had written from his post as a Local Magistrate, an appointment he had sought for filial reasons (1495.6.29). Neither Yi nor Kwŏn seem to have seen duty in the Censorate. Yi Mok's activities as a National Academy student, however, will be recalled, while Kwŏn had served as high as OSC Fifth Counselor.

49. Six prominent officials executed by Sejo when their plot to return Tanjong to the throne was exposed (1456.6.2).

50. The famous monk shown marked favor by Sejo.

51. Yi Ch'ong was a royal clansman, a great-grandson of T'aejong. Pak Kyŏng was an illegitimate son of a prominent yangban family; in the end no charges were pressed against him (1498.7.28). Yun Hyo-son and Sŏng Chung-ŏm both were then engaged in the compilation of the *Sŏngjong Sillok,* Yun in a supervisory position.

52. Kim Chong-jik was a man of Sŏnsan, North Kyŏngsang. He was first taught by his father, Kim Suk-cha, the leading disciple of Kil Chae who, rather than compromise with his principles, had refused to reenter public life after the downfall of the Koryŏ dynasty. Kil Chae, in turn, was the leading disciple of Chŏng Mong-ju, the prominent late Koryŏ official who came to be regarded as the father of Korean Neo-Confucianism. In 1459 Kim Chong-jik passed the civil examination but he was not importantly employed during Sejo's reign. In fact, in 1464 (8.6), he was dismissed from office for admonishing Sejo for being too eclectic in his approach to learning. Named a Sixth Counselor at the beginning of Sŏngjong's reign, in the course of some twenty years of on-and-off service he attained such major posts as First Royal Secretary and Minister of Punishments. Long a Deputy Director of the Office of the Royal Lectures, he was regarded with unusually high esteem by the monarch. Thus when he retired in 1491 due to illness, Sŏngjong gave him palanquin bearers for the journey home and also ordered the provincial authorities to provide food (1491.3.21, 1492.2.7). When Kim Chong-jik died in the following year (1492.8.19), he was widely mourned as the successor to the mantle of Korean Neo-Confucianist orthodoxy, as a brilliant literary talent, and as a model of temperance and probity. He was mourned in particular by a large body of disciples and one-time students or subordinates, a number of whom were ensconced in responsible positions in the central government at the time of his death.

53. Upon first reading Im Hŭi-jae's letter, Yŏnsangun remarked: "The father, Im Sa-hong, was barred from public office as an amoral man; is this man [the son] too of such a stripe? Let the father also be formally interrogated" (1498.7.14). This does not appear to have been done, however.

54. Cho Wi was the younger brother of Kim Chong-jik's wife. Cho had served as high as Second Minister of Taxation and currently was on an embassy to Ming (1498.4.11). Chŏng Sŏk-kyŏn, apparently, merely sponsored publication of Kim Chong-jik's literary collection in his official capacity as Governor of Chŏlla, where publication took place. In his deposition, Chŏng Sŏk-kyŏn claimed that he had seen merely the table of contents, not the text, and Yu Cha-gwang offered evidence that Chŏng was not a partisan of Kim Chong-jik (though he apparently was a disciple). Accordingly, Yŏnsangun stopped at discharging Chŏng from his post, which at this time probably was Second Minister of Personnel (1497.9.13, 1498.7.17 S, 7.19 S).

55. This is the date of the execution of Tanjong (1457.10.24).

56.   A number of other officials, including the OSC, took a view of Kim Chong-jik's crime a degree less grave than the consensus of high treason. Yŏnsangun found it possible to overlook this (1498.7.17 S).

57.   No Sa-sin protested that to do so would invite undue commotion. Citing the consequences of relentless punishment of cliquists in the Eastern Han, No urged that the present criminal proceedings not be permitted to ramify (1498.7.17).

58.   Many of these may legitimately be termed disciples, but some of them are noted to have been office colleagues of Kim Chong-jik, or merely to have referred questions of textual exegesis to him.

59.   Kwŏn Kyŏng-yu too was a disciple of Kim Chong-jik. He had been an OSC Fifth Counselor near the end of Sŏngjong's reign and in the first months of Yŏnsangun had served as a Local Magistrate (1495.2.28). He is not to be confused with his older brother Kwŏn Kyŏng-u (the character too is rather similar), who at the time of the purge was Second Minister of Taxation. Kwŏn Kyŏng-u was associated in his brother's guilt and was banished, but before long he won release (1499.2.18).

60.   The list that follows includes all those mentioned in the State Tribunal recommendations. It includes as well the two whose punishments had been determined earlier, and one (Cho Wi) against whom sentence subsequently was passed. Analysis reveals four main categories of purge involvement:
    (1) The former Censorate, identified by designation of post in the "Remarks" column;
    (2) Two men whose involvement is not clarified but probably was due to their participation with Kim Il-son in an OCG request in 1495 (12.30) to restore the tomb of Tanjong's mother; see 1499.1.24 S. (Yi Chu also participated in this request, which may account for Yŏnsangun increasing the severity of his sentence.) These are identified by "(?)" in the "Remarks" column;
    (3) Those involved by reason of acts incidental to official duties in the compilation of the *Sŏngjong Sillok,* identified by "(S)" in the "Remarks" column;
    (4) Those who owed their involvement to some connection, direct or remote, with Kim Chong-jik or Kim Il-son, indicated by absence of post designation or special symbol in the "Remarks" column.
Assignment to categories (3) and (4) is based in some cases on nebulous grounds or, where a man might fit into two or more categories, is perhaps arbitrary.
    Designation of sentences is abbreviated and so indicates only major degrees of severity.
    All sentences were pronounced on 1498.7.26, except where indicated by a different date in the "Remarks" column.
    An asterisk following the name indicates mention by Kim Il-son as a Kim Chong-jik disciple. It should be borne in mind that disciple status is claimed by biographers for a number of other figures of that day, including several on this list, and that twelve of those named by Kim Il-son were not punished.
    Date of civil examination final degree is appended as a rough gauge of age and of length of service in the government.

Name		Sentence	Remarks	Civil Examination
An	P'aeng-su	banishment	Fourth Inspector	1492
Cho	Hyŏng	"	Third Inspector	1485
Cho	Wi*	"	1498.9.11 S	1474
Chŏng	Hŭi-ryang	"	(S)	1495
Chŏng	Sŏk-kyŏn*	discharge	1498.7.19	1474
Chŏng	Sŭng-jo	banishment	1498.9.8; (S)	1494
Chŏng	Yŏ-ch'ang*	"		1490
Ch'oe	Pu*	"		1482

Name		Sentence	Remarks	Civil Examination
Han	Hun	banishment	1498.8.10; (?)	1494
Hong	Han	"	(S)	1485
Hŏ	Pan	execution		1498
Im	Hŭi-jae	banishment		1498
Kang	Hun	"	released 1498.8.1	1486
Kang	Kyŏm	"	(mitigated from execution)	1480
Kang	Kyŏng-sŏ	"	(S)	1477
Kang	Paek-chin*	"	1498.7.29	1477
Kim	Chong-jik	execution	1498.7.17 (posthumous)	1459
Kim	Chŏn*	discharge		1489
Kim	Il-son*	execution		1486
Kim	Koeng-p'il*	banishment		—
Kwŏn	Kyŏng-yu*	execution		1485
Kwŏn	O-bok*	"		1486
Min	Su-bok	banishment	Second Censor	1485
Pak	Han-ju*	"		1485
Pak	Kwŏn	"	Fourth Censor	1492
P'yo	Yŏn-mal*	"		1472
Sin	Chong-ho*	office warrants	(divested posthumously)	1480
Sin	Pog-ŭi	banishment	Fourth Inspector	1481
Son	Wŏl-lo	"	Third Censor	1477
Sŏng	Chung-ŏm	"	(S)	1494
Yi	Chong-jun	"		1485
Yi	Chu*	"	(increased in degree)	1488
Yi	Ch'ang-yun	"	Fourth Censor	1492
Yi	Ch'ong	"	royal clansman	—
Yi	Kye-maeng*	"	released 1498.7.28	1489
Yi	Mok	execution		1495
Yi	Su-gong	banishment	(S)	1488
Yi	Ŭi-mu	rod and corvee	(?)	1477
Yi	Wŏn*	banishment		1489
Yi	Yu-ch'ŏng	"	Second Inspector	1486
Yi	Yuk	office warrants	(divested posthumously); (S)	1464
Yu	Chŏng-su	banishment	Third Inspector	1483
Yu	Sun-jŏng*	(case in process)	(new appointment 1498.i11.8)	1487
Yun	Hyo-son	discharge	(S)	1453

61. No Sa-sin alone spoke out in opposition to some of the recommended sentences, pointing out the difference in degree between the writing of such a text as the "Lament for the Rightful Emperor" and the mere praising of it by others. Yŏnsangun brushed aside No's argument (1498.7.26 S).

62. These were, with their State Records Bureau posts as given in the presentation postface to the *Sŏngjong Sillok:* Deputy Director Ŏ Se-gyŏm and Second Deputy Directors Yi Kŭk-ton and Yu Sun, discharged; Second Deputy Director Hong Kwi-dal and Third Deputy Directors Cho Ik-chŏng, Hŏ Ch'im and An Ch'im, demoted. Yŏnsangun took this action on the ground, in brief, that they had not promptly reported to him the treasonous contents of the history drafts of Kim Il-son, Kwŏn O-bok, and Kwŏn Kyŏng-yu (the three executed by dismemberment), knowledge of which they had gained in the course of their duties (1498.7.19, 7.21, 7.26).

63. The authors of the drafts specified in this order were Kim Chong-jik, Kwŏn O-bok, Kim Il-son, and Kwŏn Kyŏng-yu.

64. These groups were linked with the recent purgees by the assertion that out of their practice of "assembling for loose discussion" had grown not only "the Kim Chong-jik evil clique," but the cliques of infamous repute in Chinese history as well (1498.8.10 S, 8.14 S, 8.16 S).

65. None of the students named in the original accusation appears to have had important family connections. Hong Sik is the most conspicuous among those implicated in the course of the proceedings; a brother of purge victim Hong Han, he had just been named Second Royal Secretary (1498.11.9). He had become involved in turn through his student son, Hong Se-p'il, who also was banished. Yi Tŭk-chŏn, a student at this time too (he passed the civil examination in 1504), and Classics Licentiate An Ch'ŏ-jung also suffered degrees of banishment.

66. This is the somewhat abbreviated version in Japanese paraphrase found in the *Chōsen shi.*

III. *The Purge of 1504*

1. Yun Ŭn-bo and several of his colleagues suffered mild punishment in the Purge of 1504 by reason of this anti-Yu Cha-gwang remonstrance (1505.2.8 S, 3.2 S, 4.6 S, 4.15 S).

2. The Censorate had called attention to these allegations of Sŏ Kŏ-jŏng in the course of the 1499 (1.22) effort against Yu but had failed to exploit the material at that time.

3. Cases in point may be found under the following dates: Yun T'ang-no – 1498.9.6; 1500.9.18, 9;27; 1504.1.6; Sin brothers – 1502.1.9, 1.13, 1.22, 1.30; 1502.9.28; 1502.11.27; Pak Wŏn-jong – 1502.6.16; 1502.9.16, 9.23; 1503.6.29; 1503.11.16, 11.23; 1503.12.25.

4. Quite the contrary. Early in his reign Yŏnsangun observed that some sovereigns of the past had been short-lived despite belief in Buddhism, while others had enjoyed long and prosperous reigns though not Buddhist believers. He had the OSC provide him with reference material on the subject, and we are told that, after reading about the unhappy circumstances of Liang Wu Ti's reign, Yŏnsangun ordered that Buddhism be suppressed and the way of Confucius promoted (1496.i3.30 S, 4.11 S).

5. See 1501.2.3.

6. See 1502.5.12.

7. See 1502.8.12. A major 1504 purge case grew out of this event. Salt had first been granted these two temples six years earlier, in accordance with a request from their monks conveyed via the Palace Supply Office. At the time, not only the censoring bodies but also the Royal Secretariat (and indeed, according to the record, the government in entirety) had attacked the award and asked punishment of Palace Supply Office personnel for the crime of memorializing the request directly to the king, i.e., for bypassing the normal government channels of communication. Although this incident continued to be the subject of remonstrance for some three months, Yŏnsangun did not give in (1496.1.1).

8. See 1502.6.3, 1503.3.1, 4.28.

9. See 1498.12.28.

10. See 1502.7.29.

11. See 1503.11.20; this remonstrance too is related to a 1504 purge case (see 1505.2.8 S).

12. Sŏng Chun had been named Commander-in-Chief of the western expedition (1499.5.9, 7.2).

13. Yŏnsangun, decidedly reluctant to call off the campaign, asked Sŏng Chun the obvious question — what accounted for his complete about-face in the matter. Sŏng was forced to admit that he simply had not been aware of the extent of the adverse supply situation (1500.1.22 S).

14. The Office of Fortifications apparently had been established the previous year, at the height of the border incidents. A number of isolated construction works already had been initiated and had drawn little fire from the Censorate (1499.7.11, 7.12, 8.7, 1500.2.9).

15. See 1503.4.28. The approach of the State Councillors stands in interesting contrast; on an earlier occasion they had asked that the hunting dogs kept in the palace not be permitted to run loose during court sessions (1501.5.6).

16. See 1502.2.16; 1503.11.6, 11.9, 11.10, 11.16, 11.20.

17. See 1502.2.5, 3.10, 4.20, 5.10, 8.30, 1503.2.19, 4.3, 5.5.

18. See 1499.9.12, 1500.10.27, 1501.1.30, 1502.3.10, 4.20, 5.10.

19. For example, when the king was urged to conduct in person certain state rituals, he replied: "That I have not yet done so is because the days are cold, and it is difficult to take a bath" (1501.12.25). Again, Yŏnsangun once cited the muggy weather as his reason for temporarily suspending the sessions of the Royal Lectures (1502.5.26).

20. Biographies of Hong Kwi-dal and Yi Se-jwa nowhere mention these events, no doubt because it would be impossible to construe them so as to reflect credit on either Hong or Yi. Perhaps it is because of this that historians have failed heretofore to date the inception of the Purge of 1504 from this incident. Accounts of the purge normally begin with the story of Yŏnsangun avenging the death of his mother (see below).

21. There are a number of instances in this purge where it is difficult, if not impossible, to obtain a clear picture of who was punished and who was not, and why; the record is simply incomplete. As an illustration of this problem, Yŏnsangun subsequently ordered punished all who had held Censorate or OSC posts from the date of Yi Se-jwa's crime (1504.3.14 S, 3.16 S, 3.17 S) and, in general, he beat and banished the Censorate officials and fined the OSC officials in lieu of the rod. But only five of the eight former Censorate officials who were named are specifically noted as having been banished (1504.3.18 S).

22. Yet, when Yi Se-jwa came to the palace upon his return from banishment to thank the king for his grace, Yŏnsangun presented him wine, saying: " 'This is the wine you spilled the other day.' Yi Se-jwa wept in gratitude" (1504.3.3 S).

23. When Yi Se-jwa was commanded to kill himself, the charge was added that he had failed to oppose vigorously the deposition of Lady Yun (1504.3.30 S). Strangely, the fact that in line of duty as Second Royal Secretary Yi had carried the poison to Yŏnsangun's mother in 1482 is mentioned for the first time rather

later and only in connection with punishment of the lower ranking official who accompanied Yi on this mission (1504.i4.26 S). One is led to conclude, therefore, that either Yŏnsangun was not yet aware of this or that he did not regard it as so serious an offense as the spilling of wine on his royal person.

Whatever the case, Yi Se-jwa was one of about a dozen victims of 1504 who suffered the full measure of posthumous indignities devised by the cruel and imaginative king. His corpse was beheaded and the head sent on display throughout the country (the king noted at this time that Yi had committed the final breach of showing anger to the royal poison-bearing messenger); the limbs were severed and gibbeted; the remains were denied burial; the bones were pulverized and scattered to the winds (1504.i4.20, 5.2, 8.17, 12.15). His house was razed, a pond dug on the site, and a stone inscribed with his crimes (1504.6.20; a blanket order already had been issued denying burial to those executed and requiring stone markers inscribed with their crimes, 1504.5.8). Laws or changes in the National Code for which he was responsible were expunged (1504.6.27); examination lists which he had certified as the responsible Minister of Rites were declared void (1504.11.24). And, finally, the king formally awarded him a title of revilement, "arch knave of *lèse majesté*" (1505.10.1).

Yi Se-jwa's father, Yi Kŭk-kam, was deleted from the merit roster; he had been a Minister of Punishments and Sejo-Enthronement Merit Subject (1504.i4.13). Subsequently the Merit Subject listing of his uncle, Yi Kŭk-ton, also was ordered expunged and the lands and slaves of his father and father's brothers confiscated (1504.5.10; this penalty applied additionally to Yi Kŭk-chŭng and Yi Kŭk-pae, it being assumed that such action already had been taken in the case of Yi Kŭk-kyun). Later, the surviving sons and grandsons of the five brothers were banished for life (1504.10.22).

In accordance with legal provisions governing cases of high treason, Yi Se-jwa's kin presently were ordered dealt with as follows: sons banished in harshest degree; wives, concubines, daughters, daughters-in-law, and grandsons enslaved; clansmen and members of families related by marriage then in office stripped of office warrants and the clansmen banished in harsh degree (1504.i4.13, i4.29, 5.15, 10.21). Before long, Yi Se-jwa's four sons were beheaded and a younger brother enslaved (1504.5.4, 7.6). This brother, Yi Se-gŏl, presently also was beheaded, the king having recalled the instigated refusal of his *kisaeng* concubine to play the harp at a palace banquet (1504.i4.27, 5.6). And Yŏnsangun even changed the name of another official surnamed Yi whose personal name contained the character "gŏl" (1504.5.9).

In the Purge of 1504 no further punishment appears to have been meted out to Hong Kwi-dal, except that his other sons were beaten and banished (1504.5.27, 6.16, 10.22) and additional kinsmen punished (1504.10.21).

24. Presently, across the board fines in lieu of beatings were levied on others found to have visited Yi Se-jwa. No and Kim fared less well because they had attempted to justify their visits on the ground that Yi Se-jwa's crime had not been one against the state. Yŏnsangun, however, interpreted these words as proof of a sympathetic attitude toward Yi (1504.3.17). No Kong-p'il was a son of No Sa-sin.

25. This was only the beginning of Yŏnsangun's revenge. The two concubines (Madame Chŏng and Madame Ŏm) and their offspring were stricken from the royal house roster; the daughters also were banished and their husbands divested of office warrants (1504.3.26). Then their parents (including the eighty-one-year-old father of one) and siblings all were beaten and banished and the property of both families confiscated (1504.3.27, 3.28). Later, the residences of the two concubines were ordered demolished and ponds dug on the sites, their remains denied burial and their bones pulverized and strewn (1504.6.27, 8.17, 12.15). The two sons of the one concubine were eventually executed (1505.6.15). Other concubines and female functionaries of the time adjudged by Yŏnsangun to bear a share of guilt were dealt with in one instance equally harshly, and in the others almost so (1504.4.23, 4.26, 5.1, 6.27, 8.17, 12.15).

26. At the end of the year, Yŏnsangun applied a favorite formula to this purge case — determining who had been the prime advocates of the noxious views presented by the group, in order to punish their greater guilt with especial severity. It was found that Kwŏn Tal-su had led the OSC and he was beheaded. But Kim Se-p'il, who

had filled the same role in the Censorate, managed to escape the death penalty and instead was beaten and enslaved in far banishment. The others were beaten again and banished in harsher degree (1504.10.8 S, 10.27 S, 10.28 S, 10.29 S, 12.2 S). Chŏng Sim, however, was let off merely with eighty strokes of the rod because of his relationship to the queen (1504.11.6. S).

27. Yi P'a had been a Fourth State Councillor under Sŏngjong. Subsequently his corpse was dismembered and publicly displayed, burial was denied, and the bones pulverized and scattered (1504.i4.20, 8.17, 12.15). Moreover, his house site, too, was converted to a pond and a stone tablet set up detailing his crime (1504.6.20). His father, Yi Kye-sun, a one-time OSC First Counselor and a Sejo-Usurpation and Sejo-Enthronement Merit Subject, was deleted from the former merit roster (1504.i4.13). His family and kin suffered alike with those of Yi Se-jwa (1504.i4.13, 7.6, 10.14).

28. These were:
Chŏng Ch'ang-son – a Sejo-Enthronement, Yejong, and Sŏngjong Merit Subject; a Chief State Councillor under Sejo and Sŏng jong.
Han Myŏng-hoe – a Sejo-Usurpation, Sejo-Enthronement, Yejong, and Sŏngjong Merit Subject; a Chief State Councillor under Sejo and Yejong; father-in-law of both Yejong and Sŏngjong.
Sim Hoe – a Sejo-Usurpation and Sŏngjong Merit Subject; grandson of a Second State Councillor and son of a Chief State Councillor, himself a Chief State Councillor under Sejo.
Chŏng In-ji – a Sejo-Usurpation, Sejo-Enthronement, Yejong, and Sŏngjong Merit Subject; a Chief State Councillor under Sejo.
Kim Sŭng-gyŏng – an Inspector-General and Second Minister of Rites under Sŏngjong.
        Subsequently the corpses of Chŏng Ch'ang-son, Han Myŏng-hoe, and Sim Hoe were beheaded and the heads gibbeted (1504.i4.20, 5.1, 5.11). Chŏng In-ji (who had died the year before the deposition and so had participated only in the preliminary discussions) and Kim Sŭng-gyŏng (who had been jailed briefly due to his staunch opposition to deposing Lady Yun) apparently suffered further only rather minor indignities (see 1504.4.22, 4.24).
        It should be noted that all concerned at the time, from High State Councillors down to National Academy students, had opposed Sŏngjong's desire to depose Lady Yun (see 1477.3.29, 1479.6.2, 6.5).

29. This sentence was recommended by high officials led by Second State Councillor Yu Sun; the Censorate's view as presented by Inspector-General Sŏng Se-myŏng contained the implication that the death penalty was favored (1504.4.18, 4.22). Presently, however, in accordance with a memorial of Yu Cha-gwang and others, poison was despatched to Yun P'il-sang's place of banishment. On the same day, provisions governing cases of high treason were applied to his family and kin (1504.i4.13, 5.23, 7.6, 9.6, 10.8, 10.14). Next, appending the charge that, in dying, Yun had asserted his innocence, Yŏnsangun ordered his corpse beheaded, dismembered, and displayed (1504.i4.20, i4.29). Later, about the same additional punishments were inflicted on Yun as on Yi Se-jwa   (1504.i4.29, 5.7, 5.15, 6.20, 7.6, 8.17, 9.6, 10.8, 12.15, 1505.3.24).

30. As in the case of Yi Se-jwa, those who had visited or associated with Yi Kŭk-kyun under certain circumstances were ascertained and punished, generally by deprivation of office warrants and banishment or by assignment to army duty in the ranks (1504.i4.19, i4.28, 5.10, 5.25, 5.27). This gave the OIG an opening to request that Yu Cha-gwang and Im Sa-hong be beheaded, on the ground of their former close association with Yi. The king actually did order them fined appropriately in lieu of far banishment and then ordered them divested of office warrants and assigned to army contingents in Kyŏnggi (1504.i4.26, i4.28). On immediate second thought, however, Yŏnsangun merely had Im fined and returned to his post and Yu fined and discharged (1504.i4.29).

31. There are other instances of punishments for acts indicating belief in or sympathy toward Buddhism (see 1504.i4.16 S, 5.26 S). Moreover, Yŏnsangun issued a number of decrees aimed at aspects of Buddhist belief

and practice: he forbade harem inmates becoming nuns (1504.4.14), returned to lay status those in Sŏngjong's harem who had become nuns (1504.i4.19), suspended the law permitting licensing of monks (1504.i4.8), and had Buddhist images removed from certain palaces (1504.i4.19). Although he had declared against Buddhism early in his reign, Yŏnsangun heretofore had evinced no disposition toward carrying out a policy of suppression. Perhaps the death at this time (1504.4.27) of his grandmother (queen of Tŏkchong), a notorious protector of the faith, removed a long-time restraining force.

32. This is the first instance of gibbeting in this purge. Presently Yŏnsangun decreed that such was to be done in all cases of beheading of a corpse (1504.i4.29). The purge cases noted here are but the first few of a procession of harsh punishments of people from all segments of the non-official, or non-yangban, class, inflicted for crimes assignable to the category of *lèse majesté* or derogation of the royal authority. Most frequently these arose out of specific acts of disobedience or disrespect; such instances may be seen at 1504.i4.8, 5.18, 6.8, 6.9, 10.15.

33. Since neither Ku Chŏn nor his son, Ku Se-gŏn, the two accused of immoral conduct, were important personages and the circumstances of the case in no way impinged upon the royal person or dignity, it may be conjectured that the remarkable severity of punishments owed to other considerations. There is an easy answer with regard to Yi Yu-nyŏng, for he was a son of royal clansman Yi Sim-wŏn and, in fact, the *Sillok* historians explain his fate in terms of this relationship, thus:

> Yi Yu-nyŏng was a fifth generation descendant of T'aejong. Fond of learning, he passed the civil examination and was selected for employment in the Office of Diplomatic Correspondence. Later he became an Assistant Section Chief in the Board of Personnel, then an OIG Fourth Inspector. [Now] he was executed in connection with the affair of Ku Se-gŏn. To begin with, Yi Yu-nyŏng's father, Yi Sim-wŏn, in a personal interview with Sŏngjong, strongly denounced the villainy of Im Sa-hong. Because of this, Im long was barred from public office. Rancor had penetrated to the marrow of his bones, but he had had no opportunity to give vent to it. Now that he had gained power, he fabricated charges and killed Yi Yu-nyŏng, together with his father and his younger brother, Yi Yu-ban. (1504.i4.20 S)

In another passage, the *Sillok* historians seem to imply that Pyŏn Hyŏng-nyang was an innocent bystander swept up by the avenging broom of Im Sa-hong, but at the same time they observe that Ku Se-gŏn was married to a niece of Yu Cha-gwang who, out of resentment, initiated the banishment phase of the case (1504.i4.19 S). Other sources hint at further sub-surface complications. Traditional accounts note that Pyŏn was one of the victims of 1504 but say very little else about him; the curious are informed merely that he studied under Kim Chong-jik, that he passed the final civil examination in 1501, that his highest post was OSC Ninth Counselor, and that he was executed in 1504 (e.g., *YK* 6.132). On the other hand, one biographical notice, despite its obvious inaccuracy, contains interesting implications: "Pyŏn Hyŏng-nyang . . . at the time of the Purge of 1498 wanted to include Kim Il-son's history drafts in the *Sŏngjong Sillok,* and . . . was executed by dismemberment" (*Kukcho inmul chi* [Seoul?, 1909], 1.220).

34. Yŏnsangun later found other instances of improper remonstrance by Sŏng Chun, and so ordered his corpse dismembered and laws he had proposed expunged (1504.5.15, 8.8, 1505.7.2). Sŏng Chun's two sons were Sŏng Chung-on and Sŏng Kyŏng-on. Both had passed the civil examination and had served in minor posts. Yŏnsangun ordered them executed in 1506 (6.15), and had the corpse of another son (who apparently died in infancy) beheaded (1506.7.1). Sŏng Chun's grandson was Han Hyŏng-yun, who was of the same lineage as Han Myŏng-hoe and hence distantly related to Yŏnsangun. He had most recently served as Second Minister of Personnel (appointed 1503.11.22). Subsequently he was punished in his own right on a count of improper remonstrance (1504.6.15).

35. It is of interest to note how the traditional biographies have distorted the charges against Chŏng In-in in his favor. These assert that once, when a Third Counselor, Chŏng composed a piece sharply critical of the king

and that, when Magistrate of Cheju, he was ordered by Yŏnsangun to find a type of horse which was unobtainable and then was killed for disobedience when he failed to procure it (*YK* 6.129; *CJJ* 1765-66). Chŏng In-in was the frightened Fourth Inspector nominated by his colleagues to indict Yu Cha-gwang at the conclusion of the Purge of 1498.

36. For details see the *Sillok* for 1504.6.

37. Censorate officials had argued that the area concerned depended upon its fishing grounds to pay the required tribute tax and that, accordingly, it would create undue hardship to take away the grounds while maintaining the taxation level unchanged. It was particularly objectionable to transfer these rights to the Palace Supply Office which, it was felt, should be abolished anyway (1501.4.21 S, 4.23 S, 4.26 S, 4.28 S). For their part, the High State Councillors of the time stressed the principle of government use of these resources rather than private or palace use (1501.5.6 S).

38. Two of these three cases were aspects of a single incident, Yŏnsangun's command that certain specially selected *kisaeng* attend a palace function "not wearing red skirts" but clothed instead in "conventional dress" (1503.6.12 S). When two Censorate officials objected that this had no sanction in traditional practice, Yŏnsangun referred the question to the Royal Secretariat. But the Royal Secretaries upheld the Censorate, citing the distinctiveness of *kisaeng* ornamentation and attire and expressing the fear that in conventional dress they might be confused with women of the palace (1503.6.13 S).

    The *Sillok* historians strongly imply that Yŏnsangun's object in ordering *kisaeng* to appear in conventional dress was precisely so that they might be indistinguishable from women of the palace, since he was desirous of taking to bed one among them and feared he would be found out. At the same time is recounted an earlier episode of Yŏnsangun leading in the rape of several young and shapely nuns; this, we are told, marks the beginning of the king's "unbridled lust" (1503.6.13 S).

    The third case in which the king apparently forbore to seek revenge was the protest of five State Councillors and (possibly) the OSC First Counselor that "Royal Stables [Administration] horses ought not be sent to the Palace Supply Office" (1504.8.8 S). This remonstrance appears to have been offered sometime in the two years preceding the Purge of 1498, but I have not been able to locate it. All of the officials concerned were deceased.

39. One of these, the Inspector-General of the time, Yi Kye-nam, had made himself indispensable to Yŏnsangun as Minister of Taxation (see 1504.8.15), and this may explain why the king was willing to drop the charges against him (see 1504.9.30 S, 10.1 S, 10.8 S). But no such likely inference can be adduced to account for Yŏnsangun's forbearance in the other cases.

40. Nam Hyo-on, it may be recalled, had broached the question of Tanjong's mother's tomb early in the previous reign (1478.4.24) and partially on this account had been involved in a minor way in the Purge of 1498 (see 1498.8.16, 8.20, 1499.10.7). He now suffered corpse dismemberment and confiscation of property, and his only son was beheaded and gibbeted. Kim Il-son had included the request to restore this tomb in a solo memorial in 1495 (5.28) and subsequently had been joined by fellow Censors Yi Chu and Han Hun in repeating the proposal (1495.12.30). Kim Il-son's father's corpse and his two illegitimate sons, both minors, were beheaded. Yi Chu's participation was punished in about the same way, while Han Hun's father, Han Ch'ung-in, escaped death only because he was a cousin of Yŏnsangun's paternal grandmother (1504.10.7 S). It is of interest that two other former Censors who are recorded as participants in the 1495.12.30 memorial on this subject were not reported as such to Yŏnsangun at this time, and so escaped involvement in the purge. These were Kim Kŭk-kyu and Yi Ŭi-mu; it has been suggested above that the latter's involvement in 1498 probably was due to his connection with this issue.

    Less than a decade later, surviving opposition to reinterring Tanjong's mother with the full rites due her as the consort of a sovereign was overwhelmed by a preponderance of government opinion, and her tomb was reestablished beside that of Munjong (1512.11.22, 11.26, 1513.3.2).

41. More than forty government officials, living and dead, were reported to Yŏnsangun as participants in one or more of some dozen instances of improper remonstrance. The great majority of them, of course, already had been victimized in earlier purge cases. The record is spotty with regard to the ultimate fate of a number of these offenders, but on the whole punishments appear to have been fixed at the rather standard rod and banishment. *Sillok* references for these purge cases are: 1505.1.6 S, 1.8 S, 2.8 S, 2.12 S, 3.2 S, 4.6 S, 4.8 S, 4.15 S.

42. The victim was one Yi Cha-hwa (not to be confused with the purged official of the same name). He was renowned for having observed the full three years mourning ritual for Sŏngjong. Earlier in the purge Yŏnsangun had ordered the State Council and Censorate to undertake the broadest inquiries to uncover such "suspiciously non-conformist" figures, but the results were negative. Similar requests, it is noted, were made repeatedly thereafter (1504.5.8, 9.26 S). Yŏnsangun, one may conjecture, would brook no rival for the title of Chosŏn's most filial son.

43. Two years later, immediately upon assuming the throne from which Yŏnsangun had been ejected, Chungjong ordered special gate insignia awarded to Yi Cha-hwa and Chŏng Sŏng-gŭn, who had been executed because "Yŏnsangun regarded their performance of three years mourning for Sŏngjong as suspiciously non-conformist." At the same time, Chungjong restored to the loyal, filial, chaste, and faithful throughout the country the gate insignia which had been torn down by Yŏnsangun (1506.9.19). And while Cho Chi-sŏ could not qualify for this particular posthumous honor, he was widely known for similar virtues. When Yŏnsangun had the two brought under arrest, beheaded, and gibbeted, he observed that both had been mentioned in the deposition of a clerk currently under interrogation in a sedition case. Yŏnsangun recalled, too, that Cho had used disrespectful words in opposing Buddhist rites for Sŏngjong (1504.i4.8 S, i4.15 S, i4.16 S, i4.17 S).

44. Cho Sun's punishment is not made explicit. After referring to Cho's diatribe against No Sa-sin, Yŏnsangun added that "even though at present, having been charged with crime, Cho Sun is not employed, further crime charges certainly ought to be added" (1504.i4.26 S). Cho probably was banished.

45. The former Copyist, Yi Hyŏn-bo, had coupled his request with another that the Recorders be moved from their tail-end station at Royal Lectures to a position in front of the Censorate officers, on the ground that it was impossible under the existing arrangement to hear what was being said. Yŏnsangun acceded to this request but denied the other, citing the absence of precedent (1502.10.28 S). In now ordering Yi Hyŏn-bo arrested on this charge, Yŏnsangun gave as his rationale only that "as a newly emerged [official] it was very improper for Yi Hyŏn-bo to offer this view" (1504.12.24 S). The nature of Yi's sentence is not clear; he had already been assigned to corvee on other charges (1504.i4.16 S).

    Some years earlier another State Records Bureau Copyist, Yi Yu-nyŏng, had made the identical request, also unsuccessfully, arguing that there should be a record of the evaluations of fitness made in the course of debate on personnel nominations (1497.7.29). Not even the fact that Yi already had suffered to the point of pulverization of his bones prevented Yŏnsangun from imposing a further sentence on this account (1505.2.8 S, 2.19 S).

46. Yŏnsangun originally ordered Yi Sim-wŏn arrested as a suspect in the "anonymous document" case, but quickly made it clear that Yi's life would be forfeit because of his "association with government officials" and as a consequence of the crimes of his son Yi Yu-nyŏng (1504.9.25 S, 9.26 S, 9.27 S). The "anonymous document," an account of an alleged denunciation of the king's capricious and cruel conduct by several female medical attendants in the palace, had been insinuated into government channels some two months earlier (1504.7.19). Yŏnsangun had gone to fantastic lengths in efforts to unmask the author (see 1504.7.20, 7.22, 7.25, 8.2) and, when these failed, he began a methodical series of arrests and interrogations of kinsmen of leading purge victims, apparently on the theory that bitterness expressing itself in such a way would most likely be found among this group (see 1504.9.6, 10.8, 11.30, 12.22).

Yi Sim-wŏn had been arrested in the Purge of 1498 and questioned about the phrase in his 1478 memorial suggesting that the Merit Subjects of Sejo were undeserving of office under Sŏngjong. He had been released, however, after explaining that his reference was to Im Wŏn-jun and his son, Im Sa-hong (1498.7.18). Neither this point nor the incident of Yi's denunciation of Im Sa-hong were remarked by Yŏnsangun in 1504. But the *Sillok* historians, biographers, and other writers on the events of this day are in complete accord in the view that Yi Sim-wŏn was the victim of a vengeful Im Sa-hong.

47. Yŏnsangun no doubt had in mind Han Ch'i-hyŏng, Sŏng Chun, and Yi Kŭk-kyun, who occupied high State Council posts during the 1498 purge investigations, and who became leading victims of 1504.

48. The punishments actually imposed on these men differed in some cases from those here decreed by the king. Kang Kyŏm was indeed executed by dismemberment (see 1504.11.9 S), but the consensus of Sŏng Chung-ŏm's biographers is that, in the latter part of 1504, he received a royal command to kill himself at his place of banishment. The execution of Kang Paek-chin is revealed at 1504.10.8 S, and Kim Koeng-p'il was beheaded and gibbeted on 1504.10.7 S. The same fate also befell Ch'oe Pu and Yi Wŏn on 1504.10.24 S, a penalty fatally more severe than that previously announced.

49. Yi Chu made this request as a Fourth Censor on 1495.11.15 S, arguing that the existing arrangements, which required Censorate officials to foregather in a narrow room or in the open, lacked dignity. Yŏnsangun's reply on this occasion was entirely sympathetic. Subsequently Yi Chu suffered extreme posthumous indignities because of his opposition to Buddhist rites for Sŏngjong and his advocacy of restoration of the tomb of Tanjong's mother (1504.6.4, 6.20, 9.30 S, 10.1 S, 10.18 S).

50. Im Hŭi-jae, it may be recalled, had become involved in the Purge of 1498 on the basis of a letter he had written to Yi Mok. Upon reading the letter, Yŏnsangun had expressed his intention to arrest Im Sa-hong as well. While there is no indication that this was done, the incident could not very well have bolstered Im Sa-hong's long shaky position, and he remained very much on the sidelines until after the inception of the Purge of 1504. Then, however, he began to receive appointments to the key posts from which he had been so long excluded. And, as we have seen, he was extraordinarily exempted from suffering the consequences of his association with Yi Kŭk-kyun, although not even so imposing a figure as Yu Cha-gwang benefitted from equal royal favor.

Immediately subsequent to this, Im Sa-hong was promoted in rank (1504.5.6) and named Minister of War (1504.5.9), a post he occupied for nearly two years. Shifted then to Minister of Personnel (1506.4.6), he shortly entered the State Council (incumbent Seventh State Councillor 1506.7.24, incumbent Sixth State Councillor 1506.7.29), where his career ended. Meanwhile, Im Hŭi-jae appears to have been released from banishment sometime in the inter-purge period; for, although Yun P'il-sang and others blocked such a move in 1499 (10.8), it may be assumed from the record of a royal command in mid-1504 (5.27) to oust Im Hŭi-jae to the provinces that he had been freed and was in Seoul at the time.

Biographers tell the story that once when Yŏnsangun visited Im Sa-hong he saw some provocative lines written on a screen and, upon inquiry, learned from Im Sa-hong that Im Hŭi-jae had written them. Angered, the king then said: "Your son is a good-for-nothing, and I should like to kill him. What would you say to this?" Im Sa-hong, on his knees, replied: "This son's character and conduct are indeed refractory, as the king has noted. I wished to inform Your Majesty of this, but as yet could not find an opportunity." Presently Im Hŭi-jae was executed, and on the very same day his father gave a party at which he ate meat and enjoyed himself as if nothing had happened. Hearing of this, Yŏnsangun more and more favored Im Sa-hong.

It would be interesting to know whether Im Sa-hong in actuality could not or would not intercede for his son. Although Im Hŭi-jae's wife (a daughter of Ku Su-yŏng, husband of a niece of Sejo and a man high in Yŏnsangun's favor) was made to suffer for her husband's crimes, being assigned to corvee (1504.10.28 S; she soon was released, 1504.12.14 S), Im Sa-hong was not. He and two surviving sons were the sole exceptions to an order ousting to the provinces the parents and brothers of "the criminals of 1498" (1504.10.25).

51. Noteworthy exceptions to this generalization, leaving aside the re-banished 1498 Censorate officials, are Chŏng Hŭi-ryang, Chŏng Sŭng-jo, Kang Kyŏng-sŏ, and Yi Chong-jun. The first three of these had been involved in 1498 in connection with their duties in the compilation of the *Sŏngjong Sillok,* not because of a relationship with Kim Chong-jik or Kim Il-son. Yi Chong-jun had been executed early in 1499 on charges stemming from his conduct while enroute to banishment (see 1498.i11.17, 12.19, 1499.3.2).

52. In addition to those already noted, Yi Mok too belongs in this category, for his house was ordered razed in 1504 (9.10 S).

53. These measures mostly were minatory or prescribed dire penalties for those divulging such information. For example, medallions to be worn by palace functionaries were struck, bearing such pointed maxims as "the mouth is the gateway of calamity, the tongue is a sword to behead the body" (1504.3.13). Later, officials of the government were required to wear an identically worded medallion (1505.1.29). Other measures sought to make it physically impossible for the taboo on palace topics to be violated. In one instance, Yŏnsangun ousted from Seoul certain kinsmen of the wives of palace functionaries, on the plausible theory that a leak might well develop here (1504.5.15). He even contemplated forcing palace servants married to women slaves in yangban homes to divorce their wives (1504.6.13). Other information on this point is found at 1504.3.19, 3.26, i4.5, 6.10, 6.16, 8.7, 8.20.

54. Further examples of Yŏnsangun's efforts to gag the official class may be seen at 1504.i4.11, i4.20, 5.3, 5.7, 5.15, 12.26.

55. We are told, however, that the evasive tactics employed by the descendants of the Merit Subjects frustrated the king's design. It was claimed, for example, that the documents of award had been lost, or that it was impossible to differentiate between merit award land and other holdings. Nevertheless, it is added, continuing exertions to recover this bounty gave rise to much bitterness (1504.5.8).

56. General information on Yŏnsangun's extravagances is seen at 1504.5.10, 5.14, 7.10, 8.15. References to the subject of the royal preserve are: 1504.7.16, 7.17, 7.22, 8.16, 8.18, 10.18, 1505.8.24, 1506.2.26. It is of interest to note that Yŏnsangun once ordered that no one mention the royal preserve to Ming envoys then on their way to Seoul (1505.6.5).

57. More than for any of the acts of misrule noted in these pages, Yŏnsangun is remembered for converting the National Academy, with its National Confucian Shrine, into a site for merrymaking (1504.7.10) and for despatching special agents throughout the country to search out beautiful young women and good fast horses (see 1505.6.16, 8.10, 9.18, 1506.1.17, 5.28).

58. One of these was Yi Chang-gon, who had been beaten and banished for no other apparent reason than that Yi Kŭk-kyun, one of Yŏnsangun's most despised victims, had once recommended him as a promising talent (1504.10.23 S, 10.24 S, 11.5 S, 1505.2.9 S, 5.22 S, 5.25 S, 1506.8.17). The circumstances of Yi Chang-gon's escape made him famous and he went on to win high office and further renown as one of the Eight Worthies of 1519.

59. The only major figures killed in the coup were Sixth State Councillor Im Sa-hong and the three brothers of the queen, Second State Councillor Sin Su-gŭn, Minister of Punishments Sin Su-yŏng, and Magistrate of Kaesŏng Sin Su-gyŏm (see 1506.9.2).

IV. *The Purge of 1519*

1. This trio is known by the special terms, "Three Great Ministers" (*samdaesin*), "Three Great Generals" (*samdaejang*), and "Three Meritorious Ones" (*samhun*). Pak and Sŏng also were promoted in post at this time, the former being named Sixth State Councillor and the latter Minister of Punishments; Yu remained temporarily as Minister of Personnel. Within little more than a month both Pak and Yu had been elevated to High State Councillor level (Pak appointed Third State Councillor 1506.9.13, Second State Councillor 1506.10.11; Yu appointed Third State Councillor 1506.10.11). Sŏng's advance upward was much slower; three years passed before he was named Third State Councillor (1509.i9.27).

2. The term, *chŏngguk kongsin,* will be rendered hereafter as Chungjong Merit Subjects. The first intention was to have only three classes, but the bulk of those originally included in the third class were downgraded to a fourth class, and "thereby reduction in the cost of rewards was made." (For the determination of reward levels see 1506.9.10 S, also 1509.6.1). A small number of additional Merit Subjects subsequently was added to this roster (see 1506.9.17, 9.20, 1507.6.17). In some cases, at least, other awards of an economic nature were made (see 1509.6.1). Fifteen fathers and sons of leading Merit Subjects were promoted to Senior Third rank or above (1506.9.23, 10.2). There were also special ceremonies held periodically to honor these (and other) Merit Subjects, on which occasions the king appears usually to have bestowed such awards as promotions in rank upon those feted or upon their sons (see, e.g., 1506.10.19, 1518.10.23).

3. Information on the enrollment and reward of these Minor Merit Subjects is found under 1506.9.16, 9.23, 11.5, 1507.3.18, 6.17, 7.21, 1508.4.7.

4. The ceremony was held 1506.7.29 S; the order that such a roster be prepared is dated 1506.4.1. The then incumbent seven State Councillors, six Board Ministers, and six Royal Secretaries make up almost the entirety of the roster (the others were the Chief Magistrate of Seoul, two Second Ministers-without-Portfolio, and Yu Cha-gwang, who seems to have held no official post at this time). Very soon after the accession of Chungjong the Respect Vows Text, understandably, was burned (1506.9.10).

5. These were Im Sa-hong, Sin Su-gŭn and Sin Su-yŏng. The third Sin brother, Su-gyŏm, was not included on the Respect Vows Text; he too was executed in the course of the coup (1506.9.2).

6. Those who can be placed rather definitely in these categories account for perhaps two-thirds of the total roster. Not a few of Chungjong's Merit Subjects played no readily discernible part in other events of the period, so that it is difficult to fit them into a schematization. It may be conjectured that those of the remaining one-third who do not belong in one of these categories were mostly undistinguished figures of military background.

7. This is not only a long but an involved controversy. It began with repeated Censorate objections to the promotions to Senior Third Rank of over one hundred Minor Merit Subjects First Class, to which protests the king paid no heed (1506.9.23, 9.27, 10.2, 10.14, 12.3). On at least one occasion, an OSC official lent support to the Censorate's demands (1506.10.3). After letting the issue lie dormant for over a year, the Censorate renewed its request that these promotions be rescinded (1508.2.21) and presently, failing to win consent, resigned (1508.4.26). As the neglected chores of the Censorate piled up, such other offices as the OSC, Royal Secretariat, and Six Boards urged the king to quickly accede to the Censorate's demands. But when Chungjong started to take steps in this direction, his High State Councillors persuaded him once more to withhold consent. The Censorate then again resigned, and the king at length rescinded some of the disputed promotions (1508.5.23). Unsatisfied, the Censorate pressed for cancellation of the promotions in rank of all the Minor Merit Subjects (First Class?) (1508.6.6, 6.11, 6.23). Chungjong not only steadfastly refused but soon found a pretext to restore the promotions he had earlier rescinded. The Censorate had

opined that the daytime visibility of Venus was due to the rejection of their remonstrance. The king, however, countered with this interpretation:

> Venus is a symbol of the negative force and that it has now become visible is because of discontent among my subjects. In my view, this natural phenomenon is the result of the recent wholesale rescission of rank promotions and accumulation of [unjudged] criminal cases in the provinces . . . The overnight and total rescission of promotions of three or four years standing has occasioned a lack of confidence in me and has unsettled men's minds . . . (1508.7.14 S)

A rebuff of such dimensions could only force the Censorate officials to resign (1508.7.14) and the State Council and Ministers of the Six Boards supported them in so acting (1508.7.17, 7.28). The king remained firm for a time but, when they failed to respond to two summons to participate in ceremonies honoring the Ming envoys then in Seoul (1508.7.22, 7.26; someone loosed an arrow at the lone Censor to accept the royal summons), Chungjong tried to conciliate them by once again rescinding a few of the disputed promotions (1508.7.28). Unmollified, the Censorate continued its walkout and, in the end, forced a large number of additional cancellations (1508.7.28, 8.7, 8.21). For several years thereafter one finds no further debate on the question of the Chungjong Merit Subjects.

8. Shortly before this date (1507.11.30), a new group of Merit Subjects had been created in the aftermath of the timely crushing of a treason plot (to be discussed below), and the Censorate request applied to this group as well. It is assumed that subsequent references to developments on this question also apply to both groups.

9. On 1508.1.5 Chungjong ordered reduced the awards of land and slaves made to "Merit Subjects Second Class and below" but the extent of the reduction is not specified. Further information on this facet of the question is found under 1507.12.26. With regard to the rank promotions, "the king in the end consented to the request of the Censorate" (1508.2.17; see also 1508.1.30).

10. It is impossible to determine the magnitude of this palace housecleaning, for the available statistics include kinsmen and slaves who were associated in the guilt of the malefactors. As one index to the number involved there is a record that, beginning on the day of the coup, "the most extreme evil-doing eunuchs and harem figures, together with their kinsmen and slaves, over one-hundred persons altogether" were sentenced either to beheading and confiscation of property or to forced settlement on the far borders (1506.9.2). Another indication is the statement appearing ten years later that "it was intended to release the evildoers of Yŏnsangun's reign and, among over six hundred names, some one hundred fifty were selected" — but not released after all (1516.5.19). Other information on this point is to be found at 1506.9.5, 10.27, 1507.7.10, 8.8.

11. In addition to the four men noted above, it may be inferred that Yŏnsangun's maternal uncle, Yun Ku, and Im Sa-hong's son, Im Sung-jae, also were killed (see 1506.9.3, 9.26). Im Sa-hong was soon subjected to posthumous beheading and confiscation of property, but Im Sung-jae was spared such severe indignities because he was a son-in-law of Sŏngjong (1506.9.26). It is of interest to note that some years later Chungjong refused a Censorate request for "explicit and formal designation of Im Sa-hong's crimes" (1509.10.20). As for the Sin brothers and Yun Ku, their sons and sons-in-law and an uncle were far banished, and other paternal and maternal kin of Sin Su-gŭn were banished in light degree (1506.9.3).

12. This was Ch'oe Hae, a minor victim of 1504. The charge, "toadying to Yŏnsangun," is not further elucidated in the record (1506.9.9 S). There is another instance of banishment on the same charge, but it occurred some ten months later (1507.7.12). The man involved was Han Sun, a brother of Yejong's queen, who had been promoted rapidly in the Royal Secretariat between 1504 and 1506; as the Second Royal Secretary his name had been included on the Respect Vows Text and he was a Merit Subject Third Class. Han Sun was requalified for public office within a year (1508.6.25) and was still serving in the government as late as 1521 (5.22).

13. There is this exception: at the same time that the "most extreme evil-doing eunuchs and harem figures" were punished, it was also ordered that "those who had become Local Magistrates by currying the favor of eunuchs and who had perpetrated evil" be discharged or otherwise relieved of their posts (1506.9.2).

14. These summary statements are based on a welter of isolated references to individual cases. Some of the more revealing instances may be found under 1506.9.16, 10.7, 10.20, 10.25, 11.16, 1507.1.7, 2.2, 7.12, 8.20, 1509.1.23, 6.1.

15. This seems a reasonable inference from the character of the clash of political forces which preceded the Purge of 1519; it is difficult to document with precision, for clearly the censoring bodies could not admit that the charge of toadying was but a pretext.

16. Not long before this, Yu had sought in vain permission to retire from public office so that he might "return to his native place and there live out his remaining years in safety." He claimed that he feared "the sinister schemes of the remnant of the Kim Chong-jik clique" and went on to criticize in veiled tones the rehabilitation of the "cliquists of 1498" (1507.2.2). It may seem strange that these pronouncements drew no fire, but into his remarks Yu had woven criticisms of the shallowness of the investigation into a political conspiracy case that had just been settled, and this may have given pause to the Censorate.

17. At the same time, Yu's two sons, a grandson, and a son-in-law were stricken from the Chungjong merit rosters and all but the son-in-law banished afar (1507.4.23). A year later the king wanted to release Yu and mitigate the banishment of Yu's sons, but he desisted in the face of Censorate and OSC opposition (1508.4.23). After Yu's death, in accordance with a request of the State Council, the king re-enrolled Yu on the Yejong merit roster and released his sons and grandson; shortly, however, the merit listing was again revoked at the behest of the censoring bodies (1512.6.15). This same sequence of re-enrolling and revoking was repeated a year or so later (1513.11.12, 1514.1.16) and again after some twenty years had passed (1533.9.8, 9.12, 9.15), and here, apparently, the matter rested. It is of interest to note in passing that Yu Cha-gwang's son seems to have been the last member of his clan to pass the civil examination.

18. It is assumed that Yi Kŭk-ton's office warrants were revoked at about this time, although verification is lacking. At any rate it was done sometime before mid-1511, at which time a son asked that the office warrants be returned, asserting that his father had been falsely charged with the crime of "divulging history matters" (1511.6.12). Although the king at first consented, the opposition of the OSC, Censorate, and Office of Royal Decrees presently forced him to revoke them once again (1511.6.12, 7.4, 7.18, 8.19, 8.26). It would appear that Yi Kŭk-ton was permanently saddled with this guilt; in 1545, when his name was proposed for pardon, it was ordered that the matter not be raised again (1545.11.24).

19. I cannot explain why this posthumous action against Yi Sŭng-gŏn was taken at such a late date. His name is bracketed with that of Yi Kŭk-ton in the reference noted above banning further inclusion on pardon lists; none of the other names similarly included are of pre-1519 figures (1545.11.24).

20. Chŏng Sŏng-gŭn later was accorded other extraordinary consideration (1508.9.6, 1514.12.11, 1517.8.12).

21. For example, there is mention of the restitution of confiscated property and reburial with proper rites of some 1504 purge victims (1506.10.5, 10.27), while the posterity of others was requalified for public office and titles were posthumously bestowed upon still others (1506.10.2, 1517.8.8). No doubt appropriate action was taken in the interests of other 1504 victims who are not included in the explicit record of redress.

22. Biographies of these three men aver that each was posthumously made a Royal Secretary by Chungjong, and in two cases the "beginning" of the reign is specified. There is a record of a request by personnel of the Office of Royal Decrees in mid-1507 that "rank be posthumously bestowed upon those executed in 1498 in connection with the history affair and their confiscated household property be returned." In response to this request the king ordered the property of Kim Il-son, Kwŏn O-bok, and Kwŏn Kyŏng-yu (and of four other 1498 victims) returned, but there is no mention here of conferral of rank (1507.6.10 S). Of possible bearing on this point is the fact that, some years later, the king rejected a request by a son of Yi Mok to posthumously confer office and rank upon his father, against whom the charges in 1498 had been less severe than in the case of Kim Il-son (1519.4.9). Yet a biography of Yi Mok too claims that "at the beginning of Chungjong's reign he was extraordinarily awarded the post of Minister of Personnel." See *Chōsen tosho kaidai* (Keijō, 1928), 384.

23. Sŏng Hŭi-an was Fourth State Councillor at this time and had just returned from an important embassy to Ming (1507.7.22, 9.7, 1508.2.3). Sŏng spoke with immediate reference to allegations (for example, of impropriety in observing mourning rites) that the Censorate was then levelling at three minor and two major current officials (1508.3.1 S). But he probably also had in mind that, in the preceding half year, the Censorate had forced the transfer or discharge of perhaps half a dozen Merit Subjects (see 1507.9.2, 11.1, 11.24, 12.18, 1508.1.5, 2.24). Most notably, Prime Merit Subjects Pak Yŏng-mun and Sin Yun-mu both had been discharged from their posts, the former under fire for having reported the contents of Censorate deliberations to Pak Wŏn-jong, who was then the Second State Councillor (see 1507.12.18, 12.26, 1508.1.5, 2.24). Although both Pak and Sin were soon requalified for office (1508.6.25), they continued to suffer Censorate attack throughout the remainder of their careers.

24. Although the Censorate failed in its efforts against Sŏng, it was not long before their attacks led the king to accept the resignation repeatedly tendered by Yu Sun (1509.i9.16). Yu Sun had been scathingly denounced by the Censorate for toadying to Yŏnsangun and for cowardly inaction at the time of the deposition coup (1509.i9.16 S, i9.17 S). On this occasion Sŏng incurred further Censorate displeasure by his defense of Yu (1509.i9.18).

25. Late in the purge year of 1504 Sŏng Hŭi-an, then Second Minister of Personnel (Junior Second Rank), was ordered demoted. According to the *Sillok*, Yŏnsangun took this action out of annoyance that Sŏng, who had made a point of telling the king that he was a dedicated student of poetry, proved to be inept at poetic composition (1504.12.17 S). Comparable acts of dissimulation were enough to bring a far worse fate to other offenders of 1504, but perhaps Sŏng was helped by the fact that his mother was a member of the royal family (a granddaughter of King Chŏngjong). At the time of the deposition coup, Sŏng held the post of a Junior Ninth Rank Military Officer of the Five Military Commands (1506.9.2).

26. Song Chil passed the civil examination in 1477 and by the end of Sŏngjong's reign had served as OSC First Counselor and entered the Royal Secretariat. He served continuously under Yŏnsangun (his involvement in 1504 was minimal and did not interrupt his career) and, as Minister of Rites, he was included on the Respect Vows Text. Enrolled by Chungjong in the Third Class of merit, he presently was appointed to the State Council. In 1512 (10.7), after a stint of mourning, at length he was elevated to High State Councillor level.

27. Pak Kyŏng was the illegitimate son of Pak Kang, a son of Pak Ŭn who was a Second State Councillor in T'aejong's reign. He had been arrested and questioned in 1498 as the alleged source of one of the defamatory items Kim Il-son wrote up in his history drafts but was quickly released (1498.7.12, 7.28, 8.20). Kim Kong-jŏ's antecedents are unknown. He had been rewarded by Yŏnsangun for the skill of his professional services, but immediately upon Chungjong's accession his rank promotion had been revoked and then he had been charged with toadying to Yŏnsangun (1501.4.5, 1506.9.5, 10.27).

28. Pak Wǒn-jong and Yu Cha-gwang, both Prime Merit Subjects, are familiar figures. No Kong-p'il, a son of No Sa-sin, had been banished in the purge of 1504. At this time he was Director of the Royal House Administration, to which post he had recently been transferred from Fifth State Councillor preparatory to undertaking a mission to Ming (1507.i1.2).

29. Nam Kon was then in mourning, while Sim Chǒng and Kim Kǔk-sǒng (Chungjong Merit Subjects Third and Fourth Class respectively) held peripheral posts of middle rank. Nam and Sim, of course, have gone down in history as two arch villains of 1519.

30. The three Yi's were brothers of the renowned Yi Chang-gon, accounted one of the Eight Worthies of 1519, but perhaps equally famed for his successful flight from Yǒnsangun's justice. Their father, Yi Sǔng-ǒn, was a disciple of Kim Chong-jik (see 1498.7.17). Yi Chang-gil had made a name for himself as a harsh tax collector when a County Magistrate near the end of Yǒnsangun's reign (see 1504.9.8). He appears to have served off and on in middle level military posts until 1531; at that time, ironically, he was ousted from the capital on charges of being a right hand man of Sim Chǒng (1531.2.25). His two brothers fled from arrest in 1507 (see 2.3 S) and are heard of no more. Cho Kwang-bo was distantly related to Cho Kwang-jo. The words he uttered while under interrogation in this case are quoted widely and with approbation, but biographers say next to nothing else about him.

31. Kim Sik was a chief lieutenant of Cho Kwang-jo and a leading victim of 1519. (He is not to be confused with another official of the same name who passed the civil examination in 1506 but whose career in the central government appears to have been of brief duration; see 1508.1.26, 1509.8.5). Cho Kwang-jwa, younger brother of Cho Kwang-bo, died in the 1521 sequel to the 1519 purge. The name Mun Sǒ-gu is clothed in no such glamor; he passed the civil examination in 1511 and enjoyed a very modest career, Great County Magistrate being the highest post he attained. Mun was not among those punished. Rather he appears to have been rewarded for telling Sim Chǒng about the plot in time to prevent its fruition (see 1507.i1.27 S).

32. The *Sillok* text of the portion of this quotation omitted in the above translation consists of but five characters, thus: 且喜接賓客 (1507.i1.25 S). I am uncertain of the meaning of this clause in this context, but it appears to make the accusation that Pak "also takes pleasure in welcoming hangers-on," that is, that he is building a private following of men personally loyal to him.

33. Chǒng Mi-su was the sole surviving descendant of King Munjong, the father of Tanjong. He is credited with saving the lives of a number of imperiled victims of 1504, through his position as Chief Magistrate of the State Tribunal. As Fourth State Councillor, Chǒng was included on the Respect Vows Text and he became a Merit Subject Third Class. At the time of this affair he does not appear to have held portfolio post.

34. Kim Kam had been little affected by the 1504 purge and, as a Second Minister-without-Portfolio, had been included on the Respect Vows Text and enrolled as a Merit Subject Second Class. Yi Kye-maeng, who narrowly missed serious involvement in 1498, had been banished in 1504. He is generally regarded as one of the men of 1519.

35. Yu Sung-jo was banished because he reported the affair only after hearing that Nam Kon and others were about to expose it. All those banished were soon released and restored to their posts and perquisites (1507.6.11, 7.4).

36. There are two further footnotes to be added to this affair. No sooner had the prosecution of the case been completed than Yu Cha-gwang, on the occasion already noted, attacked Chǒng Mi-su on the ground of

championing the "clique of 1498" for the purpose of furthering his own personal ambitions. Yu went on to request that Nam Kon, Sim Chŏng, and others be summoned for detailed questioning by the State Tribunal, for in Yu's view the investigation of the Pak Kyŏng case had not been thorough. The king did not consent (1507.2.2). Again, not long after Yu's downfall, the Censorate asked that the rank promotions awarded the informants Nam Kon, Sim Chŏng, and Kim Kŭk-sŏng be revoked, on the ground that the facts of the Pak-Kim case were extremely unclear. The king refused and, after Sŏng Hŭi-an reprimanded the Censorate for "irresponsible memorializing," he demoted eight of the Censorate officials (1507.8.23, 8.28).

37. The "1519 group," or the "men of 1519" *(kimyo in)*, is a term broadly designating the victims of the purge that began at the end of that year. The unquestioned leader of this group was Cho Kwang-jo, who was at the root of the extraordinary political turmoil that preceded this great upheaval.

38. Sin Sŏk-ho, "Kibō shika [Kimyo sahwa] no yurai ni kansuru ichi kōsatsu," *Seikyū gakusō* 20:46-47 (May 1940). This writer notes further that the connection of Cho and Kim with the Pak Kyŏng affair is nowhere visible in the accounts of the private histories. Whether this implies that the classical writers deemed the fact of no importance or, rather, that they deliberately suppressed it as detracting from the stature of these two great heroes is a question open to conjecture. I am inclined to favor the latter hypothesis. The biographies of Cho Kwang-jo and Kim Sik, too, despite their wealth of detail, pass over this subject in silence. Of Nam Kon, however, it is commonly written in this vein: "When young, Nam Kon was famed for his literary talents but, anxious for rapid advancement, when in mourning he falsely reported that Pak Kyŏng was plotting treason, thus causing his death. Because of this, Nam Kon was not countenanced by those of moral integrity and, in the end, together with Sim Chŏng, he engineered the execution of Cho Kwang-jo etc." (YK 9.48).

39. Three more from among the original conspirators were also executed and another was beaten and banished together with four men who had been implicated. All were men of little consequence and their names need not concern us. Six or seven others subjected to interrogation in the course of the inquiry were completely exonerated. Yi Ton at first was banished but, in response to the demands of the entire officialdom, which argued "the larger interests of the state," he soon was executed (1507.9.1, 10.6). In the next year, however, he was exonerated and redress made (1508.10.8).

40. Kim Chun-son was an older brother of Kim Il-son and, apparently, had been banished on this account.

41. *YK* 6.76.

42. The likely inference is that the Palace Guardsmen to whom Yi Kwa looked for support were others who were disgruntled at being omitted from this enrollment.

43. The informer was a former Guardsman named No Yŏng-son. Little seems to be known about him other than that he was illegitimate.

44. This will be treated below.

45. See note 23 above.

46. See, for example, 1509.6.11, 6.13, 7.1, 7.9, 11.4 S, 1511.10.11.

47. Hong Kyŏng-ju, also a Prime Merit Subject, was temporarily out of office, having recently resigned as Sixth State Councillor on technical grounds (1513.8.20). Min Hoe-bal was a Merit Subject Third Class.

48. Pak's two sons were strangled, the wives and daughters of both were enslaved, a brother of each was banished, and a son-in-law of Sin was discharged from his post. Pak and Sin, of course, as well as two brothers, were deleted from the merit roster. It is of interest to note, with the traditional historians, that the king accepted the totally unsupported word of a slave over the original denials of the two Prime Merit Subjects. See *YK* 7.31-33.

49. The history of the Sogyŏksŏ goes back at least to the Koryŏ period. It was the only Koryŏ "site of wine-offering rites to the heavenly bodies" which was spared destruction by the Yi (1392.11.1). During the first century of the dynasty, the Sogyŏksŏ underwent reconstruction and a change of name (to Sogyŏksŏ from Sogyŏkchŏn), but no one appears to have questioned the propriety of its existence (1396.1.10, 1402.1.27, 1417.11.17, 1466.1.15). Toward the end of Yŏnsangun's reign, a Censorate official asked that the Sogyŏksŏ be abolished because of the high cost of its rites and, although the king refused, he presently had it torn down in the course of enlarging the walled-in area of the palace grounds (1503.11.1, 1504.7.16, 1506.2.14). However, Yŏnsangun subsequently ordered that abbreviated rites be conducted at a different site (1504.7.23, 1506.1.14). One of Chungjong's first acts was to order the Sogyŏksŏ rebuilt, and to this no objection was voiced at the time (1506.10.3, 1507.10.2). In 1511 a high OSC official asked that it be abolished and in the ensuing debate the State Council and Censorate, among others, added their weight to the request (1511.5.4, 5.10, 5.15, 6.5, 7.18, 8.19). In 1516 the question was raised again (1516.6.3, 12.10).

50. See also *YK* 7.38. In accordance with the wish of his ailing mother, Chungjong subsequently reestablished the Sogyŏksŏ and had prayers offered there for her recovery (1522.12.14). The Censorate's opposition on this occasion was in vain, and further efforts to have the Sogyŏksŏ abolished once again also met with failure (1523.1.25, 3.10, 1530.4.23). It appears, however, that the Sogyŏksŏ did not remain in existence after the reign of Sŏnjo (1567-1608). *Chōsengo jiten* (Keijō, 1920), 509; see also 1555.6.16.

51. See also *YK* 7.37; *CJJ* 1612.

52. *YK* 7.37.

53. Kim Chŏng, second only to Cho Kwang-jo in prominence among the 1519 group, had passed the civil examination in 1509 and already had served as high as OSC Fifth Counselor (1510.3.6, 1514.2.14). He had requested provincial appointment for filial reasons. Pak Sang is commonly listed as one of the 1519 group but actually he was not involved in the purge. Passing the examinations in 1501, he already had seen considerable service in the lower Censorate and OSC posts.

54. Although the argument of their memorial entirely rested on moral grounds, it is widely asserted that Kim and Pak had other considerations in mind as well. All such claims, perhaps, originate in the biography of Kim contained in his literary collection. According to this source, Kim presented his views to Pak in this way: "The queen is dead and the heir still in swaddling clothes, while in the harem Madame Pak is the undisputed favorite and, moreover, has a son. If, in the manner of Lady Yun and the queen mother, both of whom rose to become queens of Sŏngjong via the harem, she should be invested as the legitimate consort, then the position of the infant heir would be difficult indeed. There is no better way to cope with this than to restore Lady Sin, thereby redressing the wrong of her being put aside though blameless and making it clear that there is no intent to make a concubine a wife." (*Ch'ungam chip* 6, Cheng-te tenth year [1515], seventh month; quoted in Sin, "Kimyo sahwa," 12).

It is noted by the *Sillok* historians that Madame Pak aspired to become queen and that Chungjong, inclined to accede to her wishes, sounded out the views of his High State Councillors but with negative results (1517.7.22 S).

55. See also *YK* 7.9.

56. *YK* 7.9, attributing the argument to Yi Haeng, expands and clarifies this point as follows: "But if Lady Sin should be restored and be blessed with a son and the question of precedence in taking the marriage vows be debated, then Lady Sin would be preferred. In what position would that put the infant heir?"

57. See also *YK* 7.10-11. The repeated protests of the State Council, the OSC, and others appear to have influenced the king to some extent, for he refused to permit interrogation by torture and commuted to a fine the further sentence of one hundred strokes of the rod recommended by the State Tribunal.

58. Cho's appointment (1515.11.20) appears to have marked the first change in the composition of the Censorate in the more than three months since the start of the Kim-Pak affair. This is a curious and unusual circumstance, but I can offer no explanation for it other than mere chance.

59. It has been said that "only Minister of Personnel An Tang stated to the king the error of the Censorate, and he then was denounced by Kwŏn Min-su and Yi Haeng, who called him 'an amoral man who would lead the state to ruin,' and was unable to speak out again" (Sin, "Kimyo sahwa," 16). But, actually, An Tang did no more than express in stronger terms what many others were saying. He deplored the violation of the freedom of remonstrance, wondering aloud who now would dare offer frank advice to the king. Noting that there were times when the Censorate too was in error, he urged that the king not always accede to their arguments (1515.8.26 S; see also 1515.9.5 S and *YK* 7.11). In other words, while An Tang felt that the view of the Censorate was mistaken, he too stopped short of criticizing its *act* of demanding prosecution of Kim and Pak; rather was he censuring the king for lack of discrimination in passing judgment on the issue.

    Yet my statement that there were none who denounced the error of the Censorate is not quite true. In the course of the civil examinations which were held at that time and which Cho Kwang-jo passed, over thirty candidates "reviled the Censorate" in their compositions and, in the final examination stage, one student (Yi Ch'ung-gŏn, a victim of 1519) took as a theme "the error of the Censorate in asking crime charges against Kim Chŏng and Pak Sang." This was indignantly reported by OSC Fourth Counselor Yi Ŏn-ho, in whose view no such candidates should have been passed (1515.9.4 S).

60. The five who favored Cho were Inspector-General Yi Chang-gon, Censor-General Kim An-guk, Fourth Censor Chang Ok, Fourth Inspector Kim Ham, and Third Censor Yi U. (*Chōsen shi* 1515.11.27 and Sin, "Kimyo sahwa," 16 erroneously record the name of the Third Censor as Pak U; see 1515.11.28 S, where Yi U is correctly called Third Censor. A brother of Pak Sang, Pak U also was an active official at this time.) The two opposed to Cho's view were Third Inspectors Yu Pu and Kim Hŭi-su (1515.11.27).

    Historians have long thought that the minority position taken by Yu Pu and Kim Hŭi-su requires explanation. The *Sillok* historians declare that the only dissenters to the otherwise unanimous condemnation of Yi Haeng and Kwŏn Min-su were Yi Ŏn-ho, Yu Pu, and Kim Hŭi-su. It was Yi Ŏn-ho, they go on to say, who persuaded the other two, with whom he had strong ties of friendship, to accept his own erroneous point of view. But beyond averring that he had been "angered" by the Kim-Pak memorial and in character was both opinionated and narrow-minded, they offer no clue as to why Yi Ŏn-ho felt as he did (1515.11.28 S).

    Sin, "Kimyo sahwa," 17-18 makes a further suggestion regarding the motivations of Yu and Kim. He notes that Yu was a nephew of Yu Sun-jŏng, one of the Three Great Generals attacked in the Kim-Pak memorial, and that Kim was a nephew of Song Chil, who had joined the Three Great Generals in demanding the ouster of Lady Sin. This argument is vitiated, I think, by two considerations. The first is that the same line of reasoning is generally useless as an explanation of the positions taken by other figures in the Kim-Pak affair. The second is that similar, if somewhat weaker, genealogical arguments can be adduced to show why Yu and Kim should not have acted as they did. And Sin, too, neglects to explain the attitude of Yi Ŏn-ho, beyond a later statement ("Kimyo sahwa," 26) grouping him together with such figures as Yi Haeng and Kwŏn Min-su as esteeming the literary attainments that the men of 1519 deemphasized.

Without attaching particular significance to it, we may point out an interesting coincidence. Some five years before the Kim-Pak issue arose, when Cho Kwang-jo was one of three National Academy students extraordinarily recommended for government employ, it was Third Censor Yi Ŏn-ho (together with Fourth Inspector Yi Pin) who persuaded the king not to so employ Cho after all. The argument of the two Yi's was that it would be a pity to take the promising young Cho away from his studies, to which he was known to be devoted (1511.4.11 S).

61.   None of the three recorded pro-Cho Censors (Pang Yu-nyŏng, Yi Wŏn-gan, Hŏ Wi) are included in the 1519 purged group, while the first two of the four fence-sitting Inspectors (Sŏng Se-ch'ang, Hong Ŏn-p'il, Pak Su-mun, Kim In-son) are commonly labeled as "men of 1519." Hong Ŏn-p'il, fresh from the OSG, had been one of the original propounders of the both right both wrong theory.

62.   It is worthwhile noting that only after Kim and Pak had been released did the same type of written offering of advice occur again for the first time since the start of the affair (see 1516.7.15). The wide concern for the principle of remonstrance was not unfounded.

63.   Yi Haeng was called back as OSC First Counselor in mid-1517 (5.15) but was quickly transferred to Headmaster of the National Academy (1517.5.28). After but two months in this post he became Second Royal Secretary (1517.7.28) and then First Royal Secretary (1517.8.4). From this position he shortly won promotion to Inspector-General (1517.8.24). Although no objection appears to have been raised to any of these earlier appointments, the *Sillok* historians tell us that despite their close daily contact no words passed between First Counselor Yi Haeng and his subordinates Kim Chŏng (appointed Fourth Counselor 1517.2.1) and Cho Kwang-jo (appointed Junior Fifth Counselor 1517.5.28). This strained situation probably accounts for the brevity of Yi's tenure as OSC First Counselor (1517.8.27 S).

64.   Little seems to be known about Yi Sŏng-ŏn, the distinguishing feature of his career being this memorial. He was a son of Yi Son, a Chungjong Merit Subject (Third Class) and had himself been enrolled in the Fourth Class. He had passed the civil examination in 1508 and had seen brief service in the Censorate (1511.6.2, 6.4, 7.5). He was named Magistrate of Suwŏn in 1515 (6.28). He next appears in a northern frontier post in 1523 (12.11). He died in 1534 while on a mission to China (1534.7.8). Sin ("Kimyo sahwa," 24) implies a relationship between the Merit Subject status of Yi Sŏng-ŏn and his father and the fact that Yi Son, as Minister of War, had joined in persuading Chungjong to put aside Lady Sin, and Yi Sŏng-ŏn's defense of Yi Haeng. It seems to me that this is stretching coincidence rather far and that exceptional motivation is more likely to be found in the ties of personal friendship which appear to have existed between the two families.

65.   With the single exception of the sixth day, the *Chōsen shi* numbering of the days of the tenth month of 1517 is in error, the actual numerical equivalents being in every case the next higher figure. Here and elsewhere I have made the appropriate correction.

66.   Inspector-General Nam Kon and Fourth Inspector Yi U had not signed the Censorate memorial on government disharmony and so were not removed from their posts at this time. Nam Kon, one of the authors of the 1519 purge, was a close friend of Yi Haeng. Sin ("Kimyo sahwa," 21) emphasizes that Yi Haeng's return to the government in the middle of this year coincided with Nam's tenure as Minister of Personnel (1516.10.16-1517.8.21 S). Yi U, it will be recalled, had backed Cho Kwang-jo's stand at the start of the controversy. On the other hand, Kim Hŭi-su, who originally had endorsed Yi Haeng's position on the Kim Chŏng-Pak Sang memorial, at this time held the post of Second Inspector, from which he was removed as one of the offending Censorate officials. And in passing it should be noted that by this time Kwŏn Min-su was deceased (1517.1.22) and thus no longer figured in the dispute.

67. One such was Yi Yu-ch'ŏng, who was quickly removed from his new post as Inspector-General after the OCG charged, principally, that he had already gone on record in opposition to the former Censorate (1517.10.26 S). Yi Yu-ch'ŏng was the father of Yi Ŏn-ho.

68. Nearly all the Censorate and OSC officials who played leading roles in this phase of the Yi Haeng controversy became victims of the 1519 purge. Among these, one important figure is Kim Chŏng who, as First Counselor, led the initial OSC denunciation of Yi Sŏng-ŏn. Presently, however, Kim Chŏng sought and received permission for a filial visit to his home and returned to the government only after the furor had died down (1517.10.10, 10.27, 12.30, i12.13). Cho Kwang-jo, too, was in the thick of things as Third Counselor (see 1517.11.18) and the four royal clansmen also were involved in the purge. Yet there are two noteworthy exceptions, Second Inspectors Pak Su-mun and Pak Ho.

69. Sin, "Kimyo sahwa," 23 avers that, because of the incessant pressure of the Censorate and OSC, "in the end the king transferred Yi Haeng and discharged Yi Sŏng-ŏn." In similar vein, *YK* 7.12 has: "In 1518 [sic] Yi Haeng was discharged; the Magistrate of Suwŏn, Yi Sŏng-ŏn, memorialized in his behalf but also was attacked and discharged." It is clear, of course, that Yi Haeng was not discharged, nor is it fair to say that he was transferred. He was, to be sure, given the different appointment of Fourth Minister of the Board of War (1518.1.5), a post carrying the same rank as Third Minister, though perhaps of lower prestige. But the record clearly indicates that at the time of this appointment the Board of Personnel made a conscious effort to insure that Yi Haeng receive a position such as would not furnish ground for speculation that he was in disfavor (see 1518.1.5 S). I prefer to think, therefore, that this was a routine change in assignment. With regard to Yi Sŏng-ŏn, the fact that he was discharged does not appear to have been recorded at the time. But that this is what befell him was noted in passing by the king some months later, in these words: "Some time ago, when Yi Sŏng-ŏn sent in a memorial, the government then too all wanted to prefer serious charges of crime against him, on the ground of scheming to destroy [the men of principle]. But because his was a memorial in response to an appeal for counsel, he was merely discharged. Cho Kye-sang's case too ought to be handled in this way" (1518.5.17 S).

70. Less exalted honors had been bestowed on Chŏng Mong-ju in earlier reigns and under Chungjong as well, and canonization itself had been proposed at least once before, to Sejo, on the basis of Chŏng's preeminence in "learning, the literary arts, and moral conduct" (1456.3.28 S).

71. Sin, "Kimyo sahwa," 27 offers the interpretation that the opposition of the High State Councillors of the time (Kim Su-dong, Yu Sun-jŏng, and Sŏng Hŭi-an) to the canonization of Chŏng Mong-ju was due simply to the fact that Chŏng was a political adversary of Yi T'aejo. I hesitate to assess the weight of such reasoning in the minds of men of that day, but at the same time I cannot accept Sin's view. A point made in later discussions of this issue is, I think, well taken. The high honor accorded Chŏng Mong-ju in T'aejong's reign (1401.1.14) was debated and determined, after all, by men who had played leading roles in the founding of the new dynasty (see 1517.8.12 S).

72. The two brief sections of this *obiter dictum* omitted in translation contain, respectively, a largely derogatory estimate of Kwŏn Chŏn's character and the king's remarks that he welcomed Kwŏn's views and intended to have the government discuss them. The relationship between the leading roles assigned here to Kwŏn, on the one hand, and to An Ch'ŏ-gyŏm and An Chŏng on the other is nowhere clarified. However, a gloss following the *Sillok* summary of the memorial presented by the National Academy students tells us that it was composed by Kwŏn (1517.8.7 S). All three, it should be remarked, passed the special civil examination sponsored by the Cho Kwang-jo group in 1519. Moreover, Kwŏn and An Ch'ŏ-gyŏm were killed and An Chŏng banished in the 1521 aftermath of the 1519 purge.

73. The essence of their argument was that Chŏng Mong-ju had served Sin U and Sin Ch'ang believing that they were in truth scions of the Koryŏ royal house. For, if otherwise, then why should Chŏng stick at transferring his allegiance to the Yi? And how could the men of early Yi, who were erstwhile close associates of Chŏng, honor him for his steadfast loyalty? (See 1517.8.11 S, 8.12 S, 8.18 S.)

74. This compromise was in close consonance with the view expressed by Personnel Minister Nam Kon, who had been absent at the time of the earlier general solicitation of views (see 1517.8.20 S). With the exception of Nam, opinions on the occasion of this re-discussion are recorded neither for the State Councillors and Six Boards Ministers nor for the OSC and Censorate officials. Nor is mention of formal expression of the royal will on the subject to be found. That Chungjong disposed of the canonization issue in the manner described is made clear, however, in subsequent *Sillok* entries (see 1517.9.17 S, 9.24 S, 9.29 S, 1519.7.30 S).

75. These anti-literary epithets are taken from Sin, "Kimyo sahwa," 8, who says they are to be found in the *Sillok* accounts of discussions at the Royal Lectures during this period. Sin gives his readers no further guidance, and I have been unable to locate specific instances of disparagement in just these terms.

76. The *wŏlgwa* was a monthly composition in some fixed format required, for example, of some OSC and Censorate officials. These were graded and prizes sometimes awarded as inducements to improving techniques. The practice, perforce abandoned under Yŏnsangun, had been revived by Chungjong (1508.2.19). Some years earlier a leading 1519 figure, Yi Cha, had been removed from the post of Second Censor for failing (but apparently not deliberately refusing) to compose the *wŏlgwa* (1514.4.19 S). Fifth Counselor Kim Ku and Junior Fifth Counselor Chŏng Ŭng, also prominent 1519 victims, joined Cho in refusing to observe the practice at this time.

   Despite his widely noted disdain for the literary arts, Cho Kwang-jo himself was an exceptionally able practitioner. The fact that he took a first in the Literary Licentiate examination testifies to this, and there is also a record that he was once awarded a prize by the king for placing first in an OSC literary competition judged by, of all people, Nam Kon and Kim Chŏn. On this occasion, the *Sillok* historians deemed Cho's achievement worth special citation (1516.11.29 S).

77. See, for example, 1517.1.21, 1519.5.19.

78. It is of interest that the idea of scrapping the existing civil examination structure and replacing it with this same Local Recommendation system was also voiced at the time of the Pak Kyŏng plot, in discussions apparently participated in by Cho Kwang-jo and Kim Sik (see 1507.i1.26 S).

79. The evidence may justify the conclusion, however, that the search for idle literati was now carried out more zealously than was the normal case. Half a year later, in response to Censorate and OSC urgings, the king formally repeated his instruction on the recommendation of idle literati (1517.8.21), and the record shows that some positive results were achieved (see 1517.10.22, 11.4, 1518.2.26).

80. A few days earlier the Second Censor, Kong Sŏ-rin, had also urged that civil examination candidates be tested by the "problem-essay" method rather than by the more usual literary forms (1518.3.8). Kong, too, is identified with the Cho group.

81. The periodic "weeding out" of officials appears to have been carried out on two distinct levels. One was the release of those whose positions were not authorized in the tables of organization (see, for example, 1511. 5.10, 1517.7.7). The other was the removal of officials on general grounds of unfitness or lack of promise (see, for example, 1511.4.24, 1514.9.28). In the present instance, sixteen lower echelon personnel had been removed as not qualified for promotion to higher office (1518.3.22 S, 3.26 S, 3.28 S).

82.   It had just been discovered that a new edition of the *Ta-Ming hui-tien* (Ming dynasty administrative codes) repeated a long-standing Ming misapprehension that Yi T'aejo was the heir of the notorious Yi In-im and had killed four Koryŏ rulers on his way to the throne. This slander had been vigorously protested by T'aejong and the Ming Board of Rites had agreed to correct it (1394.6.16, 1403.11.15, 1404.3.27). When the error was now found anew, all agreed on the necessity of making strong representations (1518.4.26). Accordingly, an embassy was appointed and, at first, Seventh State Councillor Ch'oe Suk-saeng was named to head it (1518.5.14). Protests by the Censorate and OSC, however, resulted in the designation of Nam Kon to replace Ch'oe.

Sin, "Kimyo sahwa," 34-5 suggests that the interest of the Censorate and OSC officials in having Nam Kon head the embassy may be explained by the fact that Ch'oe supported the Recommendation Examination and Nam opposed it. While I am not averse to imputing to the censoring bodies the motive of getting Nam Kon out of the way for a time, I hesitate before the conclusion that such a motive would be derived specifically from the Recommendation Examination issue, which already had been decided. It should be borne in mind in this connection that two major figures of the 1519 group (Yi Cha and Han Ch'ung) also accompanied the embassy (1518.5.14, 7.15). The mission, it may be noted, occupied nearly nine months (at least twice the time normally required for the round trip) and was only partially successful (1519.4.7).

83.   It came to be better known as the *hyŏllyang-kwa* (Examination of the Sage and Good), a term allegedly first used in ridicule by the opponents of the Recommendation Examination (1545.4.17 S).

84.   The evidence indicates that recommendations of idle literati made in response to royal instructions which antedated the very proposal of the Recommendation Examination may have been permitted to stand as valid nominations to examination candidacy. At any rate, at least two men recommended by provincial Governors late in 1517 subsequently passed the examination, and at least six others recommended prior to the announcement of procedures on 1518.6.5 also are found among the successful candidates (1517.10.22, 11.4, 1518.3.26, 5.21, 5.27, 5.30, 6.1).

85.   Just how many candidates ultimately were authorized to proceed to the examination has remained a mystery. The *Sillok* itself does not say and unofficial sources give the number as either the entire one hundred twenty, or as eighty, or as fifty-eight, tacitly admitting that it is not known which is correct (e.g., see 1518.12.1; *YK* 8.2; Kim Yuk, *Kimyo nok,* 62b; Yi Wŏn-sun, *Hwahae tangwŏn* 4 "Kimyo sahwa, pu: hyŏllyang-kwa"). It seems possible that eighty candidates may have been authorized but only fifty-eight actually sat for the examination, for cases of relinquishment of candidacy (for example, by men who passed the regular triennial examination held earlier in 1519) can be documented.

86.   Although documentation is not lacking on this point (e.g., 1516.1.23, 1518.5.2, 7.11), one must hold suspect the extravagant claims in this regard made by An's biographers (e.g., *CJJ* 235; *YK* 7.36, 9.47). The verdict of history, of course, upheld the Cho Kwang-jo group; accordingly, assertions that An recognized and championed such talents as these would reflect the more favorably on him.

87.   It is only fair to note that there were many occasions, both before and after he became a High State Councillor, on which An Tang publicly differed with, or even scathingly denounced, the views of the Cho group. To cite a few such instances, An opposed the canonization of Chŏng Mong-ju and Kim Koeng-p'il (1517.8.7); he supported the return to portfolio post of Yi Haeng (1517.10.19); he ridiculed Censorate and OSC demands for harsher punishment of Kim U-jŭng (1519.3.4; to be treated below).

88.   This was a Junior First Rank post, the step between the Senior Second Rank of Board Minister (which An Tang long had held) and the Senior First Rank of the High State Councillor positions. At the same time, Yi Kye-maeng was named Fourth State Councillor, which involved a similar promotion. For, in recommending

Yi for consideration as High State Councillor timber, Chŏng Kwang-p'il and Sin Yong-gae had observed that his rank was insufficient and had suggested that the king remove this obstacle to his candidacy (1518.1.4 S).

89. The unfortunate Recorder, Yun Ku, was banished as a result of this incident in the early aftermath of the 1519 purge. The account I have given here is substantially in accord with Yun Ku's recollections when imprisoned and interrogated nearly two years after the event. This version was corroborated in all essential points by the testimony of others whose official positions at the time had brought them first hand knowledge of what actually transpired (see 1520.3.21 S, 3.22 S, 3.27 S, 5.21 S). But it is significantly at variance with the amplifying remarks of the historical officials, which are appended to the record of the day in question. These remarks are worth quoting at length:

When Yun Ku went to ascertain [Sin's] view, the Third Diarist Yu Hŭi-ryŏng, who also had gone to Sin's house to ascertain his view on the question of the petition embassy to Ming, was able to hear what was said on this matter. The Second State Councillor said: "No one knows his subject better than the sovereign; the decision must come from the king. But in my view the choice should be made from among the three men previously memorialized. At that time the king let it be known that he regarded An Tang as suitable for High State Councillor position, but it remains my view that the choice should be made from among the three men previously memorialized."

Now Sin Yong-gae's view did not endorse An Tang, but rather inclined toward the [original] three men. But when Yun Ku was about to make his report, Royal Secretaries Yi Cha and Kim Chŏng, with eager expectation, asked: "The Second State Councillor, too, surely must have endorsed An Tang?" Whereupon Yun Ku, feeling intimidated, did not answer truthfully. Thus Sin's real view was different from that now memorialized, and the king was totally unaware that Sin's view did not endorse An Tang. (1518.5.7 S)

The weight of other evidence may justify us in dismissing these remarks of the *Sillok* historians as tendentious. But it is significant for an appreciation of the atmosphere of that day that it could be written and believed, in some quarters at least, that leading members of the Cho Kwang-jo group had been guilty of willful deceit of the sovereign in the matter of this vital appointment.

90. The *Sillok* and other historians are strangely silent on the subject, but there was a compelling legal reason why Kim Ŭng-gi had to go if An Tang were to be raised to High State Councillor position. Kim had married a sister of An Tang, and the provisions of the Yi code governing debarment from office tenancy forbade brothers-in-law occupying State Council posts at the same time (see *Kyŏngguk taejŏn* 164-165).
This is why An Tang, unlike his contemporaries of comparable stature, had continued to serve in Board Minister posts without once being named to the State Council, for Kim Ŭng-gi had been in the State Council almost without interruption since 1510. The king himself took note of the existence of this obstacle in once explaining to Nam Kon why he had been preferred for State Council position over An Tang, who was senior to Nam in length of government service (1517.8.22 S). Much earlier in his career, An had been removed as Inspector-General under these same statutes because of conflict with Kim's position as War Minister (1509.3.21).

91. See *YK* 7.36, which cites Kim Al-lo's *Yongch'ŏn tamjŏk ki.* This source, to be sure, is not likely to be sympathetic to the Cho group. But in the *Sillok,* too, there is ample record of thinly disguised efforts by members of the Cho group to call the king's attention to their predilection for An Tang (see 1518.1.10 S, 1.14 S).

92. We may recall, however, the roles of passers Kwŏn Chŏn and An Chŏng in the canonization issue. Kwŏn Chŏn, again while still a student, had joined in the effort to persuade the king to abolish the Sogyŏksŏ (1518.8.22).

93. I have not attempted to analyze this factor, but it is to be remarked that a number of unsuccessful candidates of the Recommendation Examination also were named to Censorate or OSC posts during this period.

This, perhaps, was to be expected in view of the desire expressed by the king late in 1518 (12.7 S) to employ immediately all of those recommended, "even though they have not yet passed the examination."

94. This time-honored device for making one's grievances known to the authorities was remarked several times during the years of ascendancy of the Cho Kwang-jo group (see 1516.6.28, 1517.8.16, 1518.8.21, 1519.2.11). The message attached to the arrows in the 1518 instance is said to have listed over thirty men (the names of twenty-four are recorded), all of them identified with the 1519 group, who were "convulsing the government and on the point of imperiling the state" (1518.8.21, 8.21 S).

95. Sin, "Kimyo sahwa," 42, 47-49, in addition to the three discussed in detail below, notes the names of a dozen "veteran high officials" who had been shunted into non-portfolio posts as the result of pressures exerted by the men of 1519, and of six others who, "though reviled by the literati group," still clung to State Council or Six Boards Ministers positions. Upon closer scrutiny, I find a number of objections to Sin's categorization. Tentatively I would suggest that only five (Song Chil, Kwŏn Kyun, Hong Kyŏng-ju, Hong Suk, Kang Hun) properly belong in the first category, as men who definitely owed their relegation to the sidelines to Censorate action and whom the Censorate would not likely permit to reappear in influential position. Six others (Kim Ŭng-gi, Yi Kye-maeng, Han Se-hwan, Song Ch'ŏn-hŭi, Yun Kŭm-son, Yi Son) may be classed at best as borderline cases. I would assign Kim Chŏn to the second of Sin's categories, together with Nam Kon, Ko Hyŏng-san, and possibly Chŏng Kwang-p'il. Of the remaining three in Sin's second grouping only Yi Yu-ch'ŏng really belongs there, for the records of both Yu Tam-nyŏn and Kim Kŭk-p'ip appear to be remarkably clear of adverse Censorate criticism.

Sin goes on to observe that a number of these veteran high officials were Chungjong Merit Subjects, while the others all had close ties with the merit men of 1506. This latter assertion, I fear, would prove difficult to document, nor can I accept Sin's implication that merit status itself provided the basis for the opposition between the Cho group and the higher echelons of officials. Rather, Sin's statistics are valid, I think, as a rough gauge of the power wielded by Cho Kwang-jo and his supporters, and of the revenge potential generated by the indiscriminate exercise of this power.

96. The *Sillok* historians, normally so quick to add explanatory notes to the record, pass by in silence the impeachment and ouster of Chang Sun-son. The king himself was so surprised to read the memorial which launched the attack on Chang that he summoned Censorate officials for an explanation. But he learned (from Fourth Inspector Kim Sik) only that "for some time we have wanted to indict the matter of Chang Sun-son, but had been unable to determine with certainty the circumstances [of his villainy]. Recently his evil character became more and more manifest, and also there chanced to occur a great natural disaster. It was because of these considerations that we memorialized indicting him" (1518.5.16 S).

97. The Yi Kwa Plot merit roster already had been disposed of in an earlier struggle, in 1517. King Chungjong had held firm for three months in the face of endlessly reiterated pleas from the Censorate and OSC and from high officials as well (see 1516.12.8, 12.12, 1517.3.14, 3.24). Finally the king yielded, despite the fear he expressed that rescission of this merit roster would lead to agitation in the body politic (1517.3.14 S).

98. Nine of the full quota of eleven Censorate officials are named as participating in the discussion which followed the presentation of this memorial. Of these, three (Kim Ik, Song Ho-ji, Yi Pu) had passed the Recommendation Examination, and a fourth (Cho Kwang-jwa) was an unsuccessful candidate. Still another passer (Yi Yŏn-gyŏng), if he had not been a party to the opening memorial, was named to the Censorate in the course of the debate on the Merit Subject issue (1519.11.5).

99. Granted the opportunity to state their case in person to the king, the Censorate proceeded to greatly elaborate the original theme of the baneful role of Yu Cha-gwang and, in addition, noted that merit rosters of earlier periods in the dynasty had been far more modest. They also called to the king's attention a number of specific

instances as well as general types of undeserved merit enrollment. The well-calculated argument linking the plots which studded the early years of Chungjong's reign to excessive merit enrollment in 1506 also received further stress (1519.10.25 S). This argument had been spelled out more fully by Cho Kwang-jo on an earlier occasion, in the course of the successful campaign to abolish the Yi Kwa Plot merit roster (1517.2.26 S).

100. On the original Chungjong Enthronement Merit Subject roster there were 8 Prime Merit Subjects (First Class), 13 Second Class, 31 Third Class, and 65 Fourth Class, a total of 117. The commonly encountered figure is 107 (e.g., *Chōsengo jiten* 743; *Kǔn sajǒn* 897; Ǒ Suk-kwǒn, *Kosa ch'waryo* [Keijō, 1941], 180). I do not know how to account for this statistic — it may be a simple error of character omission, or it may represent the number remaining after all deletions and reenrollments are taken into account. By 1519, thirteen of those originally enrolled had already been erased from the roster, mostly as a consequence of commission of crimes (e.g., Yu Cha-gwang, Sin Yun-mu, Pak Yǒng-mun, Kim U-jǔng).

101. The apparent unanimity of the government on this issue is puzzling. To be sure, the State Councillors and other high-level officials went on record in support of revision of the merit roster only after the censoring bodies had made unmistakably clear that they would brook no compromise. Moreover, a close look at the record strongly suggests that these high officials committed themselves with the greatest reluctance, after being sharply criticized by the censoring bodies for their failure to take a stand (see 1519.11.1 S, 11.3 S). Yet the significant fact, surely, is that in the beginning the highest officials did not oppose the Censorate but remained silent and, when at length they did commit themselves, they came down on the side of the censoring bodies, in opposition to the stubbornly resisting king.

Once having taken this position, the high officials seem to have been just as loath to compromise as were those of the Cho Kwang-jo group. It is perhaps plausible that some of those who would be expected to register objections were aware that, whatever revision was made, it would not be permitted to stand for long — that they were aware, in other words, that a purge was in the making. But Chǒng Kwang-p'il, for example, clearly could not have been privy to the secret, and in the later stages of the debate he emerges almost as the leading advocate of revision. In the previous year, on the other hand, he had strongly opposed the Censorate's demands for deletion of the merit listing of Yi Hǔi-ong, a Recorder in the Royal Secretariat in 1506 whose claim to enrollment was at least debatable (1518.4.6).

I would suggest that in this, as in many other instances, the Censorate had a good case, difficult to counter on grounds of principle, and that, accordingly, exception could be taken less to the idea proposed than to the very idea of proposing it. In other words, it might be strongly felt that the Censorate wasn't quite playing the game but, at the same time, it would be realized that, especially in this period of its heyday, open opposition to the Censorate might successfully be based only on the firmest ground.

102. The breakdown by classes reveals that the king accepted intact the revised deletion proposals; i.e., eight Second Class, twelve Third Class, and the entire Fourth Class were stricken from the roster. This left but twenty-eight Merit Subjects (five First Class, five Second Class, eighteen Third Class), among whom, it is worth noting, were purge architects Hong Kyǒng-ju and Sim Chǒng.

The question of revision of the Minor Merit Subject lists is nowhere mentioned in the record of discussion on the issue of the Merit Subjects proper. It may be that the markedly lower level of rewards received by Minor Merit Subjects put them beneath the notice of those concerned with the larger problem.

With regard to the rewards which had been given the deleted Merit Subjects, the king, snatching half a victory from seemingly total defeat, issued this order: "Although these Merit Subjects have been struck from the roster, none of the things awarded them — miscellaneous things, houses, allowances in lieu of houses — shall be repossessed" (1519.11.13 S). This order, which doubtless included within its scope such primary bounty as land and slaves, did not reduce the revision of the merit roster to a travesty. Apart from the prestige of the title, the mere fact of merit enrollment carried with it a number of desirable privileges and prospects. For example, Merit Subjects could expect favored treatment before the bar of justice, they or their eldest sons might periodically receive material awards from the king or unusual official preferment, their merit status often would serve as an avenue to participation in high government councils, their posterity would be exempted from application of corvee statutes (see *Taejŏn hoet'ong*, Chōsen sōtokufu chūsūin reprint ed. [Keijō, 1939], 365), the celebration of rites in their honor by their descendants might be continued longer at the original site (see *Taejŏn hoet'ong* 622). Moreover, it seems a reasonable inference (I have not been able to verify this point) that awards of land and slaves, even though retained by an ex-Merit Subject during his lifetime, would not be assignable to his heirs but rather would revert to the state.

Nonetheless, the king had taken a long step toward subverting the intent of the merit roster revisionists, and one wonders why the record registers no protesting voices. But perhaps there was not time. This order of the king moved the *Sillok* historians to observe that "the sophisticated [thereby] realized it would not be long before [the deletions] were restored" (1519.11.13 S); probably the sophisticated realized as well that a great storm was brewing.

103. The record of government deliberations during the first two days or so following the beginning of the purge fails to reveal a single voice raised in outspoken hostility to the Cho group. Succor came even from the mouths of those who had plotted the purge in the first place. Sim Chŏng, for example, urged that action be taken with the utmost circumspection and in consonance with "the general body of public opinion" (1519.11.16 S). Hong Kyŏng-ju too, while laying stress on the Cho group's fault of extremism, offered essentially the same advice (1519.11.16 S). Nam Kon did not participate in these deliberations, having withdrawn on the plea of illness early on the sixteenth (1519.11.16 S).

104. Angered, Chungjong ordered five leaders of the "over 150" student demonstrators jailed and had the rest driven out by troops. Those expelled from the palace precincts then asked that they be permitted to share the fate of their leaders. On the following day the students, their numbers now swelled to some 240, asked twice again to be jailed, asserting the while that Cho was innocent of crime. Representations from all sides presently brought about the release of the imprisoned students. The five arrested leaders were Yi Yak-su, Kim Su-sŏng, Pak Se-ho, Yun Ŏn-jik and Hong Sun-bok (1519.11.16 S, 11.17 S). Yi Yak-su, a Recommendation Examination candidate, also was the lead signatory of a subsequent student memorial which urged, in effect, that Cho and his fellow accused be pardoned (1519.11.19 S).

105. Chŏng Kwang-p'il and by inference An Tang and Sin Sang were quick to dissociate themselves from the implications of such royal statements. They pointed out that when they arrived on the scene in response to the royal summons (the night of the fifteenth), the bill requesting charges of crime had already been completed. They added that the prior arrivals (those who had entered the palace compound in advance through the west gate) had declared: "The king has had us request charges; this is entirely the will of the king" (1519.11.16 S; see also 11.17 S).

106. When Investigation Officers Kim Chŏn, Yi Chang-gon, and Hong Suk memorialized this as the penalty prescribed by law, they hastened to add their conviction that it was much too severe and that it would be the gravest mistake to carry out such a sentence. They noted, too, that, in the absence of uniquely applicable provisions in the Korean code, the Ming code had been used, and a gloss tells us that their reference had been to the "malicious cliquism" paragraph of the Ming code (1519.11.16 S). The use of Ming law in this way was standard procedure.

107. The OSC officials were among those removed from their posts under a blanket order issued the night the purge began, and on the following day the king had approved the discharge of eight of them. Chŏng Kwang-p'il sought to persuade Chungjong to restore to their posts both the OSC officials and the Censorate personnel who had been removed at the same time, but he succeeded in winning consent only in the case of the former (1519.11.15 S, 11.16 S).

108. Leading anti-Cho group voices among the new appointees to Censorate and OSC posts were Yi Pin (Censor-General 1519.11.20, First Counselor 1520.1.4), Yi Hang (Inspector-General 1519.11.25), Yu Kwan (Second Inspector 1519.11.26), Ch'ae Ch'im (Third Inspector 1519.11.25 and 1520.2.4), Nam Se-ju (Second Censor 1519.11.25), Cho Ch'im (Fourth Censor 1519.11.25), and Sŏ Hu (Third Inspector 1519.12.27, Second Inspector 1520.1.13). Yi Pin, Yi Hang, Ch'ae Ch'im and Cho Ch'im in particular won notoriety for their roles in intensifying the purge (see *YK* 7.56-60, 62).

109. This aspect of the purge will be reviewed in some detail below.

110. These were Ch'ungch'ŏngdo Navy Commander Han Ch'ung; Office of Royal Decrees Third Diarist Yi Ku (one of the duty officers at the outbreak of the purge); Hwanghae Governor Kim Chŏng-guk; and Ch'oe San-du, who had been a Third Inspector when the purge began. All but Yi Ku were on the list of thirty-five men of the Cho Kwang-jo clique soon to emanate from the Censorate.

111. The Censorate presented its list in two sections, of twenty-three and twelve names respectively. In submitting the former it was asserted that, while there were many other followers of Cho, these were a selected group of extreme cases. But on the next day the Censorate officials claimed that the crimes of the twelve men they now proposed to add to the list were, if anything, still more grave. The Censorate denunciation of the group of twenty-three is of peculiar interest. It says in part: "These are all of the same category as Pak Se-hŭi, etc. They cliqued together with Cho Kwang-jo, lodged at each other's houses. At times of personnel nominations, the endorsements and the condemnations they made all were determined in advance in private deliberations. This caused turmoil [in the government]" (1519.12.14 S).

112. The Censorate roster of thirty-five is as follows (arranged alphabetically in two groups, the eighteen selected for punishment on the left; asterisks indicate members of the royal clan):

An Tang	Chang Ok
Cho Kwang-jwa	Cho Ŏn-gyŏng
Chŏng Ŭng	Chŏng Sun-bung
Chŏng Wan	Han Ch'ung
Ch'oe San-du	Kim Chŏng-guk
Ch'oe Suk-saeng	Kim Kwang-bok
Kim An-guk	Ku Su-bok
Song Ho-ji	Kwŏn Chang
Song Ho-rye	Kwŏn Chŏn
Yang P'aeng-son	Sin Kwang-han
Yi Cha	*Yi Chŏng-suk
Yi Ch'ung-gŏn	*Yi Ch'ong
Yi Hŭi-min	Yi Ch'ŏng
Yi Yak-ping	*Yi Ki
Yi Yŏn-gyŏng	*Yi Kyŏng
Yu Un	*Yi Ŏm
Yu Yong-gŭn	Yu In-suk
Yun Kwang-nyŏng	

It should be noted that four of these (Chŏng Wan, Song Ho-ji, Yi Yŏn-gyŏng, Kwŏn Chŏn) were products of the Recommendation Examination and four others (Cho Kwang-jwa, Song Ho-rye, Yun Kwang-nyŏng, Kwŏn Chang) were unsuccessful candidates, as were brothers of Yi Ch'ung-gŏn, Yi Yak-ping, and Yi Yŏn-gyŏng.

Two days earlier, three students had submitted a memorial attacking Chŏng Kwang-p'il as unfit, urging the death penalty for the eight original accused, and requesting punishment of eleven others of their clique, all of whom are found also on the Censorate list (nine among the punished and another, Han Ch'ung, in judicial process) (1519.12.14). Some accounts record the lead signatory of this memorial, one Hwang Kye-ok (miswritten in the *Sillok* as Hwang I-ok), also among the five students arrested for leading the earlier pro-Cho demonstration within the palace compound (e.g., *YK* 7.53-4, 57). Biographers of the fifth student named in the *Sillok* (Hong Sun-bok) are unanimous, however, in according him this distinction. See, for example, *CJJ* 1268; *Kukcho inmul chi*, B.14; *Kimyo nok* 72; *YK* 8.14. The *Sillok* historians tell us that, although Hwang originally drafted a memorial which pleaded Cho's innocence, it was never submitted (1519.12.14 S). The Hwang Kye-ok memorial is credited with strongly influencing the king in the direction of intensifying the purge (*YK* 7.58-9, 62) or, at the least, with providing him a convenient pretext for so acting (see 1519.12.14 S).

113. See *YK* 7.63-64, 8.47; 1528.9.28, 1538.4.12. After Kim Se-p'il's experience, seven years were to pass before a kind word for the victims of 1519 was again ventured in public (see 1527.6.3).

114. Five other Investigation Officers were named in addition to Chŏng. Two of them, Nam Kon and Sim Chŏng, headed the list of those high officials against whom the alleged plot was directed (1521.10.11).

115. Both Kim Chŏng and Ki Chun had been brought up to Seoul, interrogated, beaten one hundred strokes, and returned to banishment at the height of the Kim Sik case in 1520, charged with setting a precedent for fleeing the king's justice by leaving their original places of banishment to briefly visit their aged and ailing mothers (1520.1.4, 1.14, 4.26, 5.12, 5.25, 6.17). Now the Censorate once again brought up the charge of setting an undesirable precedent, and presently both were sentenced to strangling (1521.10.17).

116. Yi Chang-gon was one of those found "sitting outside the Royal Lecture Hall" on the night the purge began. It is asserted, however, that the purge plotters beguiled him into appearing on the scene, since his presence as Minister of War was necessary to ordering out the troops. Unofficial sources go on to say that, when Yi found out that the plotters intended to kill a number of their enemies on the spot, he managed to frustrate this design and have the affair handled by normal methods of judicial procedure (*YK* 7.45, 47). It appears to have been because of this act alone that Yi Chang-gon came to be included in the designation "the Eight Worthies of 1519" (*kimyo p'arhyŏn;* see *Kimyo nok* 7b-10b). There is no other evidence significantly linking Yi's name with the men of 1519 or their program. Nor is it apparent that his ouster was related in any way to this 1521 affair, other than in timing.

It may be added in this connection that Han Ch'ung, in a statement made from prison immediately prior to the king's consent to punishment of Yi Chang-gon, averred he had once heard of the intention of three 1519 victims (Yu In-suk, Pak Yŏng, Ha Chŏng) to kill Yi. This tale, which evidently proved to be groundless, is said to have temporarily stayed the king's hand against Yi (1521.10.29, 10.30, 11.5).

117. The verdict of later generations on this affair is not clear cut; certainly most of the victims eventually were rehabilitated but the principals perhaps were not. Unofficial accounts tend to regard the affair as a frame up from beginning to end (see *YK* 8.16, 20-21). The informants, of course, were handsomely rewarded, but eventually they lost all they had gained and more (1521.10.20, 1550.1.17, 1586.9.7, 1589.10.2, 12.16).

118. Actually, Nam Kon endorsed this middle course only in the hope of appeasing the Censorate. Perhaps surprisingly, on this occasion and at least one other, Nam Kon staunchly averred that the passers of the Recommendation Examination were men of talent and that the government ought not deprive itself of their services (1519.12.3 S, 12.10 S).

119. *YK* 8.8.

120. The Recommendation Examination has no inconsiderable subsequent history, but it will suffice here to say that in 1545 revalidation of this examination list was approved by King Injong on his deathbed (1545.6.29) and the surviving passers were employed at levels reflecting their newly regained status (1545.8.1, 8.2). A little later, however, the list was again voided, as a consequence of the Purge of 1545 (1545.10.10), and it was not until early in Sŏnjo's reign that final restitution was made (1568.10.9).

It should also be noted that the Censorate was unsuccessful in its concurrent effort to have abrogated, again on grounds of unfairness, the special examination held a month before the purge (1519.10.17).

121.   By this term, the fuller form of which is *Yŏ-ssi hyangyak (Lü-shih hsiang-yüeh),* is meant the doctrine of local self-government outlined by the Sung Confucianist Lü Ta-chun, as modified by Chu Hsi and included in the *Hsiao-hsüeh.*

122.   Extension of the village code system to the capital city had been warmly urged by such men of 1519 as Ki Chun, Han Ch'ung, and An Ch'ŏ-ham. Nam Kon had opposed this, arguing that its establishment in Seoul could only lead to conflict and confusion with the central government agencies responsible for moral education and penal administration, and his view was seconded by An Tang. After listening to both sides, the king decided to accord neither legal sanction nor prohibition (1519.5.20 S, 6.8 S, 7.18 S).

123.   The arguments against the village code system advanced by the Censorate at this time were essentially those that had been voiced before, only in more fully elaborated form and related explicitly to the broader theme of the crimes of extremism and cliquism of the Cho Kwang-jo group. It is of interest to note, however, that both Cho Kwang-jo and Kim Sik had warned of the harmful effects of attempting to put the village code system into operation by coercive tactics or with undue haste (see 1519.5.19 S, 10.10 S).

124.   Efforts in Chungjong's reign to abolish or restrict the use of female musical entertainers go back to about the beginning. These efforts enjoyed widespread support among the officialdom and early met with partial success. The objections apparently were based on doctrinal and moral considerations, for the practice seems to have had specific relationship both to the propagation of Buddhism and to prostitution.

        The employment of female musical entertainers, then, had considerably declined before 1519. In that year the Censorate and OSC campaigned against the practice over a period of some three months, winning first its abolition in the provinces and ultimately its discontinuation in Seoul as well, except in the case of one type of palace function. At this time the king was willing to go farther than some of his State Councillors and other high officials but, after the purge, it was the high officials who for a time frustrated the king's desire to revive the practice. The Censorate, it may be noted, objected (in vain) to but one limited aspect of the reemployment of female musical entertainers (1509.11.11, 1510.10.21, 1517.8.3, 1519.2.6, 2.7, 2.8, 5.19, 1520.2.28, 8.7, 8.13).

125.   This probably was in revocation of the 1518 order that "recitation of the Classics be carried out henceforth on the occasion of all special [civil] examinations." This stipulation grew out of discussion on the formulation of procedures for the Recommendation Examination, but it was not a significant point of contention between the Cho group and opposing forces (1518.7.18 S, 7.21 S).

126.   Actually, Cho Kwang-jo was appointed Sixth Royal Secretary on 1518.5.2, after having served as First Counselor for nearly five months. But at the insistence of the Censorate and OSC he was returned to the more strategic OSC post after only three days (1518.5.5).

127.   The "running image" is a separation of the two constituents of the surname Cho. The trick was accomplished by outlining the desired characters on the leaf with a sweet juice. Nam Kon is sometimes blamed for this storied bit of knavery (e.g., *Kukcho inmul chi* 229, *CJJ* 1149) and, again, it is described as having been a joint project (*YK* 7.44). But the *Sillok* makes it clear that the rumor-mongers of that day ascribed it to Sim Chŏng (1520.4.16 S, 5.28 S, 6.3 S).

128.   This compounds the error already noted, for the common mistake is to call Kim Chŏn the Second Minister-without-Portfolio, the post he had held earlier in the purge year.

129. *CJJ* 1612-13. This is a Japanese paraphrase of a text contained in a compendium of obituaries of famous figures of the Yi dynasty. The compendium appears to date from the late eighteenth century, but I have not been able to inspect it to determine, if possible, the approximate date of this obituary of Cho Kwang-jo.

130. Kim Myŏng-yun may be called the black sheep among those who passed the Recommendation Examination. He was the only one to subsequently pass the normal civil examination course, in 1524, and his checkered career is distinguished chiefly by his secret report of a treason plot (1545.9.1), which gave fresh impetus to the Purge of 1545. Although duly rewarded for this service to the state, he was slow to gain preferment to the higher reaches of public office, being past sixty when he received his first Board Minister appointment (1555.5.16). He alone among the Recommendation Examination passers was still living when Sŏnjo revalidated the roster, but, by this time, in the wave of revulsion against the excesses of Myŏngjong's reign, he had been stripped of office and rank (1567.12.23). He was the son of Fourth State Councillor Kim Kŭk-p'ip.

131. The king swiftly sentenced two leaders of the plot to beating and banishment, on the charge of "seditious words" (1519.11.18). The two men were released from banishment in unusually short order, and at the same time Kim U-jŭng (the Merit Subject banished earlier in 1519 under accusation of plotting the same kind of assassination attempt) was also freed (1520.8.20). The military men involved do not appear to have been important figures.

132. Yi Hwang (T'oegye Sŏnsaeng) was sixty-seven at this time, only two years away from death. Although he did not pass the civil examination until 1534, his presence in Seoul dates from not long after the purge, for he entered the National Academy in 1523. See *CJJ* 649.

GENERAL GLOSSARY

Akhak kwebŏm 樂學軌範

Cheju 濟州
Cheng-te 正德
Chien-chou 建州
chikchŏn 職田
chinsa 進士
Chiphyŏnjŏn 集賢殿
Cho Ŭi Che mun 弔義帝文
Chosŏn 朝鮮
chŏkkae kongsin 敵愾功臣
Chŏlla 全羅
chŏngguk kongsin 靖國功臣
chŏngnan kongsin (Sejo) 靖難功臣
chŏngnan kongsin (Yi Kwa Plot) 定難功臣
chŏngsa kongsin 定社功臣
chungin 中人
chungnim ch'irhyŏn 竹林七賢
chwaik kongsin 佐翼功臣
chwamyŏng kongsin 佐命功臣
chwari kongsin 佐理功臣
Ch'ŏnan 天安
Ch'ŏngdo 清道
Ch'ŏngju 清州
ch'ŏn'gŏ-kwa 薦擧科
ch'ŏnmin 賤民
Ch'ungch'ŏng 忠清

Haeju 海州
Haep'yŏng 海平
Hamgyŏng 咸鏡
Hamyang 咸陽
han'gŭl 한글
Hanyang 漢陽
hsiang-chŭ li-hsŭan 鄉擧里選
Hsiao-hsŭeh 小學

hsien-liang fang-cheng k'o 賢良方正科
Hsing-li ta-ch'üan 性理大全
Hwach'ŏn 花川
Hwanghae 黃海
hyanggyo 鄉校
hyangni 鄉吏
hyangyak 鄉約
hyŏllyŏng 縣令
hyŏllyang-kwa 賢良科
hyŏn 縣
hyŏn'gam 縣監

iktae kongsin 翊戴功臣
Inch'ŏn 仁川

kaeguk kongsin 開國功臣
Kaesŏng 開城
Kangwŏn 江原
kapcha sahwa 甲子士禍
kimyo in 己卯人
kimyo p'arhyŏn 己卯八賢
kimyo sahwa 己卯士禍
kisaeng 妓生
kongjŏn 公田
kongsin 功臣
kongsinjŏn 功臣田
Koryŏ 高麗
Kŏje 巨濟
Kŏnch'un 建春
kun 郡
kun 君
kuŏn 求言
Kŭnjŏng 勤政
kwagŏ 科擧
kwajŏn 科田
kyŏl 結

Kyŏngbok　景福
Kyŏnggi　京畿
Kyŏngguk taejŏn　經國大典
Kyŏngsang　慶尚
kyŏngsŏmun　敬誓文
Kyŏngyŏnch'ŏng　經筵廳

Lü-shih hsiang-yüeh　呂氏鄉約

mok　牧
muo sahwa　戊午士/史禍
Muryŏng　武靈
musul chi ok　戊戌之獄

Namdo　南道

pangmok　榜目
pangnap　防納
Pukto　北道
puwŏn'gun　府院君
pyŏlsajŏn　別賜田
pyŏlsi　別試
P'yŏngan　平安

saengwŏn　生員
saengyuksin　生六臣
sahwa　士禍
sajŏn　私田
Samch'ŏk　三陟
samdaejang　三大將
samdaesin　三大臣
samhun　三勳
samp'o　三浦
samsa　三司
sangin　常人
sasaek　四色
sayuksin　死六臣
Seoul　서울

shui-liu-chai　水陸齋
Sillok　實錄
Sillokkak　實錄閣
Sinmu　神武
sipch'ŏl　十哲
sip'ye sipcho　時弊十條
Sogyŏkchŏn　昭格殿
Sogyŏksŏ　昭格署
sogyŏng　小京
sŏban　西班
sŏgyŏng　署經
sŏin　西人
sŏlchae　設齋
Sŏnsan　善山
Sŏnsŏng　宣城
sŏsa　署事
Sul chu si　述酒詩
suryuk chae　水陸齋
Suwŏn　水原

Ta-Ming hui-tien　大明會典
taedohobu　大都護府
taegan　臺諫
tangjaeng　黨爭
tohobu　都護府
tongban　東班
Tongguk t'onggam　東國通鑑
Tongguk yŏji sŭngnam　東國輿地勝覽
tongin　東人
Tongmun sŏn　東文選

ŭlsa sahwa　乙巳士禍

wŏlgwa　月課
wŏnhun　元勳
wŏnjong kongsin　原/元從功臣

Yain　野人

yangban 兩班

Yŏ-ssi hyangyak 呂氏鄉約

Yŏngch'u 迎秋

Yŏnghŭng 永興

yuil chi sa 遺逸之士

yukchin 六鎭

GLOSSARY OF NAMES OF PERSONS APPEARING IN THE TEXT

An Chǒng 安璔

An Ch'im 安琛

An Ch'ǒ-gǔn 安處謹

An Ch'ǒ-gyǒm 安處謙

An Ch'ǒ-ham 安處諴

An Ch'ǒ-jung 安處中

An Ho 安瑚

An Hyǒng 安珩

An P'aeng-su 安彭壽

An Tang 安瑭

Ansun 安順

Chang Ok 張玉

Chang Sun-son 張順孫

Changgyǒng 章敬

Cho Chi-sǒ 趙之瑞

Cho Ch'im 趙琛

Cho Ch'ung-son 趙衷孫

Cho Hyǒng 趙珩

Cho Ik-chǒng 趙益貞

Cho Kwang-bo 趙光/廣輔

Cho Kwang-jo 趙光祖

Cho Kwang-jwa 趙光/廣佐

Cho Kye-sang 曹繼商

Cho On 趙溫

Cho Ǒn-gyǒng 趙彦卿

Cho Sun 趙舜

Cho Wi 曹偉

Cho Wǒn-gi 趙元紀

Cho Yǒn 趙涓

Cho Yu-hyǒng 趙有亨

Chǒng Ch'ang-son 鄭昌孫

Chǒng Hǔi-ryang 鄭希良

Chǒng In-in 鄭麟仁

Chǒng In-ji 鄭麟趾

Chǒng Kǔg-in 丁克仁

Chǒng Kwang-p'il 鄭光弼

Chǒng, *Madame* 鄭貴人

Chǒng Mi-su 鄭眉壽

Chǒng Mong-ju 鄭夢周

Chǒng Sim 鄭沈

Chǒng Sǒk-kyǒn 鄭錫/碩堅

Chǒng Sǒng-gǔn 鄭誠謹

Chǒng Sun-bung 鄭順朋

Chǒng Sǔng-jo 鄭承祖

Chǒng Ǔng 鄭䳣

Chǒng Wan 鄭浣

Chǒng Yǒ-ch'ang 鄭汝昌

Chǒnghǔi 貞熹

Chǒnghyǒn 貞顯

Chǒngjong 定宗

Chu Hsi 朱熹

Chungjong 中宗

Ch'ae Ch'im 蔡忱

Ch'ae Se-yǒng 蔡世英

Ch'oe Hae 崔瀣

Ch'oe Kwan 崔灌

Ch'oe Pu 崔溥

Ch'oe San-du 崔山斗

Ch'oe So-ha 崔小河

Ch'oe Suk-saeng 崔淑生

Ha Chǒng 河艇/斑

Hakcho 學祖

Han Ch'i-hyǒng 韓致亨

Han Ch'ung 韓忠

Han Ch'ung-in 韓忠仁

Han Han 韓僴

Han Hun 韓訓

Han Hyo-wǒn 韓效元

Han Hyǒng-yun 韓亨允

Han Kǒn 韓健

Han Myŏng-hoe　韓明澮

Han Se-hwan　韓世桓

Han Sun　韓恂

Hong Han　洪瀚

Hong Kwi-dal　洪貴達

Hong Kyŏng-ju　洪景舟

Hong Ŏn-p'il　洪彥弼

Hong Se-p'il　洪世弼

Hong Sik　洪湜

Hong Suk　洪淑

Hong Sun-bok　洪順福

Hŏ Chong　許琮

Hŏ Ch'im　許琛

Hŏ Pan　許磐

Hŏ Wi　許渭

Hwang Kye-ok　黃季沃

Hwangbo In　皇甫仁

Hyŏn Sŏk-kyu　玄錫/碩圭

Hyŏnsuk　顯壽

I Ti　義帝

Im Hŭi-jae　任熙載

Im Kwang-jae　任光載

Im Ok-san　林玉山

Im Sa-hong　任士洪

Im Sung-jae　任崇載

Im Wŏn-jun　任元濬

Injong　仁宗

Insu　仁粹

Kang Ching　姜澂

Kang Hun　姜渾

Kang Hyŏng　姜詗

Kang Kyŏm　姜謙

Kang Kyŏng-sŏ　姜景叙

Kang Paek-chin　康伯珍

Kang Ŭng-jŏng　姜應貞

Ki Chun　奇遵

Kil Chae　吉再

Kim Al-lo　金安老

Kim An-guk　金安國

Kim Cha-wŏn　金子猿

Kim Chong-jik　金宗直

Kim Chong-sŏ　金宗瑞

Kim Chŏn　金詮/銓

Kim Chŏng　金淨

Kim Chŏng-guk　金正國

Kim Chun-son　金駿孫

Kim Ch'ŏn-nyŏng　金千齡

Kim Ham　金瑊

Kim Hŭi-su　金希壽

Kim Ik　金釴

Kim Il-son　金馹孫

Kim In-son　金麟孫

Kim Kam　金勘

Kim Koeng-p'il　金宏弼

Kim Kong-jŏ　金公著

Kim Ku　金絿

Kim Kŭk-kyu　金克愊

Kim Kŭk-p'ip　金克愊

Kim Kŭk-sŏng　金克成

Kim Kŭn-sa　金謹思

Kim Kwang-bok　金匡復

Kim Maeng-sŏng　金孟性

Kim Myŏng-yun　金明胤

Kim Ŏn-sin　金彥辛

Kim Se-p'il　金世弼

Kim Sik　金湜

Kim Su-dong　金壽童

Kim Su-gyŏng　金壽卿

Kim Su-on　金守溫

Kim Su-sŏng　金遂性

Kim Suk-cha　金淑滋

Kim Sŭng-gyŏng　金升卿

Kim U-jŭng　金友曾

Kim Ŭng-gi　金應箕

Ko Hyŏng-san 高荊山
Kong Sŏ-rin 孔瑞麟
Ku Cha-p'yŏng 丘／仇自／子平
Ku Chŏn 具詮
Ku Se-gŏn 具世健
Ku Su-bok 具壽福
Ku Su-yŏng 具壽永
Kwŏn Chang 權檣
Kwŏn Chŏn 權磌
Kwŏn Kyŏng-u 權景祐
Kwŏn Kyŏng-yu 權景裕
Kwŏn Kyun 權鈞
Kwŏn, *Madame* 權貴人
Kwŏn Min-su 權敏手
Kwŏn O-bok 權五福
Kwŏn Tal-su 權達手
Kwŏn Ye 權輗
Kyŏng Yŏn 慶延

Li Lin-fu 李林甫
Li Ssu 李斯
Lu Ch'i 盧杞
Lü Ta-chün 呂大鈞

Min Hoe-bal 閔懷發
Min Su-bok 閔壽福
Mun Sŏ-gu 文瑞龜
Munjong 文宗
Myŏngjong 明宗

Nam Hyo-on 南孝溫
Nam I 南怡
Nam Kon 南袞
Nam Se-ju 南世周
Ni Ch'ien 倪謙
No Kan 盧開
No Kong-p'il 盧公弼
No Sa-sin 盧思慎

No Yŏng-son 盧永孫
Nosan'gun 魯山君

Ŏ Se-gyŏm 魚世謙
Ŏm, *Madame* 嚴氏

Pak An-sŏng 朴安性
Pak Han-ju 朴漢柱
Pak Ho 朴壕
Pak Hun 朴薰
Pak Hyo-wŏn 朴孝元
Pak Kang 朴薑
Pak Kwang-yŏng 朴光榮
Pak Kwŏn 朴權
Pak Kyŏng 朴耕
Pak, *Madame* 朴淑儀
Pak P'aeng-nyŏn 朴彭年
Pak Sang 朴祥
Pak Se-ho 朴世豪
Pak Se-hŭi 朴世熹
Pak Su-mun 朴守紋
Pak Suk-tal 朴叔達
Pak U 朴祐
Pak Ŭn 朴訔
Pak Wŏn-jong 朴元宗
Pak Yŏng 朴英
Pak Yŏng-mun 朴永文
Pang Yu-nyŏng 方有寧
Pyŏn Hyŏng-nyang 卞亨良
P'yo Yŏn-mal 表沿沫

Sejo 世祖
Sejong 世宗
Sim Chŏng 沈貞
Sim Hoe 沈澮
Sim On 沈溫
Sim Sun-mun 沈順門
Sim Tal-wŏn 沈達源

Sin Chong-ho 申從濩
Sin Ch'ang 辛昌
Sin Kwang-han 申光漢
Sin, *Lady* 愼氏
Sin Pog-ŭi 辛服義
Sin Sang 申鏛
Sin Su-gŭn 愼守勤
Sin Su-gyŏm 愼守謙
Sin Su-yŏng 愼守英
Sin Sŭng-sŏn 愼承善
Sin U 辛禑
Sin Yong-gae 申用漑
Sin Yun-mu 辛允武
Sohye 昭惠
Son Chu 孫澍
Son Pi-jang 孫比長
Son Sun-hyo 孫舜孝
Son Wŏl-lo 孫元老
Song Chil 宋軼
Song Ch'ŏn-hŭi 宋千喜
Song Ho-ji 宋好智
Song Ho-rye 宋好禮
Sŏ Hu 徐厚
Sŏ Kŏ-jŏng 徐居正
Sŏng Chun 成俊
Sŏng Chung-on 成仲溫
Sŏng Chung-ŏm 成重淹
Sŏng Hŭi-an 成希顏
Sŏng Hyŏn 成俔
Sŏng Kyŏng-on 成景/京溫
Sŏng Mong-jŏng 成夢井
Sŏng Sam-mun 成三問
Sŏng Se-ch'ang 成世昌
Sŏng Se-myŏng 成世明
Sŏng Tam-nyŏn 成聃年
Sŏng Un 成雲
Sŏngjong 成宗
Sŏnjo 宣祖

Tanjong 端宗
Tŏkchong 德宗
T'aejo 太祖
T'aejong 太宗
T'oegye Sŏnsaeng 退溪先生

Wang (royal house) 王
Wang An-shih 王安石
Wŏlsan, *Great Prince of* 月山大君

Yang P'aeng-son 梁彭孫
Yejong 睿宗
Yi 李 (royal house)
Yi Cha 李耔
Yi Cha-hwa 李自華
Yi Chang-bae 李長培
Yi Chang-gil 李長吉
Yi Chang-gon 李長坤
Yi Chang-sŏng 李長城
Yi Chi-bang 李之芳
Yi Chong-jun 李宗準
Yi Chŏn 李恮
Yi Chŏng-suk 李正叔
Yi Chu 李胄
Yi Ch'ang-yun 李昌胤
Yi Ch'im 李忱
Yi Ch'ong 李摠.
  (Yŏnsangun reign)
Yi Ch'ong 李瀇/濴
  (Chungjong reign)
Yi Ch'ŏl-gyŏn 李鐵堅
Yi Ch'ŏng 李清
Yi Ch'ung-gŏn 李忠楗
Yi Haeng 李荇
Yi Hang 李沆
Yi Hŭi-min 李希閔
Yi Hŭi-ong 李希雍
Yi Hwang 李滉

Yi Hyŏn-bo 李賢輔

Yi In-im 李仁任

Yi Ki 李祺

Yi Kong-in 李公仁

Yi Ku 李構

Yi Kŭk-chŭng 李克增

Yi Kŭk-kam 李克堪

Yi Kŭk-ki 李克基

Yi Kŭk-kyun 李克均

Yi Kŭk-pae 李克培

Yi Kŭk-ton 李克墩

Yi Kŭm-san 李金山

Yi Kwa 李顆

Yi Kye-maeng 李繼孟

Yi Kye-nam 李季男

Yi Kye-sun 李季甸

Yi Kyŏng 李璥

Yi Mok 李穆

Yi Ŏm 李儼

Yi Ŏn-ho 李彦浩

Yi Pang-wŏn 李芳遠

Yi Pin 李蘋

Yi Pok-su 李福壽

Yi Pu 李阜

Yi P'a 李坡

Yi Se-gŏl 李世傑

Yi Se-gwang 李世匡

Yi Se-jwa 李世佐

Yi Si-ae 李施愛

Yi Sim-wŏn 李深源

Yi Son 李蓀

Yi Sŏng-dong 李成童

Yi Sŏng-gye 李成桂

Yi Sŏng-ŏn 李成彦

Yi Su-gong 李守恭

Yi Sung-wŏn 李崇元

Yi Sŭng-gŏn 李承健

Yi Sŭng-ŏn 李承彦

Yi Ton 李惇

Yi Tŏk-sung 李德崇

Yi Tŭk-chŏn 李得全

Yi U 李佑

Yi Ŭi-mu 李宜茂

Yi Wŏn 李黿

Yi Wŏn-gan 李元幹

Yi Yak-ping 李若氷

Yi Yak-su 李若水

Yi Yŏn-gyŏng 李延慶

Yi Yu-ban 李幼盤

Yi Yu-ch'ŏng 李惟清

Yi Yu-nyŏng 李幼寧

Yi Yuk 李陸

Yi Yun-t'ak 李允濯

Yŏnsangun 燕山君

Yu Cha-gwang 柳子光

Yu Chin 俞鎭

Yu Chŏng-su 柳廷秀

Yu Hŭi-jŏ 柳希渚

Yu Hŭi-ryŏng 柳希齡

Yu In-suk 柳仁淑

Yu Kwan 柳灌

Yu Kyu 柳規

Yu Pin 柳濱

Yu Pu 柳溥

Yu Sun 柳洵

Yu Sun-jŏng 柳順汀

Yu Sung-jo 柳崇祖

Yu Tam-nyŏn 柳耼年

Yu Un 柳雲

Yu Yong-gŭn 柳庸謹

Yun Cha-im 尹自任

Yun Ho 尹壕

Yun Hŭi-in 尹希仁

Yun Hyo-son 尹孝孫

Yun Ku 尹遘

(Yŏnsangun reign)

Yun Ku 尹衢
  (Chungjong reign)
Yun Kŭm-son 尹金孫
Yun Kwang-nyŏng 尹光齡
Yun, *Lady* 尹氏
Yun Ŏn-jik 尹彦直
Yun P'il-sang 尹弼商

Yun T'an 尹坦
Yun T'ang-no 尹湯老
Yun Ŭl-lo 尹殷老
Yun Ŭn-bo 尹殷輔
Yun Ŭn-p'il 尹殷弼
Yun Wŏn 尹源

BIBLIOGRAPHY

While the period of factional strife has received some over-all attention from modern scholars,*
the century of the Literati Purges, as yet, has not. Two detailed studies, however, have been made
on important aspects of the problem of the Literati Purges. Both are by the same author, the
Korean historian Sin Sŏk-ho, and both are based on the pertinent *Sillok* volumes. Sin Sŏk-ho was
in a unique position to make these studies. His official duties as a member of the Korean history
compilation project of the Japanese Government-General concerned the production of Series Four
of the massive *Chōsen shi*. The ten volumes of this series cover the first 225 years of the Yi
dynasty and the nature of his duties apparently required a thorough perusal of the entire *Sillok*
for the period of the Literati Purges.

One of these studies by Sin, "The conflict between the incoming and the established officials
in the time of Sŏngjong," discusses the major issues of contention at the Korean court in the period
1477-1497. This is the background period for the Purge of 1498 and, to a significant degree, for
the Purge of 1504 as well. As I have indicated elsewhere, the debt I owe to this study is substantial.
While I have felt it unwise to make direct use of Sin's findings, in selecting specific problems and
issues for discussion I have deviated little from the choices made by Sin.

The second article by Sin Sŏk-ho is "A study on the genesis of the Literati Purge of 1519."
This more limited inquiry is confined largely to presenting the main events of the years 1515-1519
and it stops short of treating the purge itself. This study is also of considerable value as an avenue
of approach to the embarrassing riches of the *Sillok*. There are three other studies wholly or
importantly concerned with the Literati Purges: "A discussion of the origins of factional strife
in Korea, with special reference to its relationship with the Literati Purges" (1925), by Seno
Umakuma; "The two great purge cases of the reign of Yŏnsangun" (1931), by the same author;
and "The causes of factional strife in Korea and the conditions of that time" (1916), by Kawai
Hirotami. The second of these uses *Sillok* material only sparingly and the other two not at all.
These articles were of value in the beginning stages of my research for they provided a general
introduction to the subject of the Literati Purges. Their value otherwise is limited, and I have
not had occasion to refer to them in the body of my work. I know of no studies of the purges that
have appeared in recent years, although a very few articles on limited aspects of the problem
have been published. Among these might be noted Pak Yŏng-gyu's short "Conflict between the
high officials and censorate at the beginning of Chungjong's reign" (1962), Yi Pyŏng-hyu's "Study
of the Recommendation Examination—its relationship to the background and employment of the
scholar-official class" (1967), and Kang Sin-hang's innovative investigation of "Yŏnsangun's
suppression of *han'gŭl*—skepticism as to its impact on the history of the Korean language" (1963).

---

*Three somewhat dated studies may be noted: Shidehara Hiroshi's *Account of political strife in Korea* (1907); Oda Shōgo's "Short
history of political strife in Korea" (1924); and *Investigation of political factions and Literati Purges* (1921) by Nagano Torataro
and Hosoi Hajime. A recent work is Kang Chu-jin's *A study of the history of factional strife in Yi Korea* (1971).

My discussion of the Literati Purges is based very largely on two sources, the *Sillok* and the *Chōsen shi.* For the period covered by this study, the latter is based in turn almost entirely on the *Sillok*, which it edits, condenses, and presents in Japanese paraphrase. Ideally, of course, a study of this sort should not rely on the once-removed account provided by the *Chōsen shi.* To be sure, in some cases the *Chōsen shi* simply paraphrases *Sillok* material, and in other cases it does essentially this. But all *Sillok*-based material in the *Chōsen shi* is the product of a process, often drastic, of selection and abridgement. Moreover, the *Chōsen shi* is not free from transcription and other errors. In general, it has been my aim to explore important matters of substance in the *Sillok,* but a considerable amount of work remains to be done in this direction. Nevertheless, I believe that my reliance on the *Chōsen shi* will not prove to have been misplaced in significant degree.

In addition to the *Sillok,* there are four main categories of traditional Yi dynasty sources having major relevance to the problem of the Literati Purges. The first of these consists of contemporary or near-contemporary works concerned with a single one of the purges. Most of these employ a biographical approach; one such is the *Kimyo nok* (Record of 1519) which I cite.

A second category contains works which give extensive coverage to the over-all phenomenon of Yi dynasty factionalism. These focus more on the events of the purges than on the personalities involved. The *Hwahae tangwŏn* (Origins of factionalism in China and Korea), of which I have made limited use, belongs in this category.

A third category consists of the unofficial, or private, histories. One that I cite frequently is the *Yŏllyŏsil kisul (YK),* an eighteenth century general history and encyclopedia that puts together in chronological arrangement, but with topical sub-headings, an account of the Yi dynasty to 1720. It is very largely a compendium of extracts from earlier works, the titles of some 400 of which are noted. I have used the *Yŏllyŏsil kisul* frequently to provide counterpoint to the themes of the *Sillok.* It is valuable additionally as a source of biographical data on the personages connected with the purges and also for the traditionalist point of view it represents.

Finally, there are the more general works, including literary collections, of personages who were connected with the purges or who had first-hand observations to make on the purges. The literature in this category is extensive and, potentially, of considerable value in gaining an understanding of contemporary attitudes toward the purge phenomenon. I have not yet explored this body of material, and my only contact with it has been indirect, through secondary authors. It would seem that much of what these sources have to offer the student of the Literati Purges may be found as well in the *Sillok.*

Works in all of these categories possess major defects as raw material. Most of them select and color the facts so as to present the victims of the purges in an entirely favorable light. The few that are not sympathetically disposed toward the purge heroes are guilty of committing the same offense for opposite purposes. Moreover, quite apart from the question of credibility, the traditional emphasis on the factor of personalities obstructs a more basic understanding. Although my experience in materials of these types is minimal, I feel certain that the factual basis for a study of the Literati Purges must rest on the *Sillok.*

In addition, there are a number of general biographical works containing information on many of those who figure in the story of the purges. Among these, one that I have used directly is the *Kukcho inmul chi (KIC)* (Biographies of Yi dynasty figures). I have made indirect use of a large number of others, through the entries in Japanese paraphrase in the great *Chōsen jimmei jisho (CJJ)* (Korean biographical dictionary). I have not attributed biographical information of a general nature included in the text. This information, on the whole, has been drawn from sources already noted, in particular from the *Sillok, Chōsen shi, Yŏllyŏsil kisul, Kimyo nok, Kukcho inmul chi,* and *Chōsen jimmei jisho.* In addition, I have utilized *Chōsen kokin meiken den* (Biographies of famed sages of ancient and recent Korea), *Chōsen bumbyŏ oyobi shōbu juken* (The National Confucian Shrine of Korea and the canonized Confucian sages), *Chōsen shōbu juken nempyŏ* (Chronologies of the canonized Confucian sages of Korea), and *Chōsen tosho kaidai* (Annotated Korean bibliography). For genealogical information, I have relied upon the *Mansŏng taedong po* (Korean genealogical tables.)

Chōsen jimmei jisho 朝鮮人名辭書 (Korean biographical dictionary).
 Chōsen Sōtokufu Chūsūin 朝鮮總督府中樞院 . Keijō, 1937.
Chōsengo jiten 朝鮮語辭典 (Dictionary of Korean). Chōsen Sōtokufu, Keijō, 1920.
Chōsen kokin meiken den 朝鮮古今名賢傳 (Biographies of famed sages of ancient and recent Korea). Chōsen Kōbun Sha, 朝鮮弘文社 . Keijō, 1923.
Chōsen shi 朝鮮史 (History of Korea). 37 vols. Chōsen Sōtokufu, Keijō, 1932-40.
Chōsen shōbu juken nempyŏ 朝鮮陞廡儒賢年表 (Chronologies of the canonized Confucian sages of Korea). Daitō Shibun Kai 大東斯文會 . Keijō, 1928.
Chōsen tosho kaidai 朝鮮圖書解題 (Annotated Korean bibliography). Chōsen Sōtokufu. Keijō, 1932.
Chosŏn wangjo sillok 朝鮮王朝實錄 (Veritable records of the dynasty of Chosŏn), 1187 *ts'e*, reprinted by Kuksa P'yŏnch'an Wiwŏnhoe, Seoul, 1955-58.

Han U-gŭn 韓沽劢 and Kim Ch'ŏl-chun 金哲埈 . *Kuksa kaeron* 國史概論 (Outline of Korean history). Seoul, 1954.

Kang Chu-jin 姜周鎭 . *Yijo tangjaeng-sa yŏn'gu* 李朝黨爭史研究 (A study of the history of factional strife in Yi Korea). Seoul, Seoul University Press, 1971.

Kang Sin-hang 姜信沆 ."Yonsan'gun ŏnmun kŭmap e taehan sabŭi—kugŏhak-sa-sang e mich'in kyŏnghyangŭi yumu rŭl chungsim ŭro" 燕山君 諺文禁壓 에 대한 揷疑 ······· 國語學史上에 미친 影響의 有無를 中心 으로 (Yŏnsangun's suppression of han'gŭl—skepticism as to its impact on the history of the Korean language), *Chindan hakpo* 震檀學報 no. 24: 27-62 (August 1963).

Kawai Hirotami 河合弘民 . "Chōsen ni okeru tōsō no gen'in oyobi tōji no jōkyō" 朝鮮における 黨爭の原因 及び 當時の 狀況 (The causes of factional strife in Korea and the conditions of that time), *Shigaku zasshi* 史學 雜誌 27.3:40-91 (March 1916).

Kim Al-lo 金安老 (1481-1537). *Yongch'ŏn tamjŏk ki* 龍泉談寂記 (Soliloquies at Dragon Spring).

Kim Yuk 金堉 (1580-1658). *Kimyo nok* 己卯錄 (Record of 1519).

Kukcho inmul chi 國朝人物志 (Biographies of Yi dynasty figures). 3 vols. Seoul?, 1909.

Kuksa kaesŏl 國史概說 (Outline history of Korea). Seoul Taehak Kuksa Yŏn'gu Hoe 서울大學 國史研究會 . Seoul, 1950.

Kyŏngguk taejŏn 經國大典 (National code). Reprinted by Chōsen Sōtokufu Chūsūin. Keijō, 1934.

K'ŭn sajŏn 큰 사전 (Unabridged Korean dictionary.) 6 vols. Chosŏnŏ Hakhoe 朝鮮語 學會 . Seoul, 1947-1957.

Mansŏng taedong po 萬姓大同譜 (Korean genealogical tables). 2 vols. Seoul, 1931-33.

Nagano Toratarō 長野虎太郎 and Hosoi Hajime 細井肇 . *Hōtō shika no kentō* 朋黨士禍の檢討 (Investigation of political factions and Literati Purges). Tokyo, 1921.

Oda Shōgo 小田省吾 . "Chōsen seisō ryakushi" 朝鮮政爭略史 (History of political strife in Korea), in *Bunrui shi* 分類史 (Topical history). vol. 2 of *Chōsen shi kōza* 朝鮮史講座 (Symposium on Korean history). Keijō, 1924.

——— and Ŏ Yun-jŏk 魚允迪 . *Chōsen bumbyō oyobi shōbu juken* 朝鮮文廟 及 陞廡儒賢 (The National Confucian Shrine of Korea and the canonized Confucian sages). Keijō, 1924.

Ŏ Suk-kwŏn 魚叔權 (fl. 1506-67), *Kosa ch'waryo* 攷事撮要 (Selected historical events). Reprinted by Keijō Teikoku Daigaku Hōbun Gakubu 京城帝國大學 法文學部. Keijō, 1941.

Pak Yŏng-gyu 朴榮圭. "Chosŏn Chungjong ch'o e issŏsŏ ŭi taesin kwa taegan ŭi taerip" 朝鮮中宗初에 있어서의 大臣과 臺諫의 對立 (Conflict between the high officials and censorate at the beginning of Chungjong's reign), *Kyŏngbuk-tae nonmun-jip* 慶北大 論文集 no. 5: 379-388 (1962).

Seno Umakuma 瀨野馬熊. "Chōsen tōsō no kiin o ronjite shika to no kankei ni oyobu" 朝鮮黨爭の起因を論じて士禍との關係に及ぶ (A discussion of the origins of factional strife in Korea, with especial reference to its relationship with the Literati Purges), in *Shiratori Hakase kanreki kinen Tōyō shi ronsō* 白鳥博士還曆記念 東洋史論叢 (Essays on East Asian history in commemoration of the 60th birthday of Dr. Shiratori). Tokyo, 1925.

———. "Ensan chō no ni-dai kagoku" 燕山朝の二大禍獄 (The two great purge cases of the reign of Yŏnsangun), *Seikyū gakusō* 青丘學叢 3: 40-67 (February 1931).

Shidehara Hiroshi 幣原坦. *Kankoku seisō shi* 韓國政爭志. (Account of political strife in Korea). Tokyo, 1907.

Shin, Susan S. "Land Tenure and the Agrarian Economy in Yi Dynasty Korea: 1600-1800." Ph.D. dissertation, Harvard University, 1973.

Sin Sŏk-ho 申奭鎬. "Kibō shika [Kimyo sahwa] no yurai ni kansuru ichi kōsatsu" 己卯士禍の由來に關する一考察 (A study on the genesis of the Literati Purge of 1519), *Seikyū gakusō* 青丘學叢 20:1-49 (May 1940).

Suematsu Yasukazu 末松保和, "Chōsen Giseifu kō" 朝鮮議政府考, *Chōsen gakuhō* 朝鮮學報 (Journal of Korean studies) 9:1-35 (1956).

Taejŏn hoet'ong 大典會通 (Collection of statutes). Reprinted by Chōsen Sōtokufu Chūsūin, Keijō, 1939.

Teratani Shūzō 寺谷修三 (Sin Sŏk-ho 申奭鎬). "Chōsen Seisō jidai no shin-kyū tairitsu" 朝鮮成宗時代の新舊對立 (The conflict between the incoming and the established officials in the time of Sŏngjong), in *Kindai Chōsen shi kenkyū* 朝鮮史研究 (Studies in the modern history of Korea). Chōsen Shi Henshū Kai kenkyū isan 1 朝鮮史編修會研究彙纂 Keijō, 1944.

Yi Kŭng-ik　李肯翊　(1736-1806). *Yŏllyŏsil kisul*　燃藜室記述 (Narrative of Yŏllyŏsil). Reprinted by Chosŏn Kwangmun Hoe. Kyŏngsŏng, 1912.

Yi Pyŏng-do　李丙燾.　*Kuksa taegwan*　國史大觀　(A survey of Korean history). Rev. ed. Seoul, 1955.

Yi Pyŏng-hyu　李秉烋　. "Hyŏllyangkwa yŏn'gu—saryu ŭi chint'oe mit kŭ paegyŏng kwa kwallyŏn-hayŏ"　賢良科研究士類의進退및ユ背景과關聯하여 (Study of the Recommendation Examination—its relationship to the background and employment of the scholar-official class), *Kyemyŏng sahak*　啓明史學　no. 1:9-38 (December 1967).

Yi Wŏn-sun　李源順　(1772?-1823). *Hwahae tangwŏn*　華海黨源　(Origins of factionalism in China and Korea).

HARVARD EAST ASIAN MONOGRAPHS

39.   Jerome Alan Cohen, ed., *The Dynamics of China's Foreign Relations*

40.   V. V. Vishnyakova-Akimova, *Two Years in Revolutionary China, 1925-1927,* tr. Steven I. Levine

41.   Meron Medzini, *French Policy in Japan during the Closing Years of the Tokugawa Regime*

42.   *The Cultural Revolution in the Provinces*

43.   Sidney A. Forsythe, *An American Missionary Community in China, 1895-1905*

44.   Benjamin I. Schwartz, ed., *Reflections on the May Fourth Movement: A Symposium*

45.   Ching Young Choe, *The Rule of the Taewŏn'gun, 1864-1873: Restoration in Yi Korea*

46.   W. P. J. Hall, *A Bibliographical Guide to Japanese Research on the Chinese Economy, 1958-1970*

47.   Jack J. Gerson, *Horatio Nelson Lay and Sino-British Relations, 1854-1864*

48.   Paul Richard Bohr, *Famine in China and the Missionary: Timothy Richard as Relief Administrator and Advocate of National Reform, 1876-1884*

49.   Endymion Wilkinson, *The History of Imperial China: A Research Guide*

50.   Britten Dean, *China and Great Britain: The Diplomacy of Commercial Relations, 1860-1864*

51.   Ellsworth C. Carlson, *The Foochow Missionaries, 1847-1880*

52.   Yeh-chien Wang, *An Estimate of the Land-Tax Collection in China, 1753 and 1908*

53.   Richard M. Pfeffer, *Understanding Business Contracts in China, 1949-1963*

54.   Han-sheng Chuan and Richard Kraus, *Mid-Ch'ing Rice Markets and Trade, An Essay in Price History*

55.   Ranbir Vohra, *Lao She and the Chinese Revolution*

56.   Liang-lin Hsiao, *China's Foreign Trade Statistics, 1864-1949*

57.   Lee-hsia Hsu Ting, *Government Control of the Press in Modern China, 1900-1949*

58.   Edward W. Wagner, *The Literati Purges: Political Conflict in Early Yi Korea*